Book 5 – Derivatives and Portfolio Management

SCHWESERNOTES™ 2014 CFA LEVEL II BOOK 5: DERIVATIVES AND
PORTFOLIO MANAGEMENT

©2013 Kaplan, Inc. All rights reserved.

Published in 2013 by Kaplan, Inc.

Printed in the United States of America.

ISBN: 978-1-4277-4914-7 / 1-4277-4914-0

PPN: 3200-4015

READINGS AND LEARNING OUTCOME STATEMENTS

READINGS

The following material is a review of the Derivatives and Portfolio Management principles designed to address the learning outcome statements set forth by CFA Institute.

STUDY SESSION 16

Reading Assignments

Derivatives and Portfolio Management, CFA Program Curriculum, Volume 6, Level II (CFA Institute, 2013)

STUDY SESSION 17

Reading Assignments

Derivatives and Portfolio Management, CFA Program Curriculum, Volume 6, Level II (CFA Institute, 2013)

STUDY SESSION 18

Reading Assignments

Derivatives and Portfolio Management, CFA Program Curriculum, Volume 6, Level II (CFA Institute, 2013)

LEARNING OUTCOME STATEMENTS (LOS)

The CFA Institute Learning Outcome Statements are listed below. These are repeated in each topic review; however, the order may have been changed in order to get a better fit with the flow of the review.

STUDY SESSION 16

The topical coverage corresponds with the following CFA Institute assigned reading:

51. Forward Markets and Contracts
The candidate should be able to:
a. explain how the value of a forward contract is determined at initiation, during the life of the contract, and at expiration. (page 14)
b. calculate and interpret the price and value of an equity forward contract, assuming dividends are paid either discretely or continuously. (page 17)
c. calculate and interpret the price and value of 1) a forward contract on a fixed-income security, 2) a forward rate agreement (FRA), and 3) a forward contract on a currency. (page 21)
d. evaluate credit risk in a forward contract, and explain how market value is a measure of exposure to a party in a forward contract. (page 29)

The topical coverage corresponds with the following CFA Institute assigned reading:

52. Futures Markets and Contracts
The candidate should be able to:
a. explain why the futures price must converge to the spot price at expiration. (page 37)
b. determine the value of a futures contract. (page 38)
c. explain why forward and futures prices differ. (page 39)
d. describe monetary and nonmonetary benefits and costs associated with holding the underlying asset, and explain how they affect the futures price. (page 43)
e. describe backwardation and contango. (page 44)
f. explain the relation between futures prices and expected spot prices. (page 44)
g. describe the difficulties in pricing Eurodollar futures and creating a pure arbitrage opportunity. (page 47)
h. calculate and interpret the prices of Treasury bond futures, stock index futures, and currency futures. (page 48)

STUDY SESSION 17

The topical coverage corresponds with the following CFA Institute assigned reading:

53. Option Markets and Contracts
The candidate should be able to:
a. calculate and interpret the prices of a synthetic call option, synthetic put option, synthetic bond, and synthetic underlying stock, and explain why an investor would want to create such instruments. (page 59)
b. calculate and interpret prices of interest rate options and options on assets using one- and two-period binomial models. (page 62)

c. explain and evaluate the assumptions underlying the Black–Scholes–Merton model. (page 75)

d. explain how an option price, as represented by the Black–Scholes–Merton model, is affected by a change in the value of each of the inputs. (page 77)

e. explain the delta of an option, and demonstrate how it is used in dynamic hedging. (page 80)

f. explain the gamma effect on an option's delta and how gamma can affect a delta hedge. (page 85)

g. explain the effect of the underlying asset's cash flows on the price of an option. (page 85)

h. determine the historical and implied volatilities of an underlying asset. (page 86)

i. demonstrate how put–call parity for options on forwards (or futures) is established. (page 87)

j. compare American and European options on forwards and futures, and identify the appropriate pricing model for European options. (page 89)

The topical coverage corresponds with the following CFA Institute assigned reading:

54. Swap Markets and Contracts
The candidate should be able to:

a. distinguish between the pricing and valuation of swaps. (page 99)

b. explain the equivalence of 1) interest rate swaps to a series of off-market forward rate agreements (FRAs) and 2) a plain vanilla swap to a combination of an interest rate call and an interest rate put. (page 100)

c. calculate and interpret the fixed rate on a plain vanilla interest rate swap and the market value of the swap during its life. (page 101)

d. calculate and interpret the fixed rate, if applicable, and the foreign notional principal for a given domestic notional principal on a currency swap, and estimate the market values of each of the different types of currency swaps during their lives. (page 108)

e. calculate and interpret the fixed rate, if applicable, on an equity swap and the market values of the different types of equity swaps during their lives. (page 112)

f. explain and interpret the characteristics and uses of swaptions, including the difference between payer and receiver swaptions. (page 114)

g. calculate the payoffs and cash flows of an interest rate swaption. (page 114)

h. calculate and interpret the value of an interest rate swaption at expiration. (page 115)

i. evaluate swap credit risk for each party and during the life of the swap, distinguish between current credit risk and potential credit risk, and explain how swap credit risk is reduced by both netting and marking to market. (page 116)

j. define swap spread and explain its relation to credit risk. (page 117)

The topical coverage corresponds with the following CFA Institute assigned reading:

55. Interest Rate Derivative Instruments
The candidate should be able to:

a. demonstrate how both a cap and a floor are packages of 1) options on interest rates and 2) options on fixed-income instruments. (page 127)

b. calculate the payoff for a cap and a floor, and explain how a collar is created. (page 129)

The topical coverage corresponds with the following CFA Institute assigned reading:

56. Credit Default Swaps

The candidate should be able to:

a. describe credit default swaps (CDS), single-name and index CDS, and the parameters that define a given CDS product. (page 136)

b. describe credit events and settlement protocols with respect to CDS. (page 137)

c. explain the principles underlying, and factors that influence, the market's pricing of CDS. (page 138)

d. describe the use of CDS to manage credit exposures and to express views regarding changes in shape and/or level of the credit curve. (page 141)

e. describe the use of CDS to take advantage of valuation differences among separate markets, such as bonds, loans, and equities. (page 142)

STUDY SESSION 18

The topical coverage corresponds with the following CFA Institute assigned reading:

57. Portfolio Concepts

The candidate should be able to:

a. explain mean–variance analysis and its assumptions, and calculate the expected return and the standard deviation of return for a portfolio of two or three assets. (page 151)

b. describe the minimum-variance and efficient frontiers, and explain the steps to solve for the minimum-variance frontier. (page 156)

c. explain the benefits of diversification and how the correlation in a two-asset portfolio and the number of assets in a multi-asset portfolio affect the diversification benefits. (page 160)

d. calculate the variance of an equally weighted portfolio of n stocks, explain the capital allocation and capital market lines (CAL and CML) and the relation between them, and calculate the value of one of the variables given values of the remaining variables. (page 163)

e. explain the capital asset pricing model (CAPM), including its underlying assumptions and the resulting conclusions. (page 173)

f. explain the security market line (SML), the beta coefficient, the market risk premium, and the Sharpe ratio, and calculate the value of one of these variables given the values of the remaining variables. (page 174)

g. explain the market model, and state and interpret the market model's predictions with respect to asset returns, variances, and covariances. (page 181)

h. calculate an adjusted beta, and explain the use of adjusted and historical betas as predictors of future betas. (page 183)

i. explain reasons for and problems related to instability in the minimum-variance frontier. (page 185)

j. describe and compare macroeconomic factor models, fundamental factor models, and statistical factor models. (page 186)

k. calculate the expected return on a portfolio of two stocks, given the estimated macroeconomic factor model for each stock. (page 191)

l. describe the arbitrage pricing theory (APT), including its underlying assumptions and its relation to the multifactor models, calculate the expected return on an asset given an asset's factor sensitivities and the factor risk premiums, and determine whether an arbitrage opportunity exists, including how to exploit the opportunity. (page 192)

m. explain sources of active risk, interpret tracking error, tracking risk, and the information ratio, and explain factor portfolio and tracking portfolio. (page 194)

n. compare underlying assumptions and conclusions of the CAPM and APT model, and explain why an investor can possibly earn a substantial premium for exposure to dimensions of risk unrelated to market movements. (page 198)

The topical coverage corresponds with the following CFA Institute assigned reading:

58. **Residual Risk and Return: The Information Ratio**

The candidate should be able to:

a. define the terms "alpha" and "information ratio" in both their ex post and ex ante senses. (page 216)

b. compare the information ratio and the alpha's T-statistic. (page 216)

c. explain the objective of active management in terms of value added. (page 219)

d. calculate the optimal level of residual risk to assume for given levels of manager ability and investor risk aversion. (page 221)

e. justify why the choice for a particular active strategy does not depend on investor risk aversion. (page 223)

The topical coverage corresponds with the following CFA Institute assigned reading:

59. **The Fundamental Law of Active Management**

The candidate should be able to:

a. define the terms "information coefficient" and "breadth" and describe how they combine to determine the information ratio. (page 229)

b. describe how the optimal level of residual risk of an investment strategy changes with information coefficient and breadth, and how the value added of an investment strategy changes with information coefficient and breadth. (page 232)

c. contrast market timing and security selection in terms of breadth and required investment skill. (page 232)

d. describe how the information ratio changes when the original investment strategy is augmented with other strategies or information sources. (page 233)

e. describe the assumptions on which the fundamental law of active management is based. (page 234)

The topical coverage corresponds with the following CFA Institute assigned reading:

60. The Portfolio Management Process and the Investment Policy Statement

The candidate should be able to:

a. explain the importance of the portfolio perspective. (page 241)

b. describe the steps of the portfolio management process and the components of those steps. (page 241)

c. explain the role of the investment policy statement in the portfolio management process, and describe the elements of an investment policy statement. (page 242)

d. explain how capital market expectations and the investment policy statement help influence the strategic asset allocation decision and how an investor's investment time horizon may influence the investor's strategic asset allocation. (page 242)

e. define investment objectives and constraints, and explain and distinguish among the types of investment objectives and constraints. (page 243)

f. contrast the types of investment time horizons, determine the time horizon for a particular investor, and evaluate the effects of this time horizon on portfolio choice. (page 247)

g. justify ethical conduct as a requirement for managing investment portfolios. (page 247)

FORWARD MARKETS AND CONTRACTS

EXAM FOCUS

This topic review covers the calculation of price and value for forward contracts, specifically equity forward contracts, T-bond forward contracts, currency forwards, and forward (interest) rate agreements. You need to have a good understanding of the no-arbitrage principle that underlies these calculations because it is used in the topic reviews of futures and swaps pricing as well. There are several important price and value formulas in this review. A clear understanding of the sources and timing of forward contract settlement payments will enable you to be successful on this portion of the exam without depending on pure memorization of these complex formulas. In the past, candidates have been tested on their understanding of the relationship of the payments at settlement to interest rate changes, asset price changes, and index level changes. The pricing conventions for the underlying assets have been tested separately. The basic contract mechanics are certainly "fair game," so don't overlook the easy stuff by spending too much time trying to memorize the formulas.

WARM-UP: FORWARD CONTRACTS

The party to the forward contract that agrees to buy the financial or physical asset has a **long forward position** and is called the *long*. The party to the forward contract that agrees to sell/deliver the asset has a **short forward position** and is called the *short*.

We will illustrate the basic forward contract mechanics through an example based on the purchase and sale of a Treasury bill. Note that while forward contracts on T-bills are usually quoted in terms of a discount percentage from face value, we use dollar prices here to make the example easy to follow.

Consider a contract under which Party A agrees to buy a $1,000 face value 90-day Treasury bill from Party B 30 days from now at a price of $990. Party A is the long and Party B is the short. Both parties have removed uncertainty about the price they will pay or receive for the T-bill at the future date. If 30 days from now T-bills are trading at $992, the short must deliver the T-bill to the long in exchange for a $990 payment. If T-bills are trading at $988 on the future date, the long must purchase the T-bill from the short for $990, the contract price.

Each party to a forward contract is exposed to **default risk**, the probability that the other party (the counterparty) will not perform as promised. Typically, no money changes hands at the inception of the contract, unlike futures contracts in which each party posts an initial deposit called the **margin** as a guarantee of performance.

At any point in time, including the settlement date, the party to the forward contract with the negative value will owe money to the other side. The other side of the contract will have a positive value of equal amount. Following this example, if the T-bill price is $992 at the (future) settlement date, and the short does not deliver the T-bill for $990 as promised, the short has defaulted.

 Professor's Note: For the basics of forward contracts, please see the online Schweser Library.

WARM-UP: FORWARD CONTRACT PRICE DETERMINATION

The No-Arbitrage Principle

The price of a forward contract is *not* the price to purchase the contract because the parties to a forward contract typically pay nothing to enter into the contract at its inception. Here, *price refers to the contract price of the underlying asset under the terms of the forward contract.* This price may be a U.S. dollar or euro price but it is often expressed as an interest rate or currency exchange rate. For T-bills, the price will be expressed as an annualized percentage discount from face value; for coupon bonds, it will usually be expressed as a yield to maturity; for the implicit loan in a forward rate agreement (FRA), it will be expressed as annualized London Interbank Offered Rate (LIBOR); and for a currency forward, it is expressed as an exchange rate between the two currencies involved. However it is expressed, this rate, yield, discount, or dollar amount is the forward price in the contract.

The price that we wish to determine is the forward price that makes the *values* of both the long and the short positions zero at contract initiation. We will use the *no-arbitrage principle*: there should not be a riskless profit to be gained by a combination of a forward contract position with positions in other assets. This principle assumes that (1) transactions costs are zero, (2) there are no restrictions on short sales or on the use of short sale proceeds, and (3) both borrowing and lending can be done in unlimited amounts at the risk-free rate of interest. This concept is so important, we'll express it in a formula:

forward price = price that would not permit profitable riskless arbitrage in frictionless markets

A Simple Version of the Cost-of-Carry Model

In order to explain the no-arbitrage condition as it applies to the determination of forward prices, we will first consider a forward contract on an asset that costs nothing to store and makes no payments to its owner over the life of the forward contract. A zero-coupon (pure discount) bond meets these criteria. Unlike gold or wheat, it has no storage costs; unlike stocks, there are no dividend payments to consider; and unlike coupon bonds, it makes no periodic interest payments.

The general form for the calculation of the forward contract price can be stated as follows:

$$FP = S_0 \times (1 + R_f)^T$$

or

$$S_0 = \frac{FP}{(1 + R_f)^T}$$

where:
FP = forward price
S_0 = spot price at inception of the contract $(t = 0)$
R_f = annual risk-free rate
T = forward contract term in years

Example: Calculating the no-arbitrage forward price

Consider a 3-month forward contract on a zero-coupon bond with a face value of $1,000 that is currently quoted at $500, and assume a risk-free annual interest rate of 6%. Determine the price of the forward contract under the no-arbitrage principle.

Answer:

$$T = \frac{3}{12} = 0.25$$

$$FP = S_0 \times (1 + R_f)^T = \$500 \times 1.06^{0.25} = \$507.34$$

Now, let's explore in more detail why $507.34 is the no-arbitrage price of the forward contract.

Cash and Carry Arbitrage When the Forward Contract is Overpriced

Suppose the forward contract is actually trading at $510 rather than the no-arbitrage price of $507.34. A short position in the forward contract requires the delivery of this bond three months from now. The arbitrage that we examine in this case amounts to borrowing $500 at the risk-free rate of 6%, buying the bond for $500, and simultaneously taking the short position in the forward contract on the zero-coupon bond so that we are obligated to deliver the bond at the expiration of the contract for the forward price and receive $510.

At the settlement date, we can satisfy our obligation under the terms of the forward contract by delivering the zero-coupon bond for a payment of $510, regardless of its market value at that time. We will use the $510 payment we receive at settlement from the forward contract (the forward contract price) to repay the $500 loan. The total amount to repay the loan, since the term of the loan is three months, is:

$$\text{loan repayment} = \$500 \times (1.06)^{0.25} = \$507.34$$

The payment of $510 we receive when we deliver the bond at the forward price is greater than our loan payoff of $507.34, and we will have earned an arbitrage profit of $510 – $507.34 = $2.66. Notice that this is equal to the difference between the actual forward price and the no-arbitrage forward price. The transactions are illustrated in Figure 1.

Figure 1: Cash and Carry Arbitrage When Forward is Overpriced

Today		Three Months From Today	
Spot price of bond	$500		
Forward price	$510		
Transaction	*Cash flow*	*Transaction*	*Cash flow*
Short forward	$0	Settle short position by delivering bond	$510.00
Buy bond	–$500		
Borrow at 6%	+$500	Repay loan	– $507.34
Total cash flow	$0	Total cash flow = arbitrage profit	+$2.66

Professor's Note: Here's a hint to help you remember which transactions to undertake for cash and carry arbitrage. You always want to buy underpriced assets and sell overpriced assets, so if the futures contract is overpriced, you want to take a short position that gives you the obligation to sell at a fixed price. Because you go short in the forward market, you take the opposite position in the spot market and buy the asset. You need money to buy the asset, so you have to borrow. Therefore, the first step in cash and carry arbitrage at its most basic is:

forward overpriced ⇒ short (sell) forward ⇒ long (buy) spot asset ⇒ borrow money

Reverse Cash and Carry Arbitrage When the Forward Contract is Underpriced

Suppose the forward contract is actually trading at $502 instead of the no-arbitrage price of $507.34. We reverse the arbitrage trades from the previous case and generate an arbitrage profit as follows. We sell the bond short today for $500 and simultaneously take the long position in the forward contract, which obligates us to purchase the bond in 90 days at the forward price of $502. We invest the $500 proceeds from the short sale at the 6% annual rate for three months.

In this case, at the settlement date, we receive the investment proceeds of $507.34, accept delivery of the bond in return for a payment of $502, and close out our short position by delivering the bond we just purchased at the forward price.

The payment of $502 we make as the long position in the contract is less than investment proceeds of $507.34, and we have earned an arbitrage profit of $507.34 – $502 = $5.34. The transactions are illustrated in Figure 2.

Figure 2: Reverse Cash and Carry Arbitrage When Forward is Underpriced

Today		Three Months From Today	
Spot price of bond	$500		
Forward price	$502		
Transaction	*Cash flow*	*Transaction*	*Cash flow*
Long forward	$0	Settle long position by buying bond	–$502.00
Short sell bond	+$500	Deliver bond to close short position	$0.00
Invest short-sale proceeds at 6%	–$500	Receive investment proceeds	+$507.34
Total cash flow	$0	Total cash flow = arbitrage profit	+$5.34

 Professor's Note: In this case, because the forward contract is underpriced, the trades are reversed from cash and carry arbitrage:

forward underpriced ⇒ long (buy) forward ⇒ short (sell) spot asset ⇒ invest (lend) money

We can now determine that the no-arbitrage forward price that yields a zero *value* for both the long and short positions in the forward contract at inception is the no-arbitrage price of $507.34.

 Professor's Note: This long explanation has answered the question, "What is the forward price that allows no arbitrage?" You'll have to trust me, but a very clear understanding here will make what follows easier and will serve you well as we progress to futures, options, and swaps.

Professor's Note: Day Count conventions determine how interest accrues over time. Different financial instruments use different day count conventions.

While there is some variation even within the CFA curriculum from reading-to-reading, generally the two choices to use are:

1. ***360 & Simple Interest** (multiply by days/360)*

If the question is talking about LIBOR rates or T-bills (that's generally all problems dealing with swaps, FRAs, interest rate options), that's a sign to multiply by days/360 days.

- *FRAs.*
- *Swaps.*
- *LIBOR-based derivative instruments (e.g. caps, floors, swaptions).*
- *T-bills.*

2. ***365 & Compound Interest** (raise to exponent of days/365)*

For all other instruments, use compounding and days/365.

- *Equities.*
- *Bonds.*
- *Treasury bonds.*
- *Currencies*.*
- *Options.*

* Note that days/360 is used in the currency parity and forward exchange rates relationships in the economics readings of Study Session 4 because these arbitrage relationships are based on LIBOR deposits.

LOS 51.a: Explain how the value of a forward contract is determined at initiation, during the life of the contract, and at expiration.

CFA® Program Curriculum, Volume 6, page 18

If we denote the value of the long position in a forward contract at time t as V_t, the value of the long position at contract initiation, t = 0, is:

$$V_0 \left(\text{of long position at initiation}\right) = S_0 - \left[\frac{FP}{\left(1+R_f\right)^T}\right]$$

Note that the no-arbitrage relation we derived in the prior section ensures that the value of the long position (and of the short position) at contract initiation is zero.

If $S_0 = \dfrac{FP}{\left(1+R_f\right)^T}$, then $V_0 = 0$

The value of the long position in the forward contract during the life of the contract after t years ($t < T$) have passed (since the initiation of the contract) is:

$$V_t \left(\text{of long position during life of contract}\right) = S_t - \left[\frac{FP}{\left(1 + R_f\right)^{T-t}}\right]$$

This is the same equation as above, but the spot price, S_t, will have changed, and the period for discounting is now the number of years remaining until contract expiration ($T - t$). This is a zero-sum game, so the value of the contract to the short position is the negative of the long position value:

$$V_t \left(\text{of short position during life of contract}\right) = \left[\frac{FP}{\left(1 + R_f\right)^{T-t}}\right] - S_t$$

$$= -V_t \left(\text{of long position during life of contract}\right)$$

Notice that the forward price, *FP*, is the forward price agreed to at the initiation of the contract, not the current market forward price. In other words, as the spot and forward market prices change over the life of the contract, one side (i.e., short or long position) wins and the other side loses. For example, if the market spot and forward prices increase after the contract is initiated, the long position makes money, the value of the long position is positive, and the value of the short position is negative. If the spot and forward prices decrease, the short position makes money.

Professor's Note: Unfortunately, you must be able to use the forward valuation formulas on the exam. If you're good at memorizing formulas, that prospect shouldn't scare you too much. However, if you don't like memorizing formulas, here's another way to remember how to value a forward contract. The long position will pay the forward price (FP) at maturity (time T) and receive the spot price (S_T). The value of the contract to the long position at maturity is what he will receive less what he will pay: $S_T - FP$. Prior to maturity (at time T), the value to the long is the present value of S_T (which is the spot price at

time t of S_t) less the present value of the forward price: $S_t - \left[\dfrac{FP}{\left(1 + R_f\right)^{T-t}}\right]$.

So, on the exam, think "long position is spot price minus present value of forward price."

Example: Determining value of a forward contract prior to expiration

In our 3-month zero-coupon bond contract example, we determined that the no-arbitrage forward price was $507.34. Suppose that after two months the spot price on the zero-coupon bond is $515, and the risk-free rate is still 6%. Calculate the value of the long and short positions in the forward contract.

Answer:

$$V_2 \left(\text{of long position after two months}\right) = \$515 - \frac{\$507.34}{1.06^{1/12}} = \$515 - \$504.88 = \$10.12$$

$$V_2 \left(\text{of short position after two months}\right) = -\$10.12$$

Another way to see this is to note that because the spot price has increased to $515, the current no-arbitrage forward price is:

$$FP = \$515 \times 1.06^{1/12} = \$517.51$$

The long position has made money (and the short position has lost money) because the forward price has *increased* by $10.17 from $507.34 to $517.51 since the contract was initiated. The value of the long position today is the present value of $10.17 for one month at 6%:

$$V_2 \left(\text{long position after two months}\right) = \frac{\$10.17}{1.06^{1/12}} = \$10.12$$

At contract expiration, we do not need to discount the forward price because the time left on the contract is zero. Since the long can buy the asset for *FP* and sell it for the market price S_T, the value of the long position is the amount the long position will receive if the contract is settled in cash:

$$V_T \left(\text{of long position at maturity}\right) = S_T - FP$$

$$V_T \left(\text{of short position at maturity}\right) = FP - S_T = -V_T \left(\text{of long position at maturity}\right)$$

Figure 3 summarizes the key concepts you need to remember for this LOS.

Figure 3: Forward Value of Long Position at Initiation, During the Contract Life, and at Expiration

Time	Forward Contract Valuation
At initiation	Zero, because the contract is priced to prevent arbitrage
During the life of the contract	$S_t - \left[\dfrac{FP}{(1+R_f)^{T-t}} \right]$
At expiration	$S_T - FP$

How Might Forward Contract Valuation Be Tested?

Look for these ways in which the valuation of a forward contract might appear as part of an exam question:

- To mark-to-market for financial statement reporting purposes.
- To mark-to-market because it is required as part of the original agreement. For example, the two parties might have agreed to mark-to-market a 180-day forward contract after 90 days to reduce credit risk.
- To measure credit exposure.
- To calculate how much it would cost to terminate the contract.

LOS 51.b: Calculate and interpret the price and value of an equity forward contract, assuming dividends are paid either discretely or continuously.

CFA® Program Curriculum, Volume 6, page 26

Equity Forward Contracts With Discrete Dividends

Recall that the no-arbitrage forward price in our earlier example was calculated for an asset with no periodic payments. A stock, a stock portfolio, or an equity index may have expected dividend payments over the life of the contract. In order to price such a contract, we must either adjust the spot price for the present value of the expected dividends (PVD) over the life of the contract or adjust the forward price for the future value of the dividends (FVD) over the life of the contract. The **no-arbitrage price of an equity forward contract** in either case is:

$$FP\left(\text{on an equity security}\right) = \left(S_0 - PVD\right) \times \left(1 + R_f\right)^T$$

$$FP\left(\text{on an equity security}\right) = \left[S_0 \times \left(1 + R_f\right)^T\right] - FVD$$

 Professor's Note: In practice, we would calculate the present value from the ex-dividend date, not the payment date. On the exam, use payment dates unless the ex-dividend dates are given.

For equity contracts, use a 365-day basis for calculating T if the maturity of the contract is given in days. For example, if it is a 60-day contract, T = 60 / 365. If the maturity is given in months (e.g., two months) calculate T using maturity divided by number of months (e.g., T = 2 / 12).

Example: Calculating the price of a forward contract on a stock

Calculate the no-arbitrage forward price for a 100-day forward on a stock that is currently priced at $30.00 and is expected to pay a dividend of $0.40 in 15 days, $0.40 in 85 days, and $0.50 in 175 days. The annual risk-free rate is 5%, and the yield curve is flat.

Answer:

Ignore the dividend in 175 days because it occurs after the maturity of the forward contract.

$$PVD = \frac{\$0.40}{1.05^{15/365}} + \frac{\$0.40}{1.05^{85/365}} = \$0.7946$$

$$FP = (\$30.00 - \$0.7946) \times 1.05^{100/365} = \$29.60$$

The time line of cash flows is shown in the following figure.

Pricing a 100-Day Forward Contract on Dividend-Paying Stock

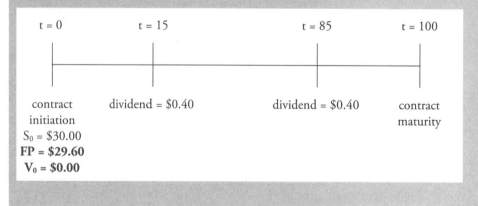

To calculate the **value of the long position in a forward contract on a dividend-paying stock**, we make the adjustment for the present value of the remaining expected discrete dividends at time t (PVD_t) to get:

$$V_t(\text{long position}) = [S_t - PVD_t] - \left[\frac{FP}{(1+R_f)^{(T-t)}}\right]$$

Professor's Note: This formula still looks like the standard "spot price minus present value of forward price." However, now the "spot price" has been adjusted by subtracting out the present value of the dividends because the long position in the forward contract does not receive the dividends paid on the underlying stock. So, now think "adjusted spot price less present value of forward price."

Example: Calculating the value of an equity forward contract on a stock

After 60 days, the value of the stock in the previous example is $36.00. Calculate the value of the equity forward contract on the stock to the long position, assuming the risk-free rate is still 5% and the yield curve is flat.

Answer:

There's only one dividend remaining (in 25 days) before the contract matures (in 40 days) as shown below, so:

$$PVD_{60} = \frac{\$0.40}{1.05^{25/365}} = \$0.3987$$

$$V_{60}\left(\text{long position}\right) = \$36.00 - \$0.3987 - \left[\frac{\$29.60}{1.05^{40/365}}\right] = \$6.16$$

Valuing a 100-Day Forward Contract After 60 Days

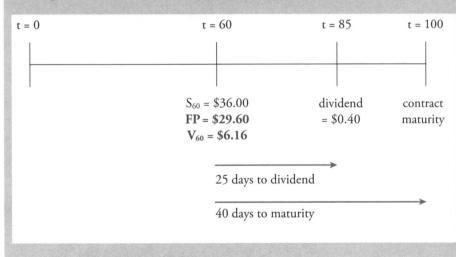

Equity Forward Contracts With Continuous Dividends

To calculate the **price of an equity index forward contract**, rather than take the present value of each dividend on (possibly) hundreds of stocks, we can make the calculation as if the dividends are paid continuously (rather than at discrete times) at the dividend yield rate on the index. Using continuous time discounting, we can calculate the no-arbitrage forward price as:

$$FP\left(\text{on an equity index}\right) = S_0 \times e^{\left(R_f^c - \delta^c\right) \times T} = \left(S_0 \times e^{-\delta^c \times T}\right) \times e^{R_f^c \times T}$$

where:
R_f^c = continuously compounded risk-free rate
δ^c = continuously compounded dividend yield

Professor's Note: The relationship between the discrete risk-free rate R_f and the continuously compounded rate R_f^c is $R_f^c = ln\left(1 + R_f\right)$. For example, 5% compounded annually is equal to ln(1.05) = 0.04879 = 4.879% compounded continuously. The 2-year 5% future value factor can then be calculated as either $1.05^2 = 1.1025$ or $e^{0.04879 \times 2} = 1.1025$.

Example: Calculating the price of a forward contract on an equity index

The value of the S&P 500 index is 1,140. The continuously compounded risk-free rate is 4.6% and the continuous dividend yield is 2.1%. Calculate the no-arbitrage price of a 140-day forward contract on the index.

Answer:

$$FP = 1,140 \times e^{(0.046 - 0.021) \times (140/365)} = 1,151$$

For the continuous time case, the **value of the forward contract on an equity index** is calculated as follows:

$$V_t\left(\text{of the long position}\right) = \left(\frac{S_t}{e^{\delta^c \times (T-t)}}\right) - \left(\frac{FP}{e^{R_f^c \times (T-t)}}\right)$$

Example: Calculating the value of a forward contract on an equity index

After 95 days, the value of the index in the previous example is 1,025. Calculate the value to the long position of the forward contract on the index, assuming the continuously compounded risk-free rate is 4.6% and the continuous dividend yield is 2.1%.

Answer:

After 95 days there are 45 days remaining on the original forward contract:

$$V_{95}\left(\text{of the long position}\right) = \left(\frac{1,025}{e^{0.021 \times (45/365)}}\right) - \left(\frac{1,151}{e^{0.046 \times (45/365)}}\right) = -122.14$$

LOS 51.c: Calculate and interpret the price and value of 1) a forward contract on a fixed-income security, 2) a forward rate agreement (FRA), and 3) a forward contract on a currency.

CFA® Program Curriculum, Volume 6, page 30

In order to calculate the no-arbitrage **forward price on a coupon-paying bond**, we can use the same formula as we used for a dividend-paying stock or portfolio, simply substituting the present value of the expected coupon payments (PVC) *over the life of the contract* for PVD, or the future value of the coupon payments (FVC) for FVD, to get the following formulas:

$$FP(\text{on a fixed income security}) = (S_0 - PVC) \times (1 + R_f)^T$$

$$\text{or}$$

$$= S_0 \times (1 + R_f)^T - FVC$$

The value of the forward contract prior to expiration is as follows:

$$V_t(\text{long position}) = [S_t - PVC_t] - \left[\frac{FP}{(1 + R_f)^{(T-t)}} \right]$$

In our examples, we assume that the spot price on the underlying coupon-paying bond includes accrued interest. For fixed income contracts, use a 365-day basis to calculate T if the contract maturity is given in days.

Example: Calculating the price of a forward on a fixed income security

Calculate the price of a 250-day forward contract on a 7% U.S. Treasury bond with a spot price of $1,050 (including accrued interest) that has just paid a coupon and will make another coupon payment in 182 days. The annual risk-free rate is 6%.

Answer:

Remember that U.S. Treasury bonds make semiannual coupon payments, so:

$$C = \frac{\$1,000 \times 0.07}{2} = \$35.00$$

$$PVC = \frac{\$35.00}{1.06^{182/365}} = \$34.00$$

The forward price of the contract is therefore:

$$FP(\text{on a fixed income security}) = (\$1,050 - \$34.00) \times 1.06^{250/365} = \$1,057.37$$

Example: Calculating the value of a forward on a fixed income security

After 100 days, the value of the bond in the previous example is $1,090. Calculate the value of the forward contract on the bond to the long position, assuming the risk-free rate is 6.0%.

Answer:

There is only one coupon remaining (in 82 days) before the contract matures (in 150 days), so:

$$PVC = \frac{\$35.00}{1.06^{82/365}} = \$34.54$$

$$V_{100}(\text{long position}) = \$1,090 - \$34.54 - \left(\frac{\$1,057.37}{1.06^{150/365}}\right) = \$23.11$$

WARM-UP: LIBOR-BASED LOANS AND FORWARD RATE AGREEMENTS

Eurodollar deposit is the term for deposits in large banks outside the United States denominated in U.S. dollars. The lending rate on dollar-denominated loans between banks is called the **London Interbank Offered Rate (LIBOR)**. It is quoted as an annualized rate based on a 360-day year. In contrast to T-bill discount yields, LIBOR is an add-on rate, like a yield quote on a short-term certificate of deposit. LIBOR is used as a reference rate for floating rate U.S. dollar-denominated loans worldwide.

Example: LIBOR-based loans

Compute the amount that must be repaid on a $1 million loan for 30 days if 30-day LIBOR is quoted at 6%.

Answer:

The add-on interest is calculated as $1 million × 0.06 × (30 / 360) = $5,000. The borrower would repay $1,000,000 + $5,000 = $1,005,000 at the end of 30 days.

LIBOR is published daily by the British Banker's Association and is compiled from quotes from a number of large banks; some are large multinational banks based in other countries that have London offices. There is also an equivalent euro lending rate called **Euribor**, or Europe Interbank Offered Rate. Euribor, established in Frankfurt, is published by the European Central Bank.

The long position in a **forward rate agreement** (FRA) is the party that would borrow the money (long the loan with the contract price being the interest rate on the loan). If the floating rate at contract expiration (LIBOR for U.S. dollar deposits and Euribor for euro deposits) is above the rate specified in the forward agreement, the long position in the contract can be viewed as the right to borrow at below market rates and the long will receive a payment. If the floating rate at the expiration date is below the rate specified in the forward agreement, the short will receive a cash payment from the long. (The right to lend at *above* market rates would have a positive value.)

> *Professor's Note: We say "can be viewed as" because an FRA is settled in cash, so there is no requirement to lend or borrow the amount stated in the contract. For this reason, the creditworthiness of the long position is not a factor in the determination of the interest rate on the FRA. However, to understand the pricing and calculation of value for an FRA, viewing the contract as a commitment to lend or borrow at a certain interest rate at a future date is helpful.*

The notation for FRAs is unique. There are two numbers associated with an FRA: the number of months until the contract expires and the number of months until the underlying loan is settled. The difference between these two is the maturity of the underlying loan. For example, a 2 × 3 FRA is a contract that expires in two months (60 days), and the underlying loan is settled in three months (90 days). The underlying rate is 1-month (30-day) LIBOR on a 30-day loan in 60 days. See Figure 4.

Figure 4: Illustration of a 2 × 3 FRA

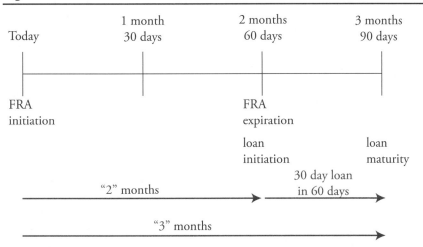

Pricing FRAs

There are three important things to remember about FRAs when we're pricing and valuing them:

1. LIBOR rates in the Eurodollar market are add-on rates and are always quoted on a 30/360 day basis in annual terms. For example, if the LIBOR quote on a 30-day loan is 6%, the actual unannualized monthly rate is 6% × (30/360) = 0.5%.

2. The long position in an FRA, in effect, is long the rate and wins when the rate increases.

3. Although the interest on the underlying loan won't be paid until the end of the loan (e.g., in three months in Figure 4), the payoff on the FRA occurs at the expiration of the FRA (e.g., in two months). Therefore, the payoff on the FRA is the present value of the interest savings on the loan (e.g., discounted one month in Figure 4).

The forward "price" in an FRA is actually a forward interest rate. The calculation of a forward interest rate is presented in Level I as the computation of forward rates from spot rates. We will illustrate this calculation with an example.

Example: Calculating the price of an FRA

Calculate the price of a 1 × 4 FRA (i.e., a 90-day loan, 30 days from now). The current 30-day LIBOR is 4% and the 120-day LIBOR is 5%.

Answer:

The actual (unannualized) rate on the 30-day loan is:

$$R30 = 0.04 \times \frac{30}{360} = 0.00333$$

The actual (unannualized) rate on the 120-day loan is:

$$R120 = 0.05 \times \frac{120}{360} = 0.01667$$

We wish to calculate the actual rate on a 90-day loan from day 30 to day 120:

$$\text{price of } 1 \times 4 \text{ FRA} = \frac{1+R120}{1+R30} - 1 = \frac{1.01667}{1.00333} - 1 = 0.0133$$

We can annualize this rate as:

$$0.0133 \times \frac{360}{90} = 0.0532 = 5.32\%$$

This is the no-arbitrage forward rate—the forward rate that will make the values of the long and the short positions in the FRA both zero at the initiation of the contract.

The time line is shown in the following figure.

Pricing a 1 × 4 FRA

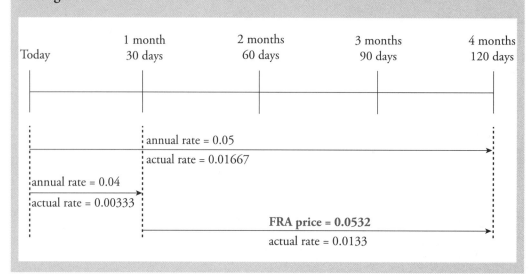

©2013 Kaplan, Inc.

Valuing an FRA at Maturity

To understand the calculation of the value of the FRA *after the initiation of the contract*, recall that in the previous example the long in the FRA has the "right" to borrow money 30 days from inception for a period of 90 days at the forward rate. If interest rates increase (specifically the 90-day forward contract rate), the long will profit as the contract has fixed a borrowing rate below the now-current market rate. These "savings" will come at the end of the loan term, so to value the FRA we need to take the present value of these savings. An example incorporating this fact will illustrate the cash settlement value of an FRA at expiration.

> **Example: Calculating value of an FRA at maturity (i.e., cash payment at settlement)**
>
> Continuing the prior example for a 1 × 4 FRA, assume a notional principal of $1 million and that, at contract expiration, the 90-day rate has increased to 6%, which is above the contract rate of 5.32%. Calculate the value of the FRA at maturity, which is equal to the cash payment at settlement.
>
> **Answer:**
>
> The interest savings at the end of the loan term (compared to the market rate of 6%) will be:
>
> $$\left[\left(0.0600 \times \frac{90}{360}\right) - \left(0.0532 \times \frac{90}{360}\right)\right] \times \$1,000,000 = \$1,700$$
>
> The present value of this amount at the FRA settlement date (90 days prior to the end of the loan term) discounted at the current rate of 6% is:
>
> $$\frac{\$1,700}{1 + \left(0.06 \times \dfrac{90}{360}\right)} = \$1,674.88$$
>
> This will be the cash settlement payment from the short to the long at the expiration of the contract. Note that we have discounted the savings in interest at the end of the loan term by the *market* rate of 6% that prevails at the contract settlement date for a 90-day term, as shown in the following figure.

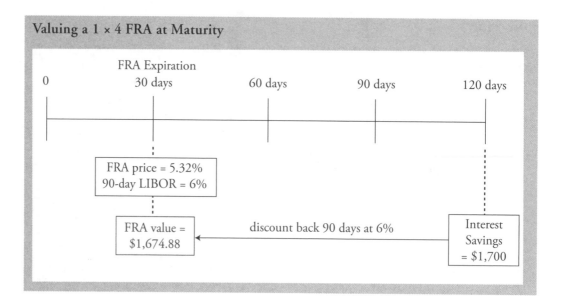

Valuing a 1 × 4 FRA at Maturity

Valuing an FRA Prior to Maturity

To value an FRA prior to the settlement date, we need to know the number of days that have passed since the initiation of the contract. For example, let's suppose we want to value the same 1 × 4 FRA ten days after initiation. Originally it was a 1 × 4 FRA, which means the FRA now expires in 20 days. The calculation of the "savings" on the loan will be the same as in our previous example, except that we need to use the "new" FRA price that would be quoted on a contract covering the same period as the original "loan." In this case the "new" FRA price is the now-current market forward rate for a 90-day loan made at the settlement date (20 days in the future). Also, we need to discount the interest savings implicit in the FRA back an extra 20 days, or 110 days, instead of 90 days as we did for the value at the settlement date.

> ### Example: Calculating value of an FRA prior to settlement
>
> Value a 5.32% 1 × 4 FRA with a principal amount of $1 million 10 days after initiation if 110-day LIBOR is 5.9% and 20-day LIBOR is 5.7%.
>
> **Answer:**
>
> *Step 1:* Find the "new" FRA price on a 90-day loan 20 days from today. This is the current 90-day forward rate at the settlement date, 20 days from now.
>
> $$\left[\frac{1+\left(0.059\times\dfrac{110}{360}\right)}{1+\left(0.057\times\dfrac{20}{360}\right)}-1\right]\times\frac{360}{90}=0.0592568$$

Step 2: Calculate the interest difference on a $1 million, 90-day loan made 20 days from now at the forward rate calculated previously compared to the FRA rate of 5.32%.

$$\left[\left(0.0592568 \times \frac{90}{360}\right) - \left(0.0532 \times \frac{90}{360}\right)\right] \times \$1,000,000 = \$1,514.20$$

Step 3: Discount this amount at the current 110-day rate.

$$\frac{\$1,514.20}{1 + \left(0.059 \times \frac{110}{360}\right)} = \$1,487.39$$

Valuing a 1 × 4 FRA Prior to Settlement

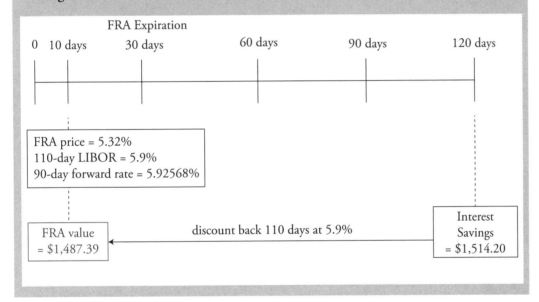

Professor's Note: I have tried to explain these calculations in such a way that you can value an FRA at any date from initiation to settlement using basic tools that you already know. Once you understand where the value of an FRA comes from (the interest savings on a loan to be made at the settlement date) and when this value is to be received (at the end of the loan), you can calculate the present value of these savings even under somewhat stressful test conditions. Just remember that if the rate in the future is less than the FRA rate, the long is "obligated to borrow" at above-market rates and will have to make a payment to the short. If the rate is greater than the FRA rate, the long will receive a payment from the short.

Pricing Currency Forward Contracts

The **price and value of a currency forward contract** is refreshingly straightforward after that last bit of mental exercise. The calculation of the currency forward rate is just an application of covered interest parity from the topic review of foreign exchange parity relations in Study Session 4.

Recall that the interest rate parity result is based on an assumption that you should make the same amount when you lend at the riskless rate in your home country as you would if you bought *one unit* of the foreign currency at the current spot rate, S_0, invested it at the foreign risk-free rate, and entered into a forward contract to exchange the proceeds of the investment at maturity for the home currency at the forward rate of F_T (both the forward and the spot rates are quoted as the price in the home currency for one unit of the foreign currency).

Covered interest rate parity gives us the no-arbitrage forward price of a unit of foreign currency in terms of the home currency for a currency forward contract of length T in years:

$$F_T \left(\text{currency forward contract} \right) = S_0 \times \frac{\left(1 + R_{DC} \right)^T}{\left(1 + R_{FC} \right)^T}$$

where:
F and S are quoted in domestic currency per unit of foreign currency
R_{DC} = domestic currency interest rate
R_{FC} = foreign currency interest rate

For foreign currency contracts use a 365-day basis to calculate T if the maturity is given in days.

Professor's Note: This is different from the way we expressed interest rate parity back in Study Session 4, in which F and S were quoted in terms of foreign currency per unit of domestic currency. The key is to remember our numerator/ denominator rule: if the spot and forward quotes are in Currency A per unit of Currency B, the Currency A interest rate should be on top and the Currency B interest rate should be on the bottom. For example, if S and F are in euros per Swiss franc, put the European interest rate on the top and the Swiss interest rate on the bottom.

Example: Calculating the price of a currency forward contract

The risk-free rates are 6% in the United States and 8% in Mexico. The current spot exchange rate is $0.0845 per Mexican peso (MXN). Calculate the forward exchange rate for a 180-day forward contract.

Answer:

$$F_T \left(\text{currency forward contract} \right) = \$0.0845 \times \frac{1.06^{180/365}}{1.08^{180/365}} = \$0.0837$$

Valuing Currency Forward Contracts

At any time prior to maturity, the value of a currency forward contract to the long will depend on the spot rate at time t, S_t, and can be calculated as:

$$V_t \left(\text{currency forward contract}\right) = \left[\frac{S_t}{\left(1 + R_{FC}\right)^{(T-t)}}\right] - \left[\frac{F_T}{\left(1 + R_{DC}\right)^{(T-t)}}\right]$$

Example: Calculating the value of a currency forward contract

Calculate the value of the forward contract in the previous example if, after 15 days, the spot rate is $0.0980 per MXN.

Answer:

$$V_{15} \left(\text{currency forward contract}\right) = \left(\frac{\$0.0980}{1.08^{165/365}}\right) - \left(\frac{\$0.0837}{1.06^{165/365}}\right) = \$0.0131$$

The continuous time price and value formulas for currency forward contracts are:

$$F_T = \left(\text{currency forward contract}\right) = S_0 \times e^{\left(R_{DC}^c - R_{FC}^c\right) \times T}$$

$$V_t \left(\text{currency forward contract}\right) = \left[\frac{S_t}{e^{R_{FC}^c \times (T-t)}}\right] - \left[\frac{F_T}{e^{R_{DC}^c \times (T-t)}}\right]$$

V_t in both cases is the value in domestic currency units for a contract covering one unit of the foreign currency. For the settlement payment in the home currency on a contract, simply multiply this amount by the notional amount of the foreign currency covered in the contract.

LOS 51.d: Evaluate credit risk in a forward contract, and explain how market value is a measure of exposure to a party in a forward contract.

CFA® Program Curriculum, Volume 6, page 41

At any date after initiation of a forward contract, it is likely to have positive value to either the long or the short. Recall that this value is the amount that would be paid to settle the contract in cash at that point in time. The party with the position that has positive value has credit risk in this amount because the other party would owe them that amount if the contract were terminated. The contract value and, therefore, the credit risk, may increase, decrease, or even change sign over the remaining term of the contract. However, at any point in time, the market values of forward contracts, as we have calculated them, are a measure of the credit risk currently borne by the party to which a cash payment would be made to settle the contract at that point. One way to reduce the credit risk in a forward contract is to mark-to-market partway through.

KEY CONCEPTS

LOS 51.a

$$V_0 \text{(of long position at initiation)} = S_0 - \left[\frac{FP}{\left(1+R_f\right)^T}\right]$$

$$V_t \text{(of long position during life of contract)} = S_t - \left[\frac{FP}{\left(1+R_f\right)^{T-t}}\right]$$

$$V_T \text{(of long postion at maturity)} = S_T - FP$$

$$V_T \text{(of short position at maturity)} = FP - S_T$$

LOS 51.b

The calculation of the forward price for an equity forward contract is different because the periodic dividend payments affect the no-arbitrage price calculation. The forward price is reduced by the future value of the expected dividend payments; alternatively, the spot price is reduced by the present value of the dividends.

$$FP \text{(on an equity security)} = \left(S_0 - PVD\right) \times \left(1+R_f\right)^T = \left[S_0 \times \left(1+R_f\right)^T\right] - FVD$$

The value of an equity forward contract to the long is the spot equity price minus the present value of the forward price minus the present value of any dividends expected over the term of the contract:

$$V_t \text{(long position)} = \left[S_t - PVD_t\right] - \left[\frac{FP}{\left(1+R_f\right)^{(T-t)}}\right]$$

We typically use the continuous time versions to calculate the price and value of a forward contract on an equity index using a continuously compounded dividend yield.

$$FP \text{(on an equity index)} = S_0 \times e^{\left(R_f^c - \delta^c\right) \times T} = \left(S_0 \times e^{-\delta^c \times T}\right) \times e^{R_f^c \times T}$$

$$V_t \text{(of the long position)} = \left(\frac{S_t}{e^{\delta^c \times (T-t)}}\right) - \left(\frac{FP}{e^{R_f^c \times (T-t)}}\right)$$

LOS 51.c

For forwards on coupon-paying bonds, the price is calculated as the spot price minus the present value of the coupons times the quantity one plus the risk-free rate.

$$FP \text{(on a fixed income security)} = \left(S_0 - PVC\right) \times \left(1+R_f\right)^T = S_0 \times \left(1+R_f\right)^T - FVC$$

The value of a forward on a coupon-paying bond t years after inception is the spot bond price minus the present value of the forward price minus the present value of any coupon payments expected over the term of the contract:

$$V_t \left(\text{long position}\right) = \left[S_t - PVC_t\right] - \left[\frac{FP}{\left(1 + R_f\right)^{\left(T-t\right)}}\right]$$

The "price" of an FRA is the implied forward rate for the period beginning when the FRA expires to the maturity of the underlying "loan."

The value of an FRA at maturity is the interest savings to be realized at maturity of the underlying "loan" discounted back to the date of the expiration of the FRA at the current LIBOR. The value of an FRA prior to maturity is the interest savings estimated by the implied forward rate discounted back to the valuation date at the current LIBOR.

For a currency forward, the price is the exchange rate implied by covered interest rate parity. The value at settlement is the gain or loss to the long from making a currency exchange in the amounts required by the contract at the contract exchange rate, rather than at the prevailing market rate:

$$F_T \left(\text{currency forward contract}\right) = S_0 \times \frac{\left(1 + R_{DC}\right)^T}{\left(1 + R_{FC}\right)^T}$$

where:
F and S are quoted in domestic currency per unit of foreign currency

Prior to settlement, the value of a currency forward is the present value of any gain or loss to the long from making a currency exchange in the amounts required by the contract at the contract exchange rate, compared to an exchange at the prevailing forward exchange rate at the settlement date.

$$V_t \left(\text{currency forward contract}\right) = \left[\frac{S_t}{\left(1 + R_{FC}\right)^{\left(T-t\right)}}\right] - \left[\frac{F_T}{\left(1 + R_{DC}\right)^{\left(T-t\right)}}\right]$$

The continuous time price and value formulas for a currency forward contract are:

$$F_T \left(\text{currency forward contract}\right) = S_0 \times e^{\left(R_{DC}^c - R_{FC}^c\right) \times T}$$

$$V_t \left(\text{currency forward contract}\right) = \left[\frac{S_t}{e^{R_{FC}^c \times \left(T-t\right)}}\right] - \left[\frac{F_T}{e^{R_{DC}^c \times \left(T-t\right)}}\right]$$

LOS 51.d
Credit risk is the risk that the counterparty will not pay when a positive amount is owed at settlement. The larger the value or the forward to one party, the greater the credit (default) risk to that party.

CONCEPT CHECKERS

1. A stock is currently priced at $30 and is expected to pay a dividend of $0.30
    20 days and 65 days from now. The contract price for a 60-day forward contract
    when the interest rate is 5% is *closest* to:
    A. $29.46.
    B. $29.70.
    C. $29.94.

2. After 37 days, the stock in Question 1 is priced at $21, and the risk-free rate is
    still 5%. The value of the forward contract on the stock to the short position is:
    A. −$8.85.
    B. +$8.85.
    C. +$9.00.

3. The contract rate (annualized) for a 3 × 5 FRA if the current 60-day rate is 4%,
    the current 90-day rate is 5%, and the current 150-day rate is 6%, is *closest* to:
    A. 6.0%.
    B. 6.9%.
    C. 7.4%.

4. A 6% Treasury bond is trading at $1,044 (including accrued interest) per $1,000
    of face value. It will make a coupon payment 98 days from now. The yield curve
    is flat at 5% over the next 150 days. The forward price per $1,000 of face value
    for a 120-day forward contract, is *closest* to:
    A. $1,014.52.
    B. $1,030.79.
    C. $1,037.13.

5. The forward price of a 200-day stock index futures contract when the spot
    index is 540, the continuous dividend yield is 1.8%, and the continuously
    compounded risk-free rate is 7% (with a flat yield curve) is *closest* to:
    A. 545.72.
    B. 555.61.
    C. 568.08.

6. An analyst who mistakenly ignores the dividends when valuing a short position
    in a forward contract on a stock that pays dividends will *most likely*:
    A. overvalue the position by the present value of the dividends.
    B. undervalue the position by the present value of the dividends.
    C. overvalue the position by the future value of the dividends.

CHALLENGE PROBLEMS

7. A portfolio manager owns Macrogrow, Inc., which is currently trading at $35 per share. She plans to sell the stock in 120 days, but is concerned about a possible price decline. She decides to take a short position in a 120-day forward contract on the stock. The stock will pay a $0.50 per share dividend in 35 days and $0.50 again in 125 days. The risk-free rate is 4%. The value of the trader's position in the forward contract in 45 days, assuming in 45 days the stock price is $27.50 and the risk-free rate has not changed, is *closest* to:
    A. $7.17.
    B. $7.50.
    C. $7.92.

8. A portfolio manager expects to receive funds from a new client in 30 days. These assets are to be invested in a basket of equities. He decides to take a long position in 20, 30-day forward contracts on the S&P 500 stock index to hedge against an increase in equity prices. The index is currently at 1,057. The continuously compounded dividend yield is 1.50%, and the discrete risk-free rate is 4%. Fifteen days later the index value is 1,103. The value of the forward position after 15 days, assuming no change in the risk-free rate or the dividend yield, is *closest* to:
    A. $831.60.
    B. $860.80.
    C. $898.60.

9. The CFO of Yellow River Company received a report from the economics department which states that short-term rates are expected to increase 50 basis points in the next 90 days. As a floating rate borrower (typically against 90-day LIBOR), the CFO recognizes that he must hedge against an increase in future borrowing costs over the next 90 days because of a potential increase in short-term interest rates. He considers many options, but decides on entering into a long forward rate agreement (FRA). The 30-day LIBOR is 4.5%, 90-day LIBOR is 4.7%, and 180-day LIBOR is 4.9%. To *best* hedge this risk, Yellow River should enter into a:
    A. 3 × 3 FRA at a rate of 4.48%.
    B. 3 × 6 FRA at a rate of 4.48%.
    C. 3 × 6 FRA at a rate of 5.02%.

10. Consider a U.K.-based company that exports goods to the EU. The U.K. company expects to receive payment on a shipment of goods in 60 days. Because the payment will be in euros, the U.K. company wants to hedge against a decline in the value of the euro against the pound over the next 60 days. The U.K. risk-free rate is 3%, and the EU risk-free rate is 4%. No change is expected in these rates over the next 60 days. The current spot rate is 0.9230 £ per €. To hedge the currency risk, the U.K. company should take a short position in a euro contract at a forward price of:
   A. 0.9205.
   B. 0.9215.
   C. 0.9244.

11. The most important measure of credit risk in a forward contract is:
   A. time to maturity.
   B. OAS.
   C. market value.

ANSWERS – CONCEPT CHECKERS

1. **C** The dividend in 65 days occurs after the contract has matured, so it's not relevant to computing the forward price.

$$PVD = \frac{\$0.30}{1.05^{20/365}} = \$0.2992$$

$$FP = (\$30.00 - \$0.2992) \times 1.05^{60/365} = \$29.94$$

2. **B** $V(\text{long position}) = \$21.00 - \left[\dfrac{\$29.94}{1.05^{23/365}}\right] = -\$8.85$

$V(\text{short position}) = +\$8.85$

3. **C** The actual (unannualized) rate on the 90-day loan is:

$$R90 = 0.05 \times \frac{90}{360} = 0.0125$$

The actual rate on the 150-day loan is:

$$R150 = 0.06 \times \frac{150}{360} = 0.025$$

The price of the 3 × 5 FRA (the 60-day forward rate in 90 days) is:

$$\left(\frac{1.025}{1.0125} - 1\right) \times \frac{360}{60} = 0.074 = 7.4\%$$

4. **B** Remember that U.S. Treasury bonds make semiannual coupon payments, so:

$$C = \frac{\$1,000 \times 0.06}{2} = \$30.00$$

$$PVC = \frac{\$30.00}{1.05^{98/365}} = \$29.61$$

The forward price of the contract is therefore:

$$FP(\text{on a fixed income security}) = (\$1,044 - \$29.61) \times (1.05)^{120/365} = \$1,030.79$$

5. **B** Use the dividend rate as a continuously compounded rate to get:

$$FP = 540 \times e^{(0.07 - 0.018) \times (200/365)} = 555.61$$

6. **B** The value of the long position in a forward contract on a stock at time t is:

$$V_t(\text{long position}) = [S_t - PVD_t] - \left[\frac{FP}{(1 + R_f)^{(T-t)}}\right]$$

If the dividends are ignored, the *long* position will be overvalued by the present value of the dividends; that means the *short* position (which is what the question asks for) will be undervalued by the same amount.

ANSWERS – CHALLENGE PROBLEMS

7. **A** The dividend in 125 days is irrelevant because it occurs after the forward contract matures.

$$PVD = \frac{\$0.50}{1.04^{35/365}} = \$0.4981$$

$$FP = (\$35 - \$0.4981) \times 1.04^{120/365} = \$34.95$$

$$V_{45}(\text{short position}) = -\left(\$27.50 - \frac{\$34.95}{1.04^{75/365}}\right) = \$7.17$$

8. **C** The discrete risk-free rate is given in the problem, so the first thing to do is calculate the continuously compounded risk-free rate and the forward price at initiation:

$$\text{continuously compounded risk-free rate} = \ln(1.04) = 0.0392$$
$$FP(\text{on an equity index}) = 1,057 \times e^{(0.0392-0.015)\times(30/365)} = 1,059.10$$

The value of one contract after 15 days is:

$$V_{15} = \left(\frac{1,103}{e^{0.015\times(15/365)}}\right) - \left(\frac{1059.10}{e^{0.0392\times(15/365)}}\right) = \$44.93$$

The value of 20 contracts is 44.93 × 20 = $898.60.

9. **C** A 3 × 6 FRA expires in 90 days and is based on 90-day LIBOR, so it is the appropriate hedge for 90-day LIBOR 90 days from today. The rate is calculated as:

$$R90 = 0.047 \times \frac{90}{360} = 0.0118$$
$$R180 = 0.049 \times \frac{180}{360} = 0.0245$$
$$\text{price of } 3 \times 6 \text{ FRA} = \left(\frac{1.0245}{1.0118} - 1\right) \times \frac{360}{90} = 0.0502 = 5.02\%$$

10. **B** The U.K. company will be receiving euros in 60 days, so it should short the 60-day forward on the euro as a hedge. The no-arbitrage forward price is:

$$F_T = £0.923 \times \frac{1.03^{60/365}}{1.04^{60/365}} = 0.9215$$

11. **C** The primary element of credit risk for a forward is the market value of the contract.

FUTURES MARKETS AND CONTRACTS

EXAM FOCUS

This topic review focuses on the no-arbitrage pricing relationships for futures contracts. The pricing of futures is quite similar, and in some cases identical, to the pricing of forwards. You should understand the basic futures pricing relation and how it is adjusted for assets that have storage costs or positive cash flows.

WARM-UP: FUTURES CONTRACTS

Futures contracts are very much like the forward contracts we learned about in the previous topic review. They are similar in that:

- Deliverable contracts obligate the long to buy and the short to sell a certain quantity of an asset for a certain price on a specified future date.
- Cash settlement contracts are settled by paying the contract value in cash on the expiration date.
- Both forwards and futures are priced to have zero value at the time the investor enters into the contract.

There are important differences, including:

- Futures are marked to market at the end of every trading day. Forward contracts are not marked to market.
- Forwards are private contracts and do not trade on organized exchanges. Futures contracts trade on organized exchanges.
- Forwards are customized contracts satisfying the needs of the parties involved. Futures contracts are highly standardized.
- Forwards are contracts with the originating counterparty; a specialized entity called a clearinghouse is the counterparty to all futures contracts.
- Forward contracts are usually not regulated. The government having legal jurisdiction regulates futures markets.

LOS 52.a: Explain why the futures price must converge to the spot price at expiration.

CFA® Program Curriculum, Volume 6, page 85

The **spot (cash) price** of a commodity or financial asset is the price for immediate delivery. The **futures price** is the price today for delivery at some future point in time (the maturity date).

At expiration, the spot price must equal the futures price because the futures price has become the price today for delivery today, which is the same as the spot. Arbitrage will force the prices to be the same at contract expiration.

Example: Why the futures price must equal the spot price at expiration

Suppose the current spot price of silver is $4.65. Demonstrate by arbitrage that the futures price of a futures silver contract that expires in one minute must equal the spot price.

Answer:

Suppose the futures price was $4.70. We could buy the silver at the spot price of $4.65, sell the futures contract, and deliver the silver under the contract at $4.70. Our profit would be $4.70 – $4.65 = $0.05. Because the contract matures in one minute, there is virtually no risk to this arbitrage trade.

Suppose instead the futures price was $4.61. Now we would buy the silver contract, take delivery of the silver by paying $4.61, and then sell the silver at the spot price of $4.65. Our profit is $4.65 – $4.61 = $0.04. Once again, this is a riskless arbitrage trade.

Therefore, in order to prevent arbitrage, the futures price at the maturity of the contract must be equal to the spot price of $4.65.

WARM-UP: FUTURES MARGINS AND MARKING TO MARKET

Each exchange has a clearinghouse. The clearinghouse guarantees that traders in the futures market will honor their obligations. The clearinghouse does this by splitting each trade once it is made and acting as the opposite side of each position. To safeguard the clearinghouse, the exchange requires both sides of the trade to post margin and settle their accounts on a daily basis. Thus, the margin in the futures markets is a performance guarantee.

Marking to market is the process of adjusting the margin balance in a futures account each day for the change in the value of the contract from the previous trading day, based on the settlement price. The futures exchanges can require a mark to market more frequently (than daily) under extraordinary circumstances.

LOS 52.b: Determine the value of a futures contract.

CFA® Program Curriculum, Volume 6, page 85

Like forward contracts, futures contracts have no value at contract initiation. Unlike forward contracts, futures contracts do not accumulate value changes over the term of the contract. Since futures accounts are marked to market daily, the value after the margin deposit has been adjusted for the day's gains and losses in contract value is always zero. The futures price at any point in time is the price that makes the value of a new contract equal to zero. The value of a futures contract strays from zero only during the trading periods between the times at which the account is marked to market:

value of futures contract = current futures price − previous mark-to-market price

If the futures price increases, the value of the long position increases. The value is set back to zero by the mark to market at the end of the mark-to-market period.

LOS 52.c: Explain why forward and futures prices differ.

CFA® Program Curriculum, Volume 6, page 86

The no-arbitrage price of a futures contract should be the same as that of a forward contract that was presented in the previous topic review:

$$FP = S_0 \times (1 + R_f)^T$$

where:
FP $\;=$ futures price
S_0 $\;=$ spot price at inception of the contract $(t = 0)$
R_f $\;=$ annual risk-free rate
T $\;=$ futures contract term in years

However, there are a number of "real-world" complications that will cause futures and forward prices to be different. If investors prefer the mark-to-market feature of futures, futures prices will be higher than forward prices. If investors would rather hold a forward contract to avoid the marking to market of a futures contract, the forward price would be higher than the futures price. From a technical standpoint, the differences between the theoretical (no-arbitrage) prices of futures and forwards center on the correlation between interest rates and the mark-to-market cash flows of futures:

- Higher reinvestment rates for gains and lower borrowing costs to fund losses lead to a preference for the mark-to-market feature of futures, and higher prices for futures than forwards, when interest rates and asset values are positively correlated.
- A preference to avoid the mark-to-market cash flows will lead to a higher price for the forward relative to the future if interest rates and asset values are negatively correlated.

A preference for the mark-to-market feature will arise from a positive correlation between interest rates and the price of the contract asset. When the value of the underlying asset increases and the mark to market generates cash, reinvestment opportunities tend to be better due to the positive correlation of asset values with higher interest rates. When the value of the underlying asset decreases and the mark to market requires cash, borrowing costs tend to be lower due to the positive correlation.

The opposite result will occur when the correlation between the price of the underlying asset and interest rates is negative. Consider forwards and futures contracts on fixed income prices. Fixed income values fall when interest rates rise, so rates and values are negatively correlated. Borrowing costs are higher when funds are needed and reinvestment rates are lower when funds are generated by the mark to market of the futures contracts. Figure 1 summarizes these results.

Figure 1: Prices of Futures versus Forward Contracts

If the correlation between the underlying asset value and interest rates is...	*Investors will...*
Positive	Prefer to go long in a **futures contract,** and the futures price will be greater than the price of an otherwise comparable forward contract
Zero	Have no preference
Negative	Prefer to go long in a **forward contract,** and the forward price will be greater than the price of an otherwise comparable futures contract

FUTURES ARBITRAGE

Professor's Note: The trades necessary to conduct futures arbitrage are the same as those for forward arbitrage as outlined in the previous topic review. The only difference is that now we are going long or short in the futures contract.

A **cash-and-carry arbitrage** consists of buying the asset, storing/holding the asset, and selling the asset at the futures price when the contract expires. The steps in a cash-and-carry arbitrage are as follows:

At the initiation of the contract:

• Borrow money for the term of the contract at market interest rates.
• Buy the underlying asset at the spot price.
• Sell (go short) a futures contract at the current futures price.

At contract expiration:

• Deliver the asset and receive the futures contract price.
• Repay the loan plus interest.

If the futures contract is overpriced, this 5-step transaction will generate a riskless profit. The futures contract is overpriced if the actual market price is greater than the no-arbitrage price.

Example: Futures cash and carry arbitrage

Assume the spot price of gold is $900/oz., that the 1-year futures price is $975/oz., and that an investor can borrow or lend funds at 7%. Ignore transaction and storage costs. Calculate the arbitrage profit.

Answer:

The futures price, according to the no-arbitrage principle, should be:

$$FP = \$900 \times 1.07 = \$963$$

Instead, it's trading at $975. That means the futures contract is overpriced, so we should conduct cash and carry arbitrage by going short in the futures contract, buying gold in the spot market, and borrowing money to pay for the purchase. If we borrow $900 to fund the purchase of gold, we must repay $900 × 1.07 = $963.

Today		1 Year from Today	
Spot price of gold	$900		
Futures price of gold	$975		
Transaction	*Cash Flow*	*Transaction*	*Cash Flow*
Short futures	$0	Settle short position by delivering gold	$975
Buy gold in spot market	−$900		
Borrow at 7%	+$900	Repay loan	−$963
Total cash flow	$0	Total cash flow = arbitrage profit	+$12

The riskless profit is equal to the difference between the futures contract proceeds and the loan payoff, or $975 − $963 = $12. Notice that this profit is equal to the difference between the actual futures price of $975 and the no-arbitrage price of $963.

If the futures price is too low (which presents a profitable arbitrage opportunity), the opposite of each step should be executed to earn a riskless profit.

This is **reverse cash-and-carry arbitrage**. The steps in reverse cash-and-carry arbitrage are as follows.

At the initiation of the contract:

- Sell the asset short.
- Lend the short sale proceeds at market interest rates.
- Buy (go long) the futures contract at the market price.

At contract expiration:

- Collect the loan proceeds.
- Take delivery of the asset for the futures price and cover the short sale commitment.

Example: Futures reverse cash and carry arbitrage

Assume gold is priced at $900/oz., that the 1-year futures price is $945/oz., and that an investor can borrow or lend funds at 7%. Ignore transaction and storage costs. Calculate the profits from arbitrage.

Answer:

The futures price, according to the no-arbitrage principle, should be:

$$FP = \$900 \times 1.07 = \$963$$

Instead, it's trading at $945. That means the futures contract is underpriced, so we should conduct reverse cash and carry arbitrage by going long in the futures contract, shorting gold, and investing the short-sale proceeds.

Today			1 Year from Today	
Spot price of gold	$900			
Futures price of gold	$945			
Transaction	*Cash Flow*		*Transaction*	*Cash Flow*
Long futures	$0		Settle long position by buying gold	−$945
Short gold	+$900		Deliver gold to close short position	
Invest short-sale proceeds at 7%	−$900		Receive investment proceeds	+$963
Total cash flow	$0		Total cash flow = arbitrage profit	+$18

The riskless profit is equal to the loan proceeds less the futures contract payment, or $963 − $945 = $18.

 Professor's Note: It may help to remember "buy low, sell high." If the futures price is "too high," sell the future and buy the spot. If the futures price is "too low," buy the future and sell the spot.

©2013 Kaplan, Inc.

LOS 52.d: Describe monetary and nonmonetary benefits and costs associated with holding the underlying asset, and explain how they affect the futures price.

CFA® Program Curriculum, Volume 6, page 90

Any positive costs associated with storing or holding the asset in a cash and carry arbitrage will increase the no-arbitrage futures price because it is costly to buy, store, and deliver the asset. Many commodities have storage costs (e.g., corn, live cattle, and gold). There also is risk of loss from spoilage (corn), disease (cattle), and fire (oil or gas). Insuring or bearing these risks adds to the cost of holding these assets.

With *financial* assets there may be a significant benefit to holding the underlying asset, but there are no storage costs other than the opportunity cost of the funds. For example, holders of dividend-paying stocks, coupon bonds, and currencies will earn dividends, coupon payments, and interest, respectively. A monetary benefit from holding the asset will *decrease* the no-arbitrage futures price because the net cost of holding the asset is reduced.

There may also be non-monetary benefits from holding an asset in short supply. For a manufacturing firm, for example, this may be the benefit of having a ready supply so that a temporary shortage of their primary input will not disrupt their operations. The return from these non-monetary benefits is called the **convenience yield**.

Recall the pricing relation we developed for spot and forward prices when there is no cost or benefit to holding the underlying asset:

$$FP = S_0 \times (1 + R_f)^T$$

If we define the net cost of holding the asset as the costs net of any non-monetary benefits, we have:

net costs (NC) = storage costs − convenience yield

The generalized no-arbitrage futures price is now:

$$FP = S_0 \times (1 + R_f)^T + FV(NC)$$

where:
$FV(NC)$ = future value, at contract expiration, of the net costs of holding the asset

Positive net costs of holding the asset increase the futures price.

When the asset generates cash flows, the net costs are negative (a net benefit), and the futures price is decreased. We can define the net benefit of holding an asset as:

NB = yield on the asset + convenience yield

In that case, the no-arbitrage futures price is:

$$FP = S_0 \times (1 + R_f)^T - FV(NB)$$

where:
$FV(NB)$ = future value, at contract expiration, of the net benefits of holding the asset

The futures price will be *lower* when the dividend or coupon yield on the underlying asset is *higher* or when the non-monetary benefits of holding the asset are higher.

LOS 52.e: Describe backwardation and contango.

CFA® Program Curriculum, Volume 6, page 95

Backwardation refers to a situation where the futures price is below the spot price. For this to occur, there must be a significant benefit to holding the asset, either monetary or non-monetary. Backwardation might occur if there are benefits to holding the asset that offset the opportunity cost of holding the asset (the risk-free rate) and additional net holding costs.

Contango refers to a situation where the futures price is above the spot price. If there are no benefits to holding the asset (e.g., dividends, coupons, or convenience yield), the futures price will be $FP = S_0(1 + R_f)^T + FV(NC)$, and contango will occur because the futures price will be greater than the spot price.

LOS 52.f: Explain the relation between futures prices and expected spot prices.

CFA® Program Curriculum, Volume 6, page 95

If both parties to a futures transaction are hedging existing risk, the futures price may be equal to expected future spot prices. In markets of hedgers, the futures price might be temporarily above or below expected future spot prices, but it would be an unbiased predictor of future spot rates.

If we view a futures contract as a transfer of risk from an asset holder to the buyer of the contract, we would expect the futures price to be lower than the expected price in the future to compensate the future buyer for accepting asset price risk. This situation is called **normal backwardation**. If the futures price is greater than the expected spot price, it is called **normal contango**.

The most likely situation in financial markets is one in which futures prices are biased predictors of spot rates (i.e., futures prices do not equal expected spot prices) and, more specifically, futures prices are less than expected spot prices (normal backwardation).

 Professor's Note: In the previous LOS, we were comparing the current futures price and the current spot price. In this LOS, we're comparing the current futures price and the expected future spot price.

WARM-UP: EURODOLLAR, TREASURY BOND, STOCK INDEX, AND CURRENCY FUTURES

A **Eurodollar futures** contract is similar to a forward rate agreement to lend US$1,000,000 for three months beginning on the contract settlement date. Buying a Eurodollar futures contract is equivalent to lending money, while selling the contract is equivalent to borrowing money. Eurodollar futures are based on 90-day LIBOR, which is an add-on yield. By convention, however, the price quotes are calculated as (100 – annualized LIBOR in percent). These contracts settle in cash, and the minimum price change is one "tick," which is a price change of 0.0001 = 0.01%, or $25 per $1 million contract.

Treasury bond (T-bond) futures are traded for T-bonds with a maturity of 15 years or more. The contract is deliverable with a face value of $100,000. T-bond futures are quoted as a percent and fractions of 1% (measured in 1/32nds) of face value.

The short in a T-bond futures contract has the option to deliver any of several bonds, which will satisfy the delivery terms of the contract. This is called a delivery option and is valuable to the short. Each bond is given a conversion factor that is used to adjust the long's payment at delivery so the more valuable bonds receive a larger payment. These factors are multipliers for the futures price at settlement. The long pays the futures price at expiration multiplied by the conversion factor.

Stock index futures are based on the level of an equity index. The most popular stock index future is the S&P 500 Index Future that trades in Chicago. Settlement is in cash and is based on a multiplier of 250. The value of a contract is 250 times the level of the index stated in the contract. With an index level of 1000, the value of each contract is $250,000. Each index point in the futures price represents a gain or loss of $250 per contract. A smaller contract on the same index has a multiplier of 50.

The **currency futures market** is smaller in volume than the forward market described in the previous topic review. In the United States, currency contracts trade on the euro, Mexican peso, and yen, among others. Contracts are set in units of the foreign currency, and the price is stated in U.S. dollars per unit of foreign currency.

WARM-UP: TREASURY BILL FUTURES PRICING

Treasury bill (T-bill) futures contracts are based on a $1 million face value 90-day (13-week) T-bill, and they settle in cash. The price quotes are 100 minus the annualized discount in percent on the T-bills. For example, a price quote of 98.52 represents an annualized discount of 1.48%, an actual discount from face of 0.0148(90 / 360) = 0.0037, and a "delivery" price of (1 – 0.0037) × $1 million = $996,300. Each change of 0.01 in the price of a T-bill futures contract is worth $25. If you took a long position at 98.52 and the price fell to 98.50, your loss is $50 per contract.

T-bill futures are priced using the no-arbitrage principle. The key to understanding the pricing of T-bill futures is to recognize that the underlying asset is a 90-day T-bill *at the maturity of the futures contract.*

For example, suppose we want to price a 77-day T-bill future. If we bought a 167-day T-bill, we could deliver it in 77 days to satisfy a short position in a 90-day T-bill futures contract. In other words, in 77 days the 167-day T-bill will be a 90-day T-bill. If the borrowing cost of the 77-day loan to finance the purchase is equal to the gains from selling the T-bill in 77 days at the futures price, there is no arbitrage opportunity.

Because a T-bill is a pure discount security, there are no cash flow benefits to consider, and we have the familiar (by now) relation:

$$FP = S_0 \times (1 + R_f)^T$$

Remember, for an asset without cash flows or storage costs, the right side of this equation is the cost of buying and holding the asset for a period of T years. The holding costs are simply the interest costs at R_f over the term of the futures contract.

Example: Calculating the price of a T-bill futures contract

A 60-day T-bill is quoted at 6%, and a 150-day bill is priced at 6.5%. Calculate the no-arbitrage price of a 60-day future on a 90-day T-bill.

Answer:

The T-bill prices as a percentage of face value are:

$$B_{60} = 1 - \left(0.060 \times \frac{60}{360}\right) = 0.9900$$

$$B_{150} = 1 - \left(0.065 \times \frac{150}{360}\right) = 0.9729$$

The cost of holding the 150-day bill for 60 days is the 60-day risk-free rate, which is the yield (not the discount) on the 60-day bill. In effect, for 60 days we're borrowing 0.99 and repaying 1.00, so the yield is the 0.01 "interest" divided by the original amount:

$$60\text{-day risk-free yield} = \frac{1.00 - 0.99}{0.99} = 0.0101$$

The 150-day T-bill is, in effect, the spot asset, because in 60 days it will be a 90-day T-bill. We calculate the no-arbitrage futures price using the price of the 150-day bill:

$$FP = S_0 \times (1 + R_f)^T = 0.9729 \times 1.0101 = 0.9827$$

Note that we used the 60-day yield from the T-bill directly—we didn't annualize it to R_f because we needed the effective rate for a 60-day loan to calculate FP.

An alternative way to get the futures price is to divide the price of the deliverable bill by the price of one that matures at contract expiration. In this example, we get the same result:

$$FP = \frac{0.9729}{0.9900} = 0.9827$$

LOS 52.g: Describe the difficulties in pricing Eurodollar futures and creating a pure arbitrage opportunity.

CFA® Program Curriculum, Volume 6, page 104

Eurodollar Futures

With T-bills, the arbitrage strategy that creates the pricing bounds is straightforward. If we sell a 77-day future on a 90-day bill, and buy a 167-day bill, we have an arbitrage. In 77 days, the bill will be a 90-day bill and its value should be equal to that of the (identical) bill covered by the contract.

Eurodollar futures do not allow such an arbitrage. The Eurodollar futures are priced as a discount yield and LIBOR is subtracted from 100 to get the quote. Every basis point (0.01%) move in (annualized) 90-day LIBOR represents a $25 gain or loss on the contract, just as with the T-bill contract.

LIBOR, however, is actually an add-on yield, the rate you would earn on the face amount of a deposit. An add-on yield account for 167 days that pays $1 at maturity can be valued at expiration (77 days later) using 90-day LIBOR 77 days from now ($L90_{t=77}$) as:

$$\frac{\$1}{1 + L90_{t=77}}$$

Prior to contract expiration, it will be worth the present value of the expectation of this value. This is important because the value of the deposit will not change $25 for every one basis point change in expected 90-day LIBOR in 77 days as does the value of the futures contract. The asset value is not perfectly hedged by the contract value as it is with the T-bill contract. While no riskless arbitrage relation exists for the Eurodollar futures contract, it is still a very useful, and widely used, hedging instrument for exposure to LIBOR.

LOS 52.h: Calculate and interpret the prices of Treasury bond futures, stock index futures, and currency futures.

CFA® Program Curriculum, Volume 6, page 105

Treasury Bond Futures

To calculate the no-arbitrage futures price for a T-bond contract, we must take account of the value of the coupon payments in constructing an arbitrage relation. To adjust the futures price for the expected coupon payments, subtract the future value of the coupon payments (FVC) from the no-arbitrage futures price on a bond with no coupon payments.

$$FP = \text{bond price} \times (1 + R_f)^T - FVC$$

Because the cost to hold the asset is reduced by the asset cash flows, the futures price that insures that a cash-and-carry arbitrage would provide no profit is lower than without the cash flows. It is cheaper to buy, hold, and deliver the asset because of the coupon payments.

> **Example: Calculating the price of a Treasury bond futures contract**
>
> Calculate the no-arbitrage futures price of a 1.2 year futures contract calling for the delivery of a specific bond, a 7% T-bond with exactly 10 years remaining to maturity and a price of $1,040, when the annual risk-free rate is 5%.
>
> **Answer:**
>
> The semiannual coupon on a single, $1,000 face-value 7% bond is $35. A bondholder will receive one payment 0.5 years from now (when there are 0.7 years left to maturity of the futures contract) and one payment 1 year from now (when there are 0.2 years until maturity). The future value of these coupons at the end of 1.2 years (the expiration date) is:
>
> $$FVC = \left(\$35 \times 1.05^{0.7}\right) + \left(\$35 \times 1.05^{0.2}\right) = \$71.56$$
>
> The futures price is then:
>
> $$FP = \left(\$1,040 \times 1.05^{1.2}\right) - \$71.56 = \$1,031.15$$

The short on the T-bond contract has the option of delivering any one of a number of different bonds. Each bond is assigned a **conversion factor** (CF), a multiplier for the futures price on the "contract" bond, to adjust the settlement payment for delivery for higher or lower coupon bonds (with identical face value). The conversion factor is used to adjust the no-arbitrage price for the "cheapest to deliver" of all the permitted bonds.

The adjustment to the futures price we calculated is:

$$FP = \left[\text{bond price} \times (1 + R_f)^T - FVC \right] \times \frac{1}{CF}$$

Example: Pricing a T-Bond futures contract with a delivery option

Suppose the futures contract from the previous example allows many different bonds to be delivered. The conversion factor of the 10-year 7% T-bond is 1.13. Calculate the appropriate no-arbitrage futures price.

Answer:

The no-arbitrage futures price is now equal to the futures price calculated from the previous example, adjusted by the conversion factor of 1.13.

$$FP = \frac{\$1,031.15}{1.13} = \$912.52$$

An arbitrage involving the cheapest-to-deliver bond may not be risk-free because the cheapest-to-deliver bond may change during the term of the contract. This offers an advantage to an arbitrageur who is short the future because the short holds the delivery option, not the long.

Stock Futures

A futures contract on an individual stock may have expected dividend payments over the life of the futures contract. To price such a contract, we must adjust for the future value of the expected dividends. The no-arbitrage futures price adjusted for the future value of the dividends (FVD) or present value of the dividends (PVD) can be written as:

$$FP(\text{on an individual stock}) = S_0 \times (1 + R_f)^T - FVD = (S_0 - PVD) \times (1 + R_f)^T$$

Example: Calculating the price of a stock futures contract

Calculate the no-arbitrage price for a 120-day future on a stock that is currently priced at $30 and is expected to pay a dividend of $0.40 in 15 days and $0.40 in 105 days. Assume the annual risk-free rate is 5% and the yield curve is flat.

Study Session 16

Answer:

The first dividend can be reinvested for 105 days and the second for 15 days, so that:

$$FVD = \left(\$0.40 \times 1.05^{105/365}\right) + \left(\$0.40 \times 1.05^{15/365}\right) = \$0.8065$$

$$FP = \left(\$30.00 \times 1.05^{120/365}\right) - \$0.8065 = \$29.68$$

Equity Index Futures

For an index contract, rather than take the present value of each dividend on (possibly) hundreds of stocks, we can make the calculation as if the dividends are paid continuously (rather than at discrete times) at the continuous time equivalent of the dividend yield rate on the index.

Using continuous time discounting, we get a no-arbitrage futures price of:

$$FP(\text{on an equity index}) = S_0 \times e^{\left(R_f^c - \delta^c\right) \times T}$$

where:

R_f^c = continuously compounded risk-free rate

δ^c = continuously compounded dividend yield

Example: Calculating the value of a futures contract on an equity index

The current value of the Nasdaq index is 1,780. The continuous dividend yield is 1.1%, and the continuously compounded risk-free rate is 3.7%. Calculate the no-arbitrage futures price of an 87-day futures contract on the Nasdaq index.

Answer:

$$FP = 1,780 \times e^{(0.037 - 0.011) \times (87/365)} = 1,791.06$$

Currency Futures

The price of a currency future is derived exactly as we did for forwards. Recall that R_{FC} and R_{DC} are the risk-free returns in the two different currencies, S_0 is the spot exchange rate, and F_T is the price of a futures contract of T years duration, with both the spot and futures price quoted in units of domestic currency per one unit of foreign currency.

$$F_T \text{ (currency futures contract)} = S_0 \times \frac{\left(1 + R_{DC}\right)^T}{\left(1 + R_{FC}\right)^T}$$

where:
DC = domestic currency
FC = foreign currency

 Professor's Note: You should recognize this as the equation of interest rate parity from Study Session 4. The key to applying this formula correctly is to remember our numerator/denominator rule from Study Session 4: if the spot and forward quotes are in Currency A/Currency B, the Currency A interest rate should be on top and the Currency B interest rate should be on the bottom. For example, if S and F are in euro per Swiss franc, put the European interest rate on the top and the Swiss interest rate on the bottom.

The continuous time version with continuously compounded interest rates is:

$$F_T = \text{(currency futures contract)} = S_0 \times e^{\left(R_{DC}^c - R_{FC}^c\right) \times T}$$

> **Example: Calculate the price of a currency futures contract**
>
> The risk-free rates are 5% in U.S. dollars ($) and 6.5% in British pounds (£). The current spot exchange rate is $1.7301/£. Calculate the no-arbitrage $ price of a 6-month £ futures contract.
>
> **Answer:**
>
> With higher short-term rates in Great Britain, the £ is expected to depreciate relative to the $.
>
> $$F_{0.5} = \$1.7301 \times \frac{1.05^{0.5}}{1.065^{0.5}} = \$1.7179 \text{ per } £$$

 Professor's Note: For details about how to exploit arbitrage opportunities when interest rate parity doesn't hold by conducting covered interest arbitrage, see the topic area on economics.

KEY CONCEPTS

LOS 52.a
At expiration of a futures contract, the spot price must equal the futures price because the futures price has become the price today for delivery today, which is the same as the spot. Arbitrage will force the prices to be the same at contract expiration.

LOS 52.b
Because futures accounts are marked to market daily, the value after the margin deposit has been adjusted for the day's gains and losses in contract value is always zero. The futures price at any point in time is the price that makes the value of a new contract equal to zero.

The futures price is a no-arbitrage price. For a future of term T on an asset with no storage costs or expected cash flows over the term of the contract, the futures price is:

$$FP = S_0 \times (1 + R_f)^T$$

LOS 52.c
When interest rates and asset values are positively correlated, higher reinvestment rates for gains and lower borrowing costs to fund losses lead to a preference for the mark to market feature of futures, and higher prices for futures than forwards. If interest rates and asset values are negatively correlated, a preference to avoid the mark-to-market cash flows will lead to a higher price for the forward relative to the future.

LOS 52.d
Futures prices are affected by the monetary costs and benefits of holding the underlying asset. Storage and insurance are costs, while any cash flows from the asset are a benefit:

$$FP = S_0 \times (1 + R_f)^T + FV(NC)$$

There can also be non-monetary benefits from holding assets and having the use of them. This non-monetary return is termed a convenience yield. In that case, the no-arbitrage futures price is:

$$FP = S_0 \times (1 + R_f)^T - FV(NB)$$

LOS 52.e
Backwardation refers to a situation where the futures price is below the spot price. For this to occur, there must be a significant benefit to holding the asset, either monetary or non-monetary. Contango refers to a situation where the futures price is above the spot price.

LOS 52.f

If the futures market consists of a balance of short and long hedgers, futures prices may be unbiased predictors of future spot rates. If the market is characterized as a transfer of asset price risk from asset holders to futures buyers, futures prices may be less than expected future spot rates. This is called normal backwardation. If the futures price is greater than the expected spot price, it is called normal contango.

LOS 52.g

Eurodollar futures are priced as a discount yield, and LIBOR-based deposits are priced as an add-on yield. The result is that the deposit value is not perfectly hedged by the Eurodollar contract, so Eurodollar futures can't be priced using the standard no-arbitrage framework.

LOS 52.h

Futures prices on coupon bonds must be adjusted for the future value of the expected coupons. For any T-bond:

$$FP = \text{bond price} \times \left(1 + R_f\right)^T - FVC$$

T-bond futures prices must be adjusted to conform to the price for the bond that is cheapest to deliver, using its conversion factor (*CF*):

$$FP = \left[\text{bond price} \times \left(1 + R_f\right)^T - FVC\right] \times \frac{1}{CF}$$

Stock index futures prices are adjusted for the future value of expected dividends:

$$FP = S_0 \times \left(1 + R_f\right)^T - FVD$$

In continuous time with a dividend yield on the index of δ, the calculation is:

$$FP\left(\text{on an equity index}\right) = S_0 \times e^{\left(R_f^c - \delta^c\right) \times T}$$

The price of currency futures is calculated as:

$$F_T\left(\text{currency futures contract}\right) = S_0 \times \frac{\left(1 + R_{DC}\right)^T}{\left(1 + R_{FC}\right)^T}$$

where:
F and S are quoted in domestic currency per unit of foreign currency

In continuous time it is $F_T = \left(\text{currency futures contract}\right) = S_0 \times e^{\left(R_{DC}^c - R_{FC}^c\right) \times T}$

CONCEPT CHECKERS

1. To initiate an arbitrage trade if the futures contract is overpriced, the trader should:
    A. borrow at the risk-free rate, short the asset, and sell the futures.
    B. short the asset, invest at the risk-free rate, and buy the futures.
    C. borrow at the risk-free rate, buy the asset, and sell the futures.

2. Backwardation refers to a situation where:
    A. spot prices are above futures prices.
    B. spot prices are below futures prices.
    C. expected future spot prices are above futures prices.

3. Forward prices are likely to be lower than futures prices when:
    A. interest rates are low.
    B. asset values are positively correlated with short rates.
    C. asset values are negatively correlated with short rates.

4. A stock index is at 965, the continuous dividend yield is 1%, and the continuous risk-free rate is 3%. The fair value for a 270-day future is *closest* to:
    A. 978.42.
    B. 979.38.
    C. 984.30.

5. A 9% Treasury bond with exactly five years to maturity is priced at $1,135. If the current risk-free rate is 5%, the no-arbitrage price of a 1.4-year futures is *closest* to:
    A. $1,122.33.
    B. $1,188.87.
    C. $1,193.33.

6. An 8-year $1,000 par Treasury bond pays a 7% semiannual coupon. The bond has a conversion factor of 1.025. The risk-free rate is 6%, and the annual yield on the bond is 7%. The bond just made a coupon payment. The price of a 15-month futures contract on this bond is *closest* to:
    A. $979.00.
    B. $1,003.47.
    C. $1,049.32.

CHALLENGE PROBLEMS

7. The discrete risk-free rates are 5.25% in the United States and 6.25% in the U.K. The spot exchange rate is $1.6500 per pound and the market price of a 75-day futures contract on the pound is $1.6498. The appropriate arbitrage strategy is to go:
    A. short in the pound futures contract at the futures price of $1.6498.
    B. short in the pound in the spot market at the spot price of $1.6468.
    C. long in the pound futures contract at the futures price of $1.6446.

8. Assuming the futures contract is trading at the no-arbitrage price, for a futures contract on an equity index with a positive dividend yield:
    A. backwardation will occur if the dividend yield is greater than the risk-free rate.
    B. contango will occur if the dividend yield is greater than the risk-free rate.
    C. contango will occur if the risk-free rate is positive.

9. An analyst has been given the following currency exchange rates and interest rates.

Country	Yield	1-year Futures Rate (USD per CAD)	Spot Exchange Rate (USD per CAD)
U.S.	6%	---	---
Canada	8%	0.70	0.72

    The profitable arbitrage is to:
    A. sell the futures at the futures price of $0.7067.
    B. sell the futures at the futures price of $0.7336.
    C. buy the futures at the futures price of $0.7000.

10. Liz Potter is analyzing futures markets in the nation of Subservia for the first time. She has noted various historical time periods with a high volume of normal backwardation trading, and other periods of time with a high volume of normal contango trading. Currently, most of the trading volume evidences normal contango pricing. Futures prices in Subservia are *most likely*:
    A. biased predictors of expected spot rates.
    B. unbiased predictors of expected spot rates.
    C. lower than expected spot rates.

ANSWERS – CONCEPT CHECKERS

1. **C** If the actual futures price is too high relative to the no-arbitrage price, sell futures, borrow at the risk-free rate, and buy the asset that can be delivered against your futures sale. At futures maturity, deliver the asset, receive the futures price, repay debt, and keep the profit.

2. **A** Backwardation refers to a situation where spot prices are higher than futures prices—significant monetary benefits of the asset or a relatively high convenience yield can lead to this result.

3. **B** When interest rates and asset values are positively correlated, higher reinvestment rates for gains and lower borrowing costs to fund losses lead to a preference for the mark-to-market feature of futures, and higher prices for futures than forwards.

4. **B** $FP = 965 \times e^{(0.03-0.01) \times (270/365)} = 979.38$

5. **A** The semiannual coupon on a single, $1,000 face-value 9% bond is $45. A bondholder will receive one payment 0.5 years from now and one payment 1 year from now. The future value of these coupons at the end of 1.4 years (the expiration date):

    $$FVC = \left(\$45 \times 1.05^{0.9}\right) + \left(\$45 \times 1.05^{0.4}\right) = \$92.91$$

    The futures price is then:

    $$FP = \left(\$1,135 \times 1.05^{1.4}\right) - \$92.91 = \$1,122.33$$

6. **A** The semiannual coupon on a $1,000 face value, 7% bond is $35. The bond will make two more coupon payments before the futures contracts matures: one in 6 months (0.5 years), and another in 12 months (1 year). The future value of these coupons at the end of 15 months (1.25 years) is:

    $$FVC = \left(\$35 \times 1.06^{0.75}\right) + \left(\$35 \times 1.06^{0.25}\right) = \$72.08$$

    The bond is trading at par because the coupon rate is equal to the annual yield, so the spot price is $1,000. The futures price (including the conversion factor of 1.025) is:

    $$FP = \left[\left(\$1,000 \times 1.06^{1.25}\right) - \$72.08\right] \times \frac{1}{1.025}$$
    $$= \$1,003.47 \times \frac{1}{1.025}$$
    $$= \$979.00$$

ANSWERS – CHALLENGE PROBLEMS

7. **A** First calculate the continuously compounded rates:

$$R_{\$}^{c} = \ln(1.0525) = 0.0512 = 5.12\%$$
$$R_{£}^{c} = \ln(1.0625) = 0.0606 = 6.06\%$$

The no-arbitrage price of the contract is:

$$F_{75} = \$1.6500 \times e^{(0.0512-0.0606) \times (75/365)} = \$1.6468$$

Notice that you get the same (rounded) answer by using the discrete interest rates and the discrete formula:

$$F_{75} = \$1.6500 \times \frac{1.0525^{75/365}}{1.0625^{75/365}} = \$1.6468$$

The futures contract is overpriced because the market price of \$1.6498 is larger than the no arbitrage price of \$1.6468. Therefore, the appropriate arbitrage strategy is to short the futures contract and go long in the pound in the spot market.

8. **A** The price of a futures contract on an equity index is:

$$FP = S_0 \times e^{\left(R_f^c - \delta\right) \times T}$$

FP will be less than S_0 (i.e., backwardation will occur) if the dividend yield (δ) is greater than the continuously compounded risk-free rate $\left(R_f^c\right)$.

9. **C** Canada: no arbitrage F = 0.72 (1.06 / 1.08) = 0.7067. The futures rate of 0.70 is "too low" (0.70 < 0.7067), so we buy the future (borrow spot CAD at 8%). Remember: "buy low, sell high."

10. **A** Based on the evidence presented, the most likely situation in the financial markets is one in which futures prices are biased predictors of spot rates. During periods of normal backwardation, the futures price is less than the expected spot prices, suggesting the presence of a positive risk premium for futures buyers.

The following is a review of the Derivative Investments: Options, Swaps, and Interest Rate Credit Derivatives principles designed to address the learning outcome statements set forth by CFA Institute. This topic is also covered in:

OPTION MARKETS AND CONTRACTS

EXAM FOCUS

This topic review covers the pricing of options. You should know how to use the binomial model to price options on stocks, equity indices, fixed income securities, and caps and floors. You should also know how to use the Black-Scholes-Merton model to value equity options.

WARM-UP: PUT-CALL PARITY FOR EUROPEAN OPTIONS

A **fiduciary call** is a portfolio consisting of:

- A long position in a European call option with an exercise price of X that matures in T years on a stock (with a price at time t of S_t).
- A long position in a pure-discount riskless bond that pays X in T years.

The cost of a fiduciary call is the cost of the call (C_0) plus the cost of the bond (the present value of X). The payoff to a fiduciary call will be X if the call is out-of-the-money and S_T if the call is in-the-money, as shown in Figure 1.

Figure 1: Payoff to a Fiduciary Call

	$S_T \leq X$ *Call is out-of- or at-the-money*	$S_T > X$ *Call is in-the-money*
Long call payoff	0	$S_T - X$
Long bond payoff	X	X
Total payoff	X	S_T

A **protective put** is a portfolio consisting of:

- A long position in a European put option with an exercise price of X that matures in T years.
- A long position in the underlying stock.

The cost of a protective put is the cost of the put option (P_0) plus the cost of the stock (S_0). The payoff to a protective put is X if the put is in-the-money and S_T if the put is out-of-the-money.

Figure 2: Payoff to a Protective Put

	$S_T < X$ *Put is in-the-money*	$S_T \geq X$ *Put is out-of- or at-the-money*
Long put payoff	$X - S_T$	0
Long stock payoff	S_T	S_T
Total payoff	X	S_T

Notice that the payoff to a fiduciary call is the same as the payoff to a protective put. Arbitrage ensures that the two should have the same cost, which leads us to **put-call parity for European options**:

$$C_0 + \left[\frac{X}{(1+R_f)^T} \right] = P_0 + S_0$$

LOS 53.a: Calculate and interpret the prices of a synthetic call option, synthetic put option, synthetic bond, and synthetic underlying stock, and explain why an investor would want to create such instruments.

CFA® Program Curriculum, Volume 6, page 167

Put-call parity is very useful because it tells us how to create a synthetic position in any one of the four instruments by combining the other three. For example, if we solve for the value of the call option, we get:

$$C_0 = P_0 + S_0 - \left[\frac{X}{(1+R_f)^T} \right]$$

Interpret the plus signs as long positions in those securities and the negative sign as a short position. That means we can create a **synthetic European call option** by:

- Buying a European put option on the same stock with the same exercise price (*X*) and the same maturity (*T*).
- Buying the stock.
- Shorting (i.e., borrowing) the present value of *X* worth of a pure-discount riskless bond.

A **synthetic European put option** is formed by:

- Buying a European call option.
- Shorting the stock.
- Buying (i.e., investing in) the discount bond.

A **synthetic stock position** is formed by:

- Buying a European call option.
- Shorting (i.e., writing) a European put option.
- Buying (i.e., investing in) the discount bond.

A **synthetic pure-discount riskless bond** is created by:

- Buying a European put option.
- Buying the stock.
- Shorting (i.e., writing) a European call option.

Example: Using put-call parity

A 1-year call option on Cross Reef Inc. with an exercise price of $60 is trading for $8. The current stock price is $62. The risk-free rate is 4%. Calculate the price of the synthetic put option implied by put-call parity.

Answer:

According to put-call parity, the price of the synthetic put option is:

$$P_0 = C_0 - S_0 + \left[\frac{X}{(1+R_f)^T} \right]$$

$$= \$8 - \$62 + \frac{\$60}{1.04}$$

$$= \$3.69$$

There are two reasons investors might want to create synthetic positions in the securities:

1. To price options by using combinations of other instruments with known prices.

2. To earn arbitrage profits by exploiting relative mispricing among the four securities. If put-call parity doesn't hold, an arbitrage profit is available, as discussed in the next section.

USING PUT-CALL PARITY FOR ARBITRAGE

As with all arbitrage trades, you want to "buy low and sell high." If put-call parity doesn't hold (if the cost of a fiduciary call does not equal the cost of a protective put), then you buy (go long in) the underpriced position and sell (go short) in the overpriced position.

Example: Exploiting violations of put-call parity

The stock of ArbCity Inc. is trading for $75. A 3-month call option with an exercise price of $75 is selling for $4.50, and a 3-month put at $75 is selling for $3.80. The risk-free rate is 5%. Calculate the no-arbitrage price of the put option, and illustrate how the violation of put-call parity can be exploited to earn arbitrage profits.

Answer:

First, calculate what the put option should be selling for, given the other prices:

$$P_0 = C_0 - S_0 + \left[\frac{X}{(1+R_f)^T}\right] = \$4.50 - \$75.00 + \left[\frac{\$75}{1.05^{0.25}}\right]$$

$$= \$4.50 - \$75.00 + \$74.09 = \$3.59$$

Put-call parity doesn't hold because the actual market price of the put is $3.80, not the no-arbitrage price of $3.59:

$$C_0 + \left[\frac{X}{(1+R_f)^T}\right] \neq P_0 + S_0$$

$$\$4.50 + \$74.09 \neq \$3.80 + \$75$$

$$\$78.59 \neq \$78.80$$

The fiduciary call (the left side of the equation) is relatively underpriced, and the protective put (the right side) is relatively overpriced. Therefore, the arbitrage strategy is to buy the fiduciary call (and pay $78.59) and short-sell the protective put (and receive $78.80). The arbitrage profits from this trade are $78.80 – $78.59, or $0.21 per share. The net cash flow at maturity will be zero, so we've produced cash flow of $0.21 today with no cash outflow obligation in the future—that's what we call an arbitrage profit. The cash flows are shown in the following table.

| Today | | *Three Months from Today* | | | |
| | | *If Stock Price < $75* | | *If Stock Price > $75* | |
Transaction	*Cash Flow*	*Transaction*	*Cash Flow*	*Transaction*	*Cash Flow*
Long call option	–$4.50			Exercise call and buy stock	–$75.00
Invest in zero coupon bond	–$74.09	Proceeds from bond	+$75.00	Proceeds from bond	+$75.00
Cost of fiduciary call	–$78.59				
Short put option	+$3.80	Put exercised, obligation to buy stock	–$75.00		
Short stock	+$75.00	Settle short position by delivering stock	$0.00	Settle short position by delivering stock	$0.00
Proceeds from protective put	+$78.80				
Total cash flow = arbitrage profit	$0.21	Total cash flow	$0.00	Total cash flow	$0.00

In a frictionless market, these violations will be eliminated very quickly as arbitrageurs jump in to exploit them.

LOS 53.b: Calculate and interpret prices of interest rate options and options on assets using one- and two-period binomial models.

CFA® Program Curriculum, Volume 6, page 174

A **binomial model** is based on the idea that, over the next period, some value will change to one of two possible values (binomial). To construct a binomial model, we need to know the beginning asset value, the size of the two possible changes, and the probabilities of each of these changes occurring.

One-Period Binomial Model

Imagine that a share of stock is currently priced at $30. The size of the possible price changes, and the probability of these changes occurring, are as follows:

$$U = \text{size of up move} = 1.333$$

$$D = \text{size of down move} = \frac{1}{U} = \frac{1}{1.333} = 0.75$$

$$\pi_U = \text{probability of an up-move} = 0.55$$

$$\pi_D = \text{probability of a down-move} = 1 - \pi_U = 1 - 0.55 = 0.45$$

Note that the down-move factor is the reciprocal of the up-move factor, and the probability of an up-move is one minus the probability of a down-move. The one-period binomial tree for the stock is shown in Figure 3. The beginning stock value of $30 is to the left, and to the right are the two possible paths the stock can take, based on the starting point and the size of an up- and down-move. If the stock increases by a factor of 1.333 (a return of 33.3%), it ends up at $40.00; if it falls by a factor of 0.75 (a return of –25%), it ends up at $22.50.

Figure 3: One-Period Binomial Tree

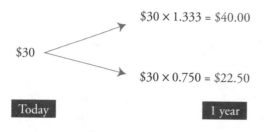

©2013 Kaplan, Inc.

The probabilities of an up-move and a down-move are calculated based on the size of the moves and the risk-free rate as:

$$\pi_U = \text{risk-neutral probability of an up-move} = \frac{1 + R_f - D}{U - D}$$

$$\pi_D = \text{risk-neutral probability of a down-move} = 1 - \pi_U$$

where:
R_f = risk-free rate
U = size of an up-move
D = size of a down-move

Professor's Note: These two probabilities are not the actual probability of an up- or down-move. They are risk-neutral pseudo probabilities that are consistent with investor risk-neutrality. The distinction between actual probabilities and risk-neutral probabilities is not part of the Level II curriculum, so you don't need to worry about it for the exam.

We can calculate the value of an option on the stock by:

- Calculating the payoff of the option at maturity in both the up-move and down-move states.
- Calculating the expected value of the option in one year as the probability-weighted average of the payoffs in each state.
- Discounting the expected value back to today at the risk-free rate.

Example: Calculating call option value with a one-period binomial tree

Use the binomial tree in Figure 3 to calculate the value today of a one-year call option on the stock with an exercise price of $30. Assume the risk-free rate is 7%, the current value of the stock is $30, and the size of an up-move is 1.333.

Answer:

First, we have to calculate the parameters—the size of a down-move and the probabilities:

$$D = \text{size of a down-move} = \frac{1}{U} = \frac{1}{1.333} = 0.75$$

$$\pi_U = \text{risk-neutral probability of an up-move} = \frac{1 + 0.07 - 0.75}{1.333 - 0.75} = 0.55$$

$$\pi_D = \text{risk-neutral probability of a down-move} = 1 - 0.55 = 0.45$$

Next, determine the payoffs to the option in each state. If the stock moves up to $40, a call option with an exercise price of $30 will pay off $10. If the stock moves down to $22.50, the call option will be worthless. The option payoffs are illustrated in the following figure.

Let the stock values for the up-move and down-move be S_1^+ and S_1^- and for the call values, C_1^+ and C_1^-.

One-Period Call Option with X = $30

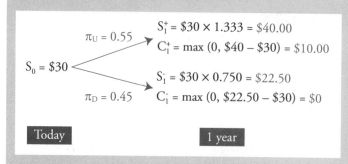

The expected value of the option in one period is:

E(call option value in 1 year) = ($10 × 0.55) + ($0 × 0.45) = $5.50

The value of the option today, discounted at the risk-free rate of 7%, is:

$$C_0 = \frac{\$5.50}{1.07} = \$5.14$$

We can use the same basic framework to **value a one-period put option**. The only difference is that the payoff to the put option will be different from the call payoffs.

Example: Valuing a one-period put option on a stock

Use the information in the previous two examples to calculate the value of a put option on the stock with an exercise price of $30.

Answer:

If the stock moves up to $40, a put option with an exercise price of $30 will be worthless. If the stock moves down to $22.50, the put option will be worth $7.50.

The risk-neutral probabilities are 0.55 and 0.45 for an up- and down-move, respectively. The expected value of the put option in one period is:

E(put option value in 1 year) = ($0 × 0.55) + ($7.50 × 0.45) = $3.375

The value of the option today, discounted at the risk-free rate of 7%, is:

$$P_0 = \frac{\$3.375}{1.07} = \$3.154$$

ARBITRAGE WITH A ONE-PERIOD BINOMIAL MODEL

If the price of the one-period $30 call option from the previous example is not $5.14, there is an arbitrage opportunity. This arbitrage will involve the call option and shares of stock. If the option is overpriced, we would short the option and buy a fractional share of the stock for each option we shorted. If the option is underpriced, we would purchase the option and short a fractional share of stock for each option share.

The fractional share of stock in the arbitrage trade (commonly referred to as the hedge ratio) for each option traded is derived from the option's delta, which is calculated in the one-period model as:

$$\text{Delta} = \frac{C_1^+ - C_1^-}{S_1^+ - S_1^-}$$

The concept of delta will be explained more fully later on in this topic review. For now, the main point is that delta provides you with the information required to calculate a hedge ratio.

> **Example: Calculating arbitrage profit**
>
> Assume the option in the previous example is actually selling for $6.50. Illustrate how this arbitrage opportunity can be exploited to earn an arbitrage profit. Assume we trade 100 call options.

Answer:

Because the option is overpriced, we will short 100 options and purchase a certain number of shares of stock determined by the hedge ratio:

$$\text{Delta} = \frac{\$10 - \$0}{\$40 - \$22.50} = 0.5714 \text{ shares per option}$$

total shares of stock to purchase $= 100 \times 0.5714 = 57.14$

A portfolio that is long 57.14 shares of stock at $30 per share and short 100 calls at $6.50 per call has a net cost of:

net portfolio cost = $(57.14 \times \$30) - (100 \times \$6.50) = \$1,064$

The values of this portfolio at maturity if the stock moves up to $40 or down to $22.50 are:

portfolio value in up-move = $(57.14 \times \$40) - (100 \times \$10) = \$1,286$

portfolio value in down-move = $(57.14 \times \$22.50) - (100 \times \$0) = \$1,286$

The return on the portfolio in either state is:

$$\text{portfolio return} = \frac{\$1,286}{\$1,064} - 1 = 0.209 = 20.9\%$$

This is a true arbitrage opportunity! We've created a portfolio that earns a return of 20.9% no matter what happens next period. That means it's risk free. The actual risk-free rate in the market is 7%. The profitable arbitrage trades are to:

- Borrow $1,064 at 7% for one year. In one year, we'll owe $1,064 \times 1.07 = $1,138.48.
- Buy the hedged portfolio for $1,064.
- In one year, collect the $1,286, repay the loan at $1,138.48, and keep the arbitrage profits of $147.52.

Two-Period Binomial Model

Valuing an option using a **two-period binomial model** requires a little more work, but the basic steps are still the same:

- Calculate the stock values at the end of two periods (there are three possible outcomes because an up-then-down move gets you to the same place as a down-then-up move).
- Calculate three possible option payoffs at the end of two periods.
- Calculate the expected option values at the end of two periods (t = 2) using the up- and down-move probabilities.
- Discount the expected option values (t = 2) back one period at the risk-free rate to find the option values at the end of the first period (t = 1).

- Calculate the expected option value at the end of one period (t = 1) using up- and down-move probabilities.
- Discount the expected option value at the end of one period (t = 1) back one period at the risk-free rate to find the option value today.

Let's look at an example to illustrate the steps involved.

Example: Valuing a call option on a stock with a two-period model

Suppose you have a stock currently priced at $50, and a two-period European call option is available with a strike price of $45. The size of an up-move is 1.25. The risk-free rate per period is 7%. Compute the value of the call option using a two-period binomial model.

Answer:

First compute the size and probability of up- and down-moves, and then compute the theoretical value of the stock in each period:

$$D = \frac{1}{1.25} = 0.80$$

$$\pi_U = \frac{1.07 - 0.80}{1.25 - 0.80} = 0.6$$

$$\pi_D = 1 - 0.6 = 0.4$$

The two-period binomial tree for the stock is shown in the following figure.

Two-Period Binomial Tree for Stock Price

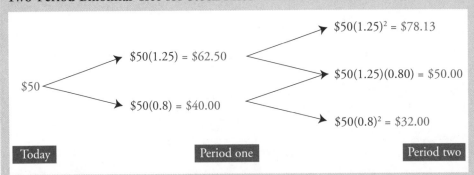

We know the value of the option at expiration in each state is equal to max (0, stock price – exercise price):

$$C_2^{++} = \max\left(0, \$78.13 - \$45.00\right) = \$33.13$$

$$C_2^{-+} = \max\left(0, \$50.00 - \$45.00\right) = \$5.00$$

$$C_2^{+-} = \max\left(0, \$50.00 - \$45.00\right) = \$5.00$$

We will approach this problem by using the single-period binomial model and applying this model to each period. Using this method, we can compute the value of the call option in the up-state in period one as follows:

$$C_1^{+} = \frac{\left(\pi_U \times C_2^{++}\right) + \left(\pi_D \times C_2^{+-}\right)}{1 + R_f} = \frac{E\left(\text{call option value}\right)}{1 + R_f}$$

$$= \frac{\left(0.6 \times \$33.13\right) + \left(0.4 \times \$5.00\right)}{1.07}$$

$$= \frac{\$21.88}{1.07} = \$20.45$$

The value of the call in the down-state in period one is computed as:

$$C_1^{-} = \frac{\left(\pi_U \times C_2^{-+}\right) + \left(\pi_D \times C_2^{--}\right)}{1 + R_f} = \frac{E\left(\text{call option value}\right)}{1 + R_f}$$

$$= \frac{\left(0.6 \times \$5.00\right) + \left(0.4 \times \$0.00\right)}{1.07}$$

$$= \frac{\$3.00}{1.07} = \$2.80$$

Now we know the value of the option in both the up-state (C_1^+) and the down-state (C_1^-) one period from now. To get the value of the option today, we simply apply our methodology one more time. Therefore, bringing (C_1^+) and (C_1^-) back one more period to the present, the *value of the call option today* is:

$$C_0 = \frac{\left(\pi_U \times C^+\right) + \left(\pi_D \times C^-\right)}{1+R_f} = \frac{E\left(\text{call option value}\right)}{1+R_f}$$

$$= \frac{\left(0.6 \times \$20.45\right) + \left(0.4 \times \$2.80\right)}{1.07}$$

$$= \frac{\$13.39}{1.07} = \$12.51$$

The binomial tree for the call option is shown below.

Two-Period Binomial Tree for Option Price

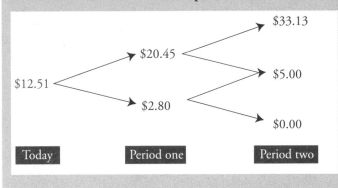

WARM-UP: BINOMIAL INTEREST RATE TREES

An interest rate model makes assumptions about interest rate volatility along with a set of paths that interest rates may follow over time. This set of possible interest rate paths is referred to as an interest rate tree. The set of possible interest rate paths that are used to value bonds with a binomial model is called a **binomial interest rate tree**. The diagram in Figure 4 depicts a two-period binomial interest rate tree.

Figure 4: Two-Period Binomial Interest Rate Tree

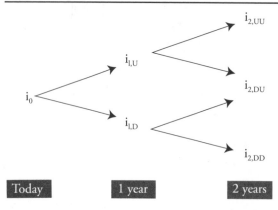

A node is a point in time when interest rates can take one of two possible paths: an upper path, U, or a lower path, D. Now consider the node on the right side of the diagram where the interest rate $i_{2,DU}$ appears. This is the rate that will occur if the initial rate, i_0, follows the lower path from Node 0 to Node 1 to become $i_{1,D}$, then follows the upper of the two possible paths to Node 2, where it takes on the value $i_{2,DU}$. At the risk of stating the obvious, the upper path from a given node leads to a higher rate than the lower path. Notice also that an upward move followed by a downward move gets us to the same place on the tree as a down-then-up move, so $i_{2,DU} = i_{2,UD}$.

The interest rates at each node in this interest rate tree are one-period forward rates corresponding to the nodal period. Beyond the root of the tree, there is more than one one-period forward rate for each nodal period (i.e., at year 1, we have two 1-year forward rates, $i_{1,U}$ and $i_{1,D}$). The relationship among the set of rates associated with each individual nodal period is a function of the interest rate volatility assumption of the model being employed to generate the tree. A change in the assumed interest rate volatility will affect the rates at every node in the tree.

The construction of an interest rate tree, binomial or otherwise, is a tedious process, one you will not have to do on the exam. In practice, the interest rate tree is usually generated using specialized computer software. There is one underlying rule governing the construction of an interest rate tree—*the values for on-the-run issues generated using an interest rate tree should prohibit arbitrage opportunities*. This means that the value of an on-the-run issue produced by the interest tree must equal the value of its market price. It should be noted that in accomplishing this, the interest rate tree must maintain the interest rate volatility assumption of the underlying model.

Options on Fixed Income Securities

To price options on bonds, we need a binomial interest rate tree that shows possible future one-period interest rates. We can then calculate the payoffs for a bond or an interest rate option using the interest rate outcomes. Once we have payments for each node, we can take the probability-weighted present value of these payments, just as we did in the stock call example.

The difference is that the risk-free rate is not constant. Interest rate trees are straight-forward when interest rates are fixed. Because the tree gives us a series of one-period rates, we need to discount the payments by one or more of these rates, depending on how many periods the payoff is out (to the right) on the tree.

There are three basic steps to valuing an option on a fixed-income instrument using a binomial tree:

Step 1: Price the bond at each node using the projected interest rates.
Step 2: Calculate the intrinsic value of the option at each node at the maturity of the option.
Step 3: Bring the terminal option values determined in Step 2 back to today.

The risk-neutral probability of an up- and down-move in the interest rate tree is always 50%, unlike with equity options, where the probabilities depend on the risk-free rate and the size of the up- and down-moves.

Example: Calculating value of a call option on a coupon bond

You want to value a European call option with two years to expiration and a strike price (call price) of $100.00. The underlying bond is a $100 par value, 7% annual coupon bond with three years to maturity. The following figure represents the first two years of the binomial tree for valuing the underlying bond.

Fill in the missing data in the binomial tree, and calculate the value of the European call option (note that because the option is European, it can only be exercised at the end of year 2).

Two-Period Binomial Tree for Option Price

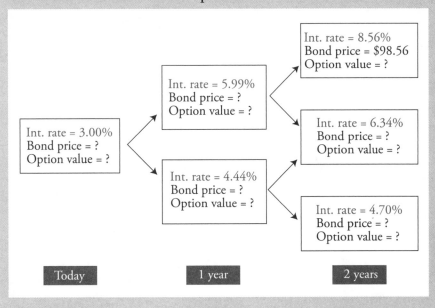

Answer:

Step 1: *Calculate the bond prices* at each node using the backward induction methodology.

At the middle node in year 2, the price is $100.62. You can calculate this using your calculator by noting that at the end of year 2, the bond has one year left to maturity:

$$N = 1; I/Y = 6.34; PMT = 7; FV = 100; CPT \rightarrow PV = 100.62$$

At the bottom node in year 2, the price is $102.20, calculated as follows:

$$N = 1; I/Y = 4.70; PMT = 7; FV = 100; CPT \rightarrow PV = 102.20$$

At the top node in year 1, the price is $100.57, calculated as follows:

$$\text{price} = \frac{\left[(\$98.56 + \$7) \times 0.5\right] + \left[(\$100.62 + \$7) \times 0.5\right]}{1.0599} = \$100.57$$

Note: Don't forget the coupon payment ($7 in this example).

At the bottom node in year 1, the price is $103.80, calculated as follows:

$$\text{price} = \frac{\left[(\$100.62 + \$7) \times 0.5\right] + \left[(\$102.20 + \$7) \times 0.5\right]}{1.0444} = \$103.80$$

Today the price is $106.00, calculated as follows:

$$\text{price} = \frac{\left[(\$100.57 + \$7) \times 0.5\right] + \left[(\$103.80 + \$7) \times 0.5\right]}{1.03} = \$106.00$$

As shown here, the price at a given node is the average of the present value of the cash flows associated with the two nodes that "feed" into the given node. The discount rate applied is the prevailing interest rate at the given node. Note that because this is a European option, you really only need the bond prices at the maturity date of the option (end of year 2) if you are given the arbitrage-free interest rate tree. However, it is good practice to compute all the bond prices.

Step 2: *Determine the intrinsic value of the option* at maturity in each node. For example, the intrinsic value of the option at the bottom node at the end of year 2 is $2.20 (= $102.20 – $100.00). At the top node in year 2, the intrinsic value of the option is zero because the bond price is less than the call price.

Step 3: Calculate the option value at each node prior to expiration. For example, at the top node for year 1, the option price is $0.29, calculated as follows:

$$\text{price} = \frac{(\$0.00 \times 0.5) + (\$0.62 \times 0.5)}{1.0599} = \$0.29$$

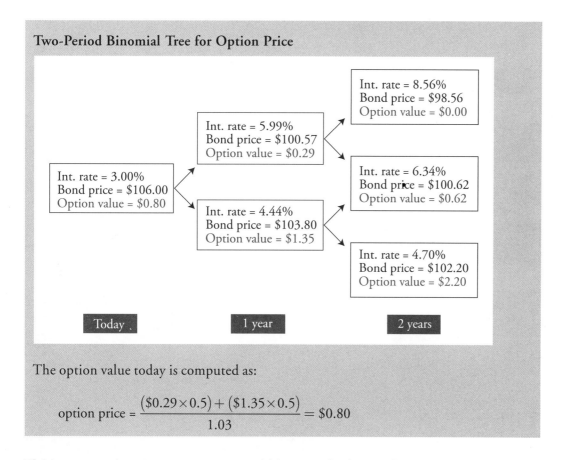

Two-Period Binomial Tree for Option Price

Int. rate = 8.56%
Bond price = $98.56
Option value = $0.00

Int. rate = 5.99%
Bond price = $100.57
Option value = $0.29

Int. rate = 3.00%
Bond price = $106.00
Option value = $0.80

Int. rate = 6.34%
Bond price = $100.62
Option value = $0.62

Int. rate = 4.44%
Bond price = $103.80
Option value = $1.35

Int. rate = 4.70%
Bond price = $102.20
Option value = $2.20

Today   1 year   2 years

The option value today is computed as:

$$\text{option price} = \frac{(\$0.29 \times 0.5) + (\$1.35 \times 0.5)}{1.03} = \$0.80$$

If this were an American option, we would have to check to make sure that the option value at each node was not less than the intrinsic value of the option. For example, the lowest node at year 1 shows an option value of $1.35. However, the intrinsic value of the option at that node (if the option were exercisable) is $3.80 (= 103.80 − 100). Hence, if the option were American style, arbitrage would be possible (i.e., buy the option for $1.35, and exercise immediately for a profit of $3.80 − $1.35 = $2.45). Challenge Problem 15 at the end of this topic asks you to value this same option assuming it is an American option. If you need to value an American option, the value at any node will be equal to the greater of the present value of the future payoffs or the current intrinsic value.

Options on Interest Rates: Caps and Floors

Interest rate caps and floors are bundles of European-style options on interest rates, called **caplets** and **floorlets**. The value of a cap or floor is the sum of the values of the individual caplets or floorlets.

An interest rate caplet is similar to a call option on interest rates. The value of a caplet is:

$$\text{expiration value of caplet} = \frac{\max\ \{0,\ [(\text{one-year rate} - \text{cap rate}) \times \text{notional principal}]\}}{1 + \text{one-year rate}}$$

Likewise, an interest rate floorlet is equivalent to a put option on interest rates:

$$\text{expiration value of floorlet} = \frac{\max\ \{0,\ [(\text{floor rate} - \text{one-year rate}) \times \text{notional principal}]\}}{1 + \text{one-year rate}}$$

To value a cap (floor), you simply value each caplet (floorlet) and then add them up.

 Professor's Note: Caps and floors pay in arrears: the payoff occurs one period after the expiration of the cap or floor. The basics of caps and floors are discussed in the next topic review.

Example: Valuing an interest rate cap

Suppose you purchase a 2-year cap with annual reset and a strike rate of 5.0% on a notional principal of $25 million. This represents a bundle containing a 1-year option and a 2-year option. Fill in the binomial trees, and calculate the value of the 2-year caplet, the 1-year caplet, and the 2-year cap.

2-Year Caplet

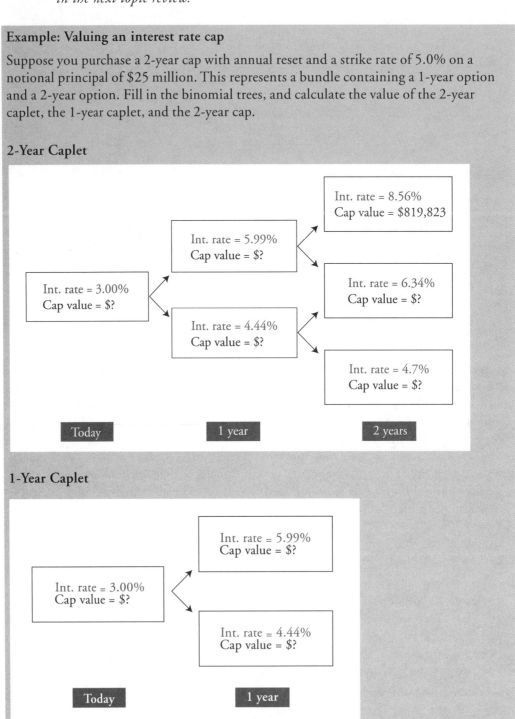

©2013 Kaplan, Inc.

Step 1: Replicate the previous procedure for the 1-year caplet.

Value of a 1-Year Caplet

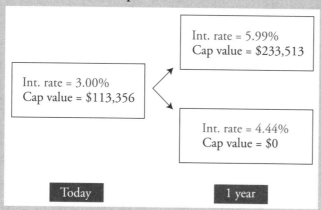

Int. rate = 5.99%
Cap value = $233,513

Int. rate = 3.00%
Cap value = $113,356

Int. rate = 4.44%
Cap value = $0

Today   1 year

For example, the caplet value in the top box at the end of year 1 was determined as follows:

$$\text{caplet value} = \frac{\max\left\{0,\left[\$25,000,000\times(0.0599-0.0500)\right]\right\}}{1.0599} = \frac{\$247,500}{1.0599} = \$233,513$$

$$\text{1-year caplet} = \frac{(\$233,513\times0.5)+(\$0\times0.5)}{1.0300} = \$113,356$$

Step 2: Add the two values together to get the value of the cap:

value of 2-year cap = $113,356 + $333,094 = $446,450

The procedure for the valuation of a floor is identical, except that the expiration value of each floorlet is:

$$\text{expiration value of floorlet} = \frac{\max\left\{0,\left[(\text{floor rate}-\text{one-year rate})\times\text{notional principal}\right]\right\}}{1+\text{one-year rate}}$$

LOS 53.c: Explain and evaluate the assumptions underlying the Black–Scholes–Merton model.

CFA® Program Curriculum, Volume 6, page 191

The **Black-Scholes-Merton** (BSM) **model** values options in continuous time and is derived from the same no-arbitrage assumption used to value options with the binomial model. In the binomial model, the hedge portfolio is riskless over the next period, and the no-arbitrage option price is the one that guarantees that the hedge portfolio will yield the risk-free rate. To derive the BSM model, an "instantaneously" riskless portfolio (one that is riskless over the next instant) is used to solve for the option price based on the same logic.

The assumptions underlying the Black-Scholes-Merton model and the model's limitations are shown in Figure 5.

Figure 5: Black-Scholes-Merton Model Assumptions and Limitations

Assumption	Limitation
*The price of the underlying asset follows a lognormal distribution.**	Not applicable.
The (continuous) risk-free rate is constant and known.	The BSM model is not useful for pricing options on bond prices and interest rates. In those cases, interest rate volatility is a key factor in determining the value of the option.
The volatility of the underlying asset is constant and known. Option values depend on the volatility of the price of the underlying asset or interest rate.	In practice, the volatility is not known and must be estimated. The bigger problem is that volatility is often not constant over time and the BSM model is not useful in these situations. More sophisticated models have been developed to handle this issue; but fortunately for us, they are not part of the Level II curriculum.
Markets are "frictionless." There are no taxes, no transactions costs, and no restrictions on short sales or the use of short-sale proceeds.	Model is less realistic and less useful. More sophisticated models developed to address this issue are outside the scope of the Level II curriculum.
The underlying asset has no cash flow, such as dividends or coupon payments.	The BSM model can be easily altered if we relax the assumption of no cash flows on the underlying asset.
The options valued are European options, which can only be exercised at maturity.	The model does not correctly price American options. Binomial option pricing models are more appropriate for pricing American options.

*A variable that is lognormally distributed is one where the logs of the values (in this case, the continuous returns) are normally distributed. It has a minimum of zero and conforms to prices better than the normal distribution (which would produce negative prices).

 Professor's Note: While we don't anticipate candidates being asked to use the BSM model to actually value a call option, we have presented the formula anyway so that you are familiar with it and will recognize it if you see it.

The formula for the BSM model is:

$$C_0 = \left[S_0 \times N(d_1)\right] - \left[X \times e^{-R_f^c \times T} \times N(d_2)\right]$$

where:

$$d_1 = \frac{\ln\left(\dfrac{S_0}{X}\right) + \left[R_f^c + \left(0.5 \times \sigma^2\right)\right] \times T}{\sigma \times \sqrt{T}}$$

$$d_2 = d_1 - \left(\sigma \times \sqrt{T}\right)$$

T = time to maturity (as % of a 365-day year)

S_0 = asset price

X = exercise price

R_f^c = continuously compounded risk-free rate

σ = volatility of continuously compounded returns on the stock

$N(\bullet)$ = cumulative normal probability of value in parentheses

We've given you the formulas for the call value. However, remember that you can always use put-call parity (with continuously compounded interest rates) to calculate the put value:

$$P_0 = C_0 - S_0 + \left(X \times e^{-R_f^c \times T}\right)$$

LOS 53.d: Explain how an option price, as represented by the Black–Scholes–Merton model, is affected by a change in the value of each of the inputs.

CFA® Program Curriculum, Volume 6, page 195

There are five inputs to the BSM model: asset price, exercise price, asset price volatility, time to expiration, and the risk-free rate. The relationship between each input and the option price (except exercise price) is captured by a sensitivity factor designated as one of the "Greeks."

Delta describes the relationship between asset price and option price. Call option deltas are positive because as the underlying asset price increases, call option value also increases. In contrast, the delta of a put option is negative because the put value falls as the asset price increases. See Figure 6.

Figure 6: Call and Put Delta: The Relationship Between Option Price and Underlying Asset Price

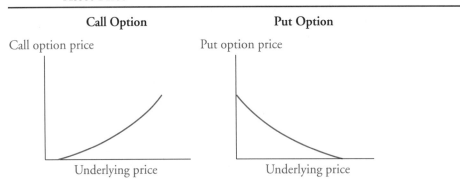

Vega measures the sensitivity of the option price to changes in the volatility of returns on the underlying asset, as shown in Figure 7. Both call and put options are more valuable, all else equal, the higher the volatility, so vega is positive for calls and puts. Volatility is a very important input to any option valuation model (and *vega is an important sensitivity measure*) because option values can be very sensitive to changes in volatility. Also, vega gets larger as the option gets closer to being at-the-money.

Figure 7: Call and Put Vega: The Relationship Between Option Price and Volatility

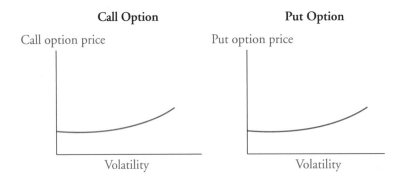

Rho measures the sensitivity of the option price to changes in the risk-free rate, as shown in Figure 8. The price of a European call or put option does not change much if we use different inputs for the risk-free rate, so rho is not a very important sensitivity measure. Call options increase in value as the risk-free rate increases (the rho of a call option is positive). You can see this by looking at the BSM model. As the risk-free rate increases, the second term decreases, and the value of the call option increases.

$$C_0 = \left[S_0 \times N(d_1) \right] - \left[X \times e^{-R_f^c \times T} \times N(d_2) \right]$$

Put options decrease in value as the risk-free rate increases (the rho of a put option is negative).

Figure 8: Call and Put Rho: The Relationship Between Option Price and the Risk-Free Rate

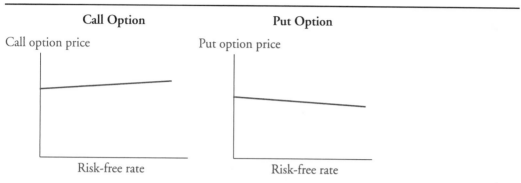

Theta measures the sensitivity of the option price to the passage of time, as shown in Figure 9. As time passes and a call option approaches maturity, its value declines, all else equal. This is called "time decay." This is also true for *most* put options (deep in-the-money put options close to maturity may actually increase in value as time passes). Notice that because it is described as a measure of "time decay," *theta is less than zero*: as time passes and the option approaches the maturity date, its value decreases.

Figure 9: Call and Put Theta: The Relationship Between Option Price and the Time to Expiration

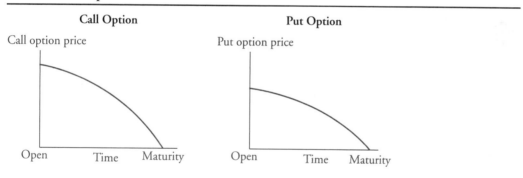

Professor's Note: The statement that theta is less than zero is counterintuitive to many Level II candidates because there are two ways to state the relationship between time and option value:

- *The relationship between option value and **time to maturity** is positive: all else equal, shorter maturity options have lower values.*
- *The relationship between option value and the **passage of time** is negative: all else equal, as time passes and the option approaches maturity, the value of the option decays.*

The key to understanding why theta is less than zero is to recognize that it is capturing the intuition of the second statement.

Figure 10: Direction of BSM European Option Prices for a Change in the Five Model Inputs

Sensitivity Factor ("Greek")	Input	Calls	Puts
Delta	Asset price (S)	Positively related Delta > 0	Negatively related Delta < 0
Vega	Volatility (σ)	Positively related Vega > 0	Positively related Vega > 0
Rho	Risk-free rate (r)	Positively related Rho > 0	Negatively related Rho < 0
Theta	Time to expiration (T)	Value → $0 as call → maturity Theta < 0	Value usually →$0 as put → maturity Theta <0*
	Exercise price (X)	Negatively related	Positively related

* There is an exception to the general rule that European put option thetas are negative. The put value may increase as the option approaches maturity if the option is deep in-the-money and close to maturity.

 Professor's Note: Remember that these relationships are for European options on assets with no cash flows (e.g., dividends).

LOS 53.e: Explain the delta of an option, and demonstrate how it is used in dynamic hedging.

CFA® Program Curriculum, Volume 6, page 195

Delta is the change in the price of an option for a one-unit change in the price of the underlying security:

$$\text{delta}_{\text{call}} = \frac{C_1 - C_0}{S_1 - S_0} = \frac{\Delta C}{\Delta S}$$

where:
ΔC = *change in* the price of the call over a short time interval
ΔS = *change in* the price of the underlying stock over a short time interval

> **Example: Calculating delta**
>
> During the last ten minutes of trading, call options on Commart Inc. common stock have risen from $1.20 to $1.60. Shares of the underlying stock have risen from $51.30 to $52.05 during the same time interval. Calculate the delta of the call option.

Answer:

The call option delta can be estimated as:

$$\text{delta}_{call} = \frac{\$1.60 - \$1.20}{\$52.05 - \$51.30} = \frac{\$0.40}{\$0.75} = 0.533$$

Usually, however, we want to estimate the change in the value of the call given the change in the value of the stock and the option's delta. The BSM model helps us out because a call option's delta for small changes in S is $N(d_1)$ from the BSM model, while a put option's delta is $N(d_1) - 1$. However, because we're now using a linear relationship to estimate a non-linear change, the following relationships are only approximations:

$$\Delta C \approx N(d_1) \times \Delta S$$

$$\Delta P \approx [N(d_1) - 1] \times \Delta S$$

where:
ΔP = change in put price

The approximations are close for small changes in stock price, but the approximation gets worse as the ΔS gets larger. Notice that $N(d_1)$ is less than 1, so $N(d_1) - 1$, the put option delta, must be less than zero.

Example: Calculating change in option price

$N(d_1)$ from the BSM model is 0.58. Calculate the approximate change in the price of a call option on the stock if the stock price increased by $0.75.

Answer:

$$\Delta C \approx 0.58 \times \$0.75 = \$0.435$$

Interpreting Delta

The payoff diagrams for a European call option before and at expiration are shown in Figure 11. The "at expiration" diagram represents the call option's intrinsic value:

- Zero when the call option is out-of-the-money.
- Stock price minus exercise price when the option is in-the-money.

Prior to expiration, the option also has time value, so the prior-to-expiration curve lies above the at-expiration diagram by the amount of the time value.

Figure 11: European Call Option Payoff Diagrams

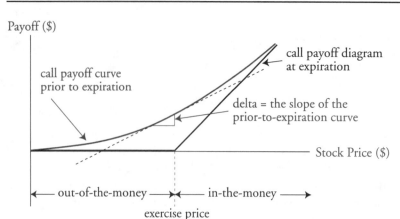

The slope of the "prior-to-expiration" curve is the change in call price per unit change in stock price. Sound familiar? It should—that's also the definition of delta. That means *delta is the slope of the prior-to-expiration curve.* The delta of the put option is also the slope of the *prior-to-expiration* put curve.

Let's review some basic facts about call and put options:

- The value of a call option increases as the underlying stock price increases. This means the delta of a call option is greater than zero.
- The value of a put option decreases as the underlying stock price increases. This means the delta of a put option is less than zero.

We know that an option's delta is equal to the *slope* of the prior-to-expiration curve (see Figure 11). You can see that the slope of the call option curve is positive. This is consistent with our observations. You can also see why delta approximates the change in call price only for small changes in stock price. As the change in stock price increases, the dotted line gets further away from the "call payoff curve prior to expiration."

Take a closer look at Figure 11. When the call option is deep out-of-the-money, the slope of the at-expiration curve is close to zero, which means the call delta will be close to zero. For deep out-of-the-money call options (when the stock price is low), the option price does not change much for a given change in the underlying stock. When the call option is in-the-money (when the stock price is high), the slope of the at-expiration curve is close to 45 degrees, which means the call delta is close to one. In this case, the call option price will change almost one-for-one given a change in the underlying stock price.

The bottom line is that *a call option's delta will increase from 0 to +1 as stock price increases.*

For a put option, the put delta is close to zero when the put is out-of-the-money (when the stock price is high). When the put option is in-the-money (the stock price is close to zero), the put delta is close to −1.

The bottom line is that *a put option's delta will increase from −1 to 0 as stock price increases.*

> **Example: Interpreting call and put deltas**
>
> The current stock price of Com.Net is $60. Call and put options with exercise prices of $100 are currently trading. Compare and contrast the change in the price of each option for a $1 increase in the stock price.
>
> **Answer:**
>
> The call option is deep out-of-the-money and must have a delta close to zero. The put option is deep in-the-money and will have a delta close to –1. Therefore, the value of the out-of-the-money call will *increase* by a very small amount, and the value of the in-the-money put will *decrease* by close to $1. The put price will fall by more than the call price will increase.

We can also consider what happens to delta as the option approaches maturity, even if the underlying stock price doesn't change. The effects for call and put options are different and depend on whether the options are in or out-of-the-money.

Remember that a call option delta is between 0 and 1. If the call option is:

- **Out-of-the-money** (stock price is less than exercise price), the call delta **moves closer to 0** as time passes, assuming the underlying stock price doesn't change.
- **In-the-money** (stock price is greater than exercise price), the call delta **moves closer to 1** as time passes, assuming the underlying stock price doesn't change.

Remember that a put option delta is between –1 and 0. If the put option is:

- **Out-of-the-money** (stock price is greater than exercise price), the put delta **moves closer to 0** as time passes, assuming the underlying stock price doesn't change.
- **In-the-money** (stock price is less than exercise price), the put delta **moves closer to –1** as time passes, assuming the underlying stock price doesn't change.

Dynamic Hedging

The goal of a **delta-neutral portfolio (or delta-neutral hedge)** is to combine a long position in a stock with a short position in a call option so that the value of the portfolio does not change when the value of the stock changes. A delta-neutral portfolio is a risk-free combination of a long stock position and short calls where the number of calls to sell is equal to:

$$\textit{number of options} \text{ needed to delta hedge} = \frac{\textit{number of shares} \text{ hedged}}{\textit{delta} \text{ of call option}}$$

Delta neutral portfolios are best illustrated with an example.

Example: Hedging with call options, part 1

You own 60,000 shares of Arthurall Company common stock that is currently selling for $50. A call option on Arthurall with a strike price of $50 is selling at $4 and has a delta of 0.60. Determine the number of call options necessary to create a delta-neutral hedge.

Answer:

In order to determine the number of call options necessary to hedge against instantaneous movements in Arthurall's stock price, we calculate:

$$\text{number of options needed to delta hedge} = \frac{60,000}{0.60}$$

$$= 100,000 \text{ options, or } 1,000 \text{ option contracts}$$

Because we are long the stock, we need to short the options.

Example: Hedging with call options, part 2

Calculate the effect on portfolio value of a $1.00 increase in the price of Arthurall stock.

Answer:

Assuming the price of Arthurall stock increased instantly by $1.00, the value of the call options would decrease by $0.60 because you're *short* (or have sold) the call option contracts. Recall that when you're short an asset, as the underlying price rises, you lose, and when the price falls, you win. Therefore, the net impact of the price change would be zero:

total value of increase in stock position 60,000 × $1 = $60,000

total value of decrease in option position = 100,000 × –$0.60 = –$60,000

total change in portfolio value = $60,000 – $60,000 = $0

A key consideration in delta-neutral hedging is that the delta-neutral position only holds for very small changes in the value of the underlying stock. Hence, the delta-neutral portfolio must be continually rebalanced to maintain the hedge. This is called a dynamic hedge. As the underlying stock price changes, so does the delta of the call option. As the delta changes, the number of calls that need to be sold to maintain a risk-free position changes. Hence, continuously maintaining a delta-neutral position can be very costly in terms of transaction costs.

LOS 53.f: Explain the gamma effect on an option's delta and how gamma can affect a delta hedge.

CFA® Program Curriculum, Volume 6, page 198

Gamma measures the *rate of change in delta* as the underlying stock price changes. Call and put options on the same underlying asset with the same exercise price and time to maturity will have equal gammas. Long positions in calls and puts have positive gammas.

For example, a gamma of 0.04 implies that a $1.00 increase in the price of the underlying stock will cause a call option's delta to increase by 0.04, making the call option more sensitive to changes in the stock price.

Gamma is largest when a call or put option is at-the-money and close to expiration, as shown in Figure 12. In other words, delta is very sensitive to changes in the underlying stock price when call and put options are at-the-money and close to expiration. If the option is either deep in- or deep out-of-the-money, gamma approaches zero because changes in the underlying stock price do not have a significant effect on delta.

Figure 12: Call and Put Gamma

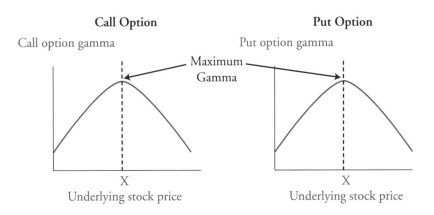

In this context, gamma can be viewed as a measure of how poorly a dynamic hedge will perform when it is not rebalanced in response to a change in the asset price. Hedges with at-the-money options will have higher gammas, and consequently small changes in stock price will lead to large changes in delta and frequent rebalancing. In contrast, hedges with deep in- or deep out-of-the money options will have small gammas, and stock price changes will not affect the delta of the hedge significantly. This lowers rebalancing and transaction costs.

LOS 53.g: Explain the effect of the underlying asset's cash flows on the price of an option.

CFA® Program Curriculum, Volume 6, page 203

All else equal, the existence of cash flows on the underlying asset will:

- Decrease the value of a call option.
- Increase the value of a put option.

For example, consider an option on a stock that generates cash flows (i.e., dividends). The Gordon growth model (expected return equals dividend yield plus growth rate) suggests that a higher dividend yield for the stock will reduce the growth rate in the stock price (all else equal). Because option values are based on the change in the stock price, and a lower stock price decreases the value of a call and increases the value of a put, dividends will make call options less valuable and put options more valuable, all else equal.

We can see this by looking at the BSM Model. Just as we subtracted the present value of cash flows expected to occur during the option's life from the asset price when valuing forwards and futures, we can subtract it from the asset price in the BSM model. Because the BSM model is in continuous time, in practice $S_0 \times e^{-\delta T}$ is substituted for S_0 in the BSM formula, where δ is equal to the continuously compounded rate of dividend payment. Over time, the asset price is discounted by a greater amount to account for the greater amount of cash flows.

We can also revise put-call parity for options on underlying assets with cash flows by adjusting S for the present value of the cash flows (PVCF):

$$C_0 + \frac{X}{\left(1 + R_F\right)^T} = P_0 + \left(S_0 - PVCF\right)$$

LOS 53.h: Determine the historical and implied volatilities of an underlying asset.

CFA® Program Curriculum, Volume 6, page 205

The steps in computing **historical volatility** for use as an input in the BSM continuous-time options pricing model are:

Step 1: Convert a time series of N prices to returns:

$$R_i = \frac{P_i - P_{i-1}}{P_{i-1}}, \, i = 1 \text{ to } N$$

Step 2: Convert the returns to continuously compounded returns:

$$R_i^c = \ln\left(1 + R_i\right), \, i = 1 \text{ to } N$$

Step 3: Calculate the variance and standard deviation of the continuously compounded returns:

$$\sigma^2 = \frac{\displaystyle\sum_{i=1}^{N}\left(R_i^c - \overline{R}_i^c\right)^2}{N - 1}$$

$$\sigma = \sqrt{\sigma^2}$$

Implied volatility is the value for standard deviation of continuously compounded rates of return that is "implied" by the market price of the option. Of the five inputs into the BSM model, four are observable: stock price, exercise price, risk-free rate, and time to maturity. If we use these four inputs in the formula and set the BSM formula equal to market price, we can solve for the volatility that satisfies the equality.

Volatility enters into the equation in a complex way, and there is no closed-form solution for the volatility that will satisfy the equation. Rather, it must be found by iteration (trial and error). If a value for volatility makes the value of a call calculated from the BSM model lower than the market price, it needs to be increased (and vice versa) until the model value equals market price (remember, option value and volatility are positively related).

LOS 53.i: Demonstrate how put–call parity for options on forwards (or futures) is established.

CFA® Program Curriculum, Volume 6, page 208

 Professor's Note: The LOS says to "demonstrate," which means to derive put-call parity, but don't let this intimidate you. We're going to use a no-arbitrage argument by forming two portfolios that have the same payoffs and arguing that they must have the same cost to prevent arbitrage.

We will use the method of equivalent portfolios to get an equality that establishes **put-call parity for options on forwards (or futures)**.

The first portfolio (Portfolio 1) consists of:

- A call option on the forward contract with an exercise price of X that matures at time T on a forward contract at F_T (the price of a forward on the asset at time T).
- A pure-discount bond that pays $(X – F_T)$ at time T.

The cost of this portfolio is:

$$C_0 + \frac{X - F_T}{\left(1 + R_f\right)^T}$$

The payoff for this portfolio at expiration will depend on whether the option is in- or out-of-the-money; the bond will always pay $(X – F_T)$:

- If the call option is out-of-the-money ($S_T \leq X$), the payoff will just be from the bond $(X – F_T)$:

    Portfolio 1 payoff if call is out-of-the-money = $X – F_T$

- If the call option is in-the-money ($S_T > X$), the option will be worth $(S_T – X)$, and the bond will be worth $(X – F_T)$:

    Portfolio 1 payoff if call is in-the-money = $(S_T – X) + (X – F_T) = S_T – F_T$

An equivalent portfolio (Portfolio 2) can be constructed by combining:

- A put option on the forward contract with an exercise price of X.
- A long position in the forward contract.

The cost of this portfolio is P_0, the cost of the option, because it's costless to enter into a forward contract.

The payoff for this portfolio at the expiration will depend on whether the option is in- or out-of-the-money; the long position in the forward contract will always pay $(S_T - F_T)$:

- If the put option is in-the-money $(S_T < X)$, the option will be worth $(X - S_T)$, and the forward contract will be worth $(S_T - F_T)$:

$$\text{Portfolio 2 payoff if put is in-the-money} = (X - S_T) + (S_T - F_T) = X - F_T$$

- If the put option is out-of-the-money $(S_T \geq X)$, the payoff will just be from the forward contract:

$$\text{Portfolio 2 payoff if put is out-of-the-money} = S_T - F_T$$

Because the call is in-the-money when the put is out-of-the-money, and vice versa, the payoffs to the two positions are identical. A portfolio that is long one and short the other must have a zero up-front cost, which means the cost of Portfolio 1 must equal the cost of Portfolio 2:

$$C_0 + \frac{X - F_T}{\left(1 + R_f\right)^T} = P_0$$

or

$$C_0 + \frac{X - F_T}{\left(1 + R_f\right)^T} - P_0 = 0$$

or

$$F_T = \left(C_0 - P_0\right)\left(1 + R_f\right)^T + X$$

For an asset with no cash flows or storage costs, the forward contract price is:

$$F_T = S_0 \left(1 + R_f\right)^T$$

Substituting in the parity relation, we get the familiar put-call parity for all options:

$$C_0 + \frac{X}{\left(1 + R_f\right)^T} = P_0 + S_0$$

 Professor's Note: Because the forward price in relation to the spot price is $F_T = S_0 (1+R)^T$, it is also true that $S_0 = F_T / (1+R_f)^T$. Replacing S_0 with $F_T / (1+R_f)^T$ in option put-call parity produces a parity relation for options on forwards that includes the price of the forward at time 0. If you need only the forward parity relation, this would be a quicker way to get it than the equivalent portfolio derivation.

LOS 53.j: Compare American and European options on forwards and futures, and identify the appropriate pricing model for European options.

CFA® Program Curriculum, Volume 6, page 212

There is a benefit to early exercise of *options on futures* when they are deep in-the-money. Exercising the option (either a put or call) early will generate cash from the mark to market. This cash can earn interest, while the futures position will gain or lose from movements in the futures price. These price movements between early exercise and option expiration will mirror those of the deep in-the-money option. For this reason, *American options on futures are more valuable than comparable European options.*

Because there is no mark to market on forwards, early exercise does not accelerate the payment of any gains. With no reason for early exercise, *the value of American and European options on forwards are the same.*

THE BLACK MODEL

The Black model can be used to price European options on forwards and futures:

$$C_0 = e^{-R_f^c \times T} \left[F_T \times N(d_1) - X \times N(d_2) \right]$$

$$d_1 = \frac{\ln\left(F_T / X \right) + \left(\frac{\sigma^2}{2} \right) T}{\sigma \sqrt{T}}$$

$$d_2 = d_1 - \sigma \sqrt{T}$$

where:
σ = standard deviation of returns on the futures contract
F_T = futures price

The Black model is just the BSM model with $e^{-R_f^c \times T} F_T$ substituted for S_0. In fact, the price of a European option on a forward or futures contract is equal to an option on the underlying asset if the options and the forward/futures contract expire at the same time.

KEY CONCEPTS

LOS 53.a

Put-call parity for European options says that the cost of a fiduciary call must be equal to the cost of a protective put:

$$C_0 + \frac{X}{(1+R_f)^T} = P_0 + S_0$$

Put-call parity can be used to demonstrate how to create synthetic instruments. For example, a synthetic call is a long put, a long stock position, and a short position in a pure-discount risk-free bond. Investors create these synthetic securities to exploit relative mispricing among the four securities.

LOS 53.b

To value an option using a two-period binomial model:

- Calculate the stock values at the end of two periods (there are three possible outcomes because an up-down move gets you to the same place as a down-up move).
- Calculate option payoffs at the end of two periods.
- Calculate expected values at the end of two periods using the up- and down-move probabilities. Discount these back one period at the risk-free rate to find the option values at the end of the first period.
- Calculate expected value at the end of period one using the up- and down-move probabilities. Discount this back one period to find the option value today.

To price an option on a bond using a binomial tree, (1) price the bond at each node using projected interest rates, (2) calculate the intrinsic value of the option at each node at maturity of the option, and (3) calculate the value of the option today.

The value of an interest rate cap or floor is the sum of the values of the individual caplets or floorlets.

$$\text{expiration value of caplet} = \frac{\max\left\{0, \left[(\text{one-year rate} - \text{cap rate}) \times \text{notional principal}\right]\right\}}{1 + \text{one-year rate}}$$

$$\text{expiration value of floorlet} = \frac{\max\left\{0, \left[(\text{floor rate} - \text{one-year rate}) \times \text{notional principal}\right]\right\}}{1 + \text{one-year rate}}$$

As the period covered by a binomial model is divided into arbitrarily small, discrete time periods, the model results converge to those of the continuous-time model.

LOS 53.c

The assumptions underlying the BSM model are:

- The price of the underlying asset follows a lognormal distribution.
- The (continuous) risk-free rate is constant and known.
- The volatility of the underlying asset is constant and known.
- Markets are "frictionless."
- The underlying asset generates no cash flows.
- The options are European.

Because of the limitations of its assumptions, the BSM model is not appropriate:

- For valuing interest rate options because the assumption of a constant and known risk-free rate is violated.
- When the assumption of a constant and known volatility of underlying asset returns is violated.
- In cases where taxes and transactions costs are significant.
- For pricing American options.

LOS 53.d

Direction of BSM option price for an increase in the five model inputs:

Sensitivity Factor ("Greek")	Input	Calls	Puts
Delta	Asset price (S)	Positively related Delta > 0	Negatively related Delta < 0
Vega	Volatility (σ)	Positively related Vega > 0	Positively related Vega > 0
Rho	Risk-free rate (r)	Positively related Rho > 0	Negatively related Rho < 0
Theta	Time to expiration (T)	Value → $0 as call → maturity Theta < 0	Value usually →$0 as put → maturity Theta <0
	Exercise price (X)	Negatively related	Positively related

LOS 53.e

Delta is the change in the price of an option for a one-unit change in the price of the underlying security. $N(d_1)$ from the BSM model is the delta of a call option for small changes in stock price. $N(d_1) - 1$ is the put option delta. The following approximations are reasonably accurate for small changes in stock price:

$$\Delta C \approx N(d_1) \times \Delta S$$

$$\Delta P \approx [N(d_1) - 1] \times \Delta S$$

Call option deltas will increase from zero to +1 as the underlying asset price increases. Put option deltas will increase from −1 to zero as the stock price increases.

The goal of a delta-neutral portfolio (or delta-neutral hedge) is to combine a long position in a stock with a short position in a call option so that the portfolio value does not change when the stock value changes.

A delta-neutral portfolio is a risk-free combination of a long stock position and short calls where the number of calls to sell is equal to number of shares hedged divided by delta of the call option.

A key consideration in delta-neutral hedging is that the delta-neutral position only holds for very small changes in the value of the underlying stock. Hence, the delta-neutral portfolio must be continually rebalanced to maintain the hedge. This is called a dynamic hedge. As the underlying stock price changes, so does the delta of the call option.

LOS 53.f
Gamma measures how much delta changes as the asset price changes and, thus, offers a measure of how poorly a fixed hedge will perform as the price of the underlying asset changes.

LOS 53.g
Cash flows on the underlying asset decrease call prices and increase put prices.

LOS 53.h
Historical volatility is the standard deviation of a past series of continuously compounded returns for the underlying asset. Implied volatility is the volatility that, when used in the Black-Scholes formula, produces the current market price of the option.

LOS 53.i
Put-call parity for options on forwards and futures is as follows:

$$C_0 + \frac{X - F_T}{(1 + R_f)^T} = P_0$$

American options on futures are more valuable than European options because early exercise provides mark to market funds on the futures, which can earn interest. Americans and European options on forward contracts are equivalent because there is no mark to market.

LOS 53.j
There is a benefit to early exercise of options on futures when they are deep in the money. Exercising the option (either a put or call) early will generate cash from the mark to market. This cash can earn interest, while the futures position will gain or lose from movements in the futures price. These price movements between early exercise and option expiration will mirror those of the deep in the money option. For this reason, *American options on futures are more valuable than comparable European options.*

Because there is no mark to market on forwards, early exercise does not accelerate the payment of any gains. With no reason for early exercise, *the value of American and European options on forwards are the same.*

The Black model can be used to price European options on forwards and futures.

CONCEPT CHECKERS

1. Compare the call and put prices on a stock that doesn't pay a dividend (NODIV) with comparable call and put prices on another stock (DIV) that is the same in all respects except it pays a dividend. Which of the following statements is *most accurate*? Price of:
    A. DIV call will be less than price of NODIV call.
    B. NODIV call will equal price of NODIV put.
    C. NODIV put will be greater than price of DIV put.

2. In a one-period binomial model, the hedge ratio is 0.35. To construct a riskless arbitrage involving 1,000 call options if the option is "overpriced," what is the appropriate portfolio?

	Calls	Stock
A.	Buy 1,000 options	Short 350 shares
B.	Buy 1,000 options	Short 2,857 shares
C.	Sell 1,000 options	Buy 350 shares

3. Which of the following statements is *least accurate*? The value of a:
    A. call option will decrease as the risk-free rate increases.
    B. put option will decrease as the exercise price decreases.
    C. call option will decrease as the underlying stock price decreases.

4. Which of the following inputs into the Black-Scholes-Merton model is *least likely* to have opposite effects on put and call prices?
    A. Volatility.
    B. Strike price.
    C. Risk-free rate.

5. Which of the following statements is *most accurate*? Implied volatility:
    A. requires market prices.
    B. requires a series of past returns.
    C. is equal for otherwise identical options with different maturities.

6. The delta of a put is –0.43. If the price of the underlying stock increases from $40 to $44, the price of the put option:
    A. increases by approximately 4.3%.
    B. decreases by approximately 4.3%.
    C. decreases by approximately $1.72.

7. A synthetic European put option is created by:
    A. buying the discount bond, buying the call option, and short-selling the stock.
    B. buying the call option, short-selling the discount bond, and short-selling the stock.
    C. short-selling the stock, buying the discount bond, and selling the call option.

CHALLENGE PROBLEMS

8. Which of the following is not an assumption underlying the Black-Scholes-Merton options pricing model?
   A. The underlying asset does not generate cash flows.
   B. Continuously compounded returns are lognormally distributed.
   C. The option can only be exercised at maturity.

Use the following information to answer Questions 9 and 10.

Stock ABC trades for $60 and has 1-year call and put options written on it with an exercise price of $60. ABC pays no dividends. The annual standard deviation estimate is 10%, and the continuously compounded risk-free rate is 5%. The value of the call is $4.09.

Chefron Inc. common stock trades for $60 and has a 1-year call option written on it with an exercise price of $60. The annual standard deviation estimate is 10%, the continuous dividend yield is 1.4%, and the continuously compounded risk-free rate is 5%.

9. The value of the put on ABC stock is *closest* to:
   A. $1.16.
   B. $3.28.
   C. $4.09.

10. The value of the call on Chefron stock is *closest* to:
    A. $3.51.
    B. $4.16.
    C. $5.61.

11. The stock price is currently $80. The stock price will move up by 15% or down by a certain amount each period. The value of a two-period call option with an exercise price of $62 if the risk-free rate is 4% per period is *closest* to:
    A. $19.17.
    B. $22.99.
    C. $27.11.

12. The current stock price of Heart, Inc., is $80. Call and put options with exercise prices of $50 and 15 days to maturity are currently trading. Which of these scenarios is *most likely* to occur if the stock price falls by $1?

	Call value	Put value
A.	Decrease by $0.94	Increase by $0.08
B.	Decrease by $0.76	Increase by $0.96
C.	Decrease by $0.07	Increase by $0.89

13. A put option with an exercise price of $45 is trading for $3.50. The current stock price is $45. What is the *most likely* effect on the option's delta and gamma if the stock price increases to $50?
    A. Both delta and gamma will increase.
    B. Both delta and gamma will decrease.
    C. One will increase and the other will decrease.

14. From the Black-Scholes-Merton model, $N(d_1) = 0.42$ for a 3-month call option on Panorama Electronics common stock. If the stock price falls by $1.00, the price of the call option will:
    A. decrease by less than the increase in the price of the put option.
    B. increase by more than the decrease in the price of the put option.
    C. decrease by the same amount as the increase in the price of the put option.

15. An analyst has calculated the value of a 2-year European call option to be $0.80. The strike price of the option is 100.00, and the underlying asset is a 7% annual coupon bond with three years to maturity. The two-period binomial tree for the European option is shown in the figure.

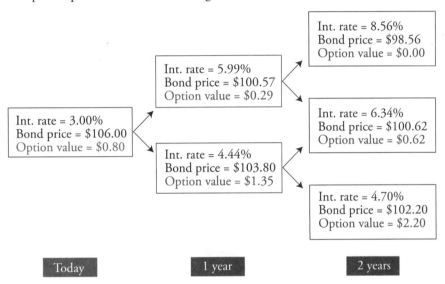

The value of the comparable 2-year American call option (exercisable after 1 year) with a strike price of 100.00 is *closest* to:
    A. $1.56.
    B. $2.12.
    C. $3.80.

16. A CFA candidate is trying to recall the derivation of the put-call parity formula for forwards. When correctly derived, the formula is best expressed as:
    A. $F_t = (C_o - P_o)(1 + R_f)^T + X$
    B. $F_t = S_o(1 + R_f)^T - P_o - C_o$
    C. $F_t = S_o(1 + R_f)^T - P_o + C_o$

ANSWERS – CONCEPT CHECKERS

1. **A**   The dividend affects option values because if you own the option, you do not have access to the dividend. Hence, if the firm pays a dividend during the life of the option, this must be considered in the valuation formula. Dividends decrease the value of call options all else equal, and they increase the value of put options.

2. **C**   The hedge ratio in a one-period model is equivalent to a delta, the ratio of the call price change to the stock price change. We will sell the 1,000 calls because they are overpriced. Buying 350 shares of stock will produce a riskless hedge. The payoff at expiration will return more than the riskless rate on the net cost of the hedge portfolio. Borrowing to finance the hedge portfolio and earning a higher rate than the borrowing rate produces arbitrage profits.

3. **A**   The value of a call and the risk-free rate are positively related, so as the risk-free rate increases, the value of the call will increase.

4. **A**   Volatility increases will increase the values of both puts and calls.

5. **A**   Implied volatility is the volatility that produces market option prices from the BSM model. Its use for pricing options is limited because it is based on market prices. Past returns are used to calculate historical volatility.

6. **C**   The put option will decrease in value as the underlying stock price increases: $-0.43 \times \$4 = -\$1.72$.

7. **A**   A synthetic European put option is formed by:
    - Buying a European call option.
    - Short-selling the stock.
    - Buying (i.e., investing) the present value of the exercise price worth of a pure-discount riskless bond.

ANSWERS – CHALLENGE PROBLEMS

8. **B**   To derive the BSM model, we need to assume no arbitrage is possible, and:
    - Asset price (not returns) follows a lognormal distribution.
    - The (continuous) risk-free rate is constant.
    - The volatility of the underlying asset is constant.
    - Markets are "frictionless."
    - The asset has no cash flows.
    - The options are European (i.e., they can only be exercised at maturity).

9. **A**   According to put/call parity, the put's value is:

$$P_0 = C_0 - S_0 + \left(X \times e^{-R_c^f \times T} \right) = \$4.09 - \$60.00 + \left[\$60.00 \times e^{-(0.05 \times 1.0)} \right] = \$1.16$$

10. **A**   ABC and Chefron stock are identical in all respects except Chefron pays a dividend. Therefore, the call option on Chefron stock must be worth less than the call on ABC (i.e., less than $4.09). $3.51 is the only possible answer.

11. **B** Stock Tree

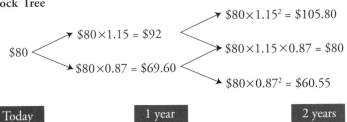

Option Tree

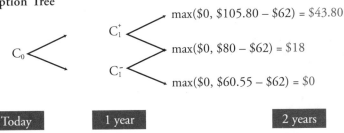

$U = 1.15$

$D = \dfrac{1}{1.15} = 0.87$

$\pi_U = \dfrac{1.04 - 0.87}{1.15 - 0.87} = 0.61$

$\pi_D = 1 - 0.61 = 0.39$

$C_2^{++} = \$43.80$

$C_2^{++} = C_2^{-+} = \$18.00$

$C_2^{--} = \$0$

$C_1^{+} = \dfrac{(0.61 \times \$43.80) + (0.39 \times \$18.00)}{1.04} = \$32.44$

$C_1^{-} = \dfrac{(0.61 \times \$18.00) + (0.39 \times \$0)}{1.04} = \$10.56$

$C_0 = \dfrac{(0.61 \times \$32.44) + (0.39 \times \$10.56)}{1.04} = \$22.99$

12. **A**   The call option is deep in-the-money and must have a delta close to one. The put option is deep out-of-the-money and will have a delta close to zero. Therefore, the value of the in-the-money call will decrease by close to $1 (e.g., $0.94), and the value of the out-of-the-money put will increase by a much smaller amount (e.g., $0.08). The call price will fall by more than the put price will increase.

13. **C**   The put option is currently at-the-money because its exercise price is equal to the stock price of $45. As stock price increases, the put option's delta (which is less than zero) will increase toward zero, becoming less negative. The put option's gamma, which measures the rate of change in delta as the stock price changes, is at a maximum when the option is at-the-money. Therefore, as the option moves out-of-the-money, its gamma will fall.

14. **A**   If $\Delta S = -\$1.00$, $\Delta C \approx 0.42 \times (-1.00) = -\$0.42$, and $\Delta P \approx (0.42 - 1) \times (-1.00) = \$0.58$.

   The call will decrease by less ($0.42) than the increase in the price of the put ($0.58).

15. **B**   In the upper node at the end of the first year the European option is worth $0.29, but the American option can be exercised and a profit of $0.57 realized (the difference between the bond price of $100.57 and the exercise price of $100).

   In the lower node at the end of the first year, the European option is worth $1.35, but the American option can be exercised and a profit of $3.80 realized (the difference between the bond price of $103.80 and the exercise price of $100).

   The value of the American option today is therefore:

   $$\text{American option price} = \frac{(\$0.57 \times 0.5) + (\$3.80 \times 0.5)}{1.03} = \$2.12$$

16. **A**   The put/call parity formula for a forward is $F_t = (C_o - P_o)(1 + R_f)^T + X$. Note that you do not need to know the derivation—just the relationship to put-call parity.

SWAP MARKETS AND CONTRACTS

Study Session 17

EXAM FOCUS

The main focus of this topic review is describing swaps in terms of equivalent securities. You should understand how to construct and value these equivalent portfolios and the comparable swaps prior to and at expiration. In addition, pay close attention to swaptions.

LOS 54.a: Distinguish between the pricing and valuation of swaps.

CFA® Program Curriculum, Volume 6, page 254

The distinction between the price and the value of a swap is the same one we made for forward contracts. Remember that the price of a forward contract is the forward rate that yields a zero value for the contract at initiation. After contract initiation, as rates or prices change, the contract will likely have value to either the long or the short.

Consider a plain vanilla interest rate swap. One party agrees to pay floating (borrow at the floating rate) and receive fixed (lend at a fixed rate). At initiation of the swap, the fixed rate is selected so that the present value of the floating-rate payments is equal to the present value of the fixed-rate payments, which means the swap value is zero to both parties. This fixed rate is called the **swap rate**. Determining the swap rate is equivalent to "pricing" the swap.

As short-term rates (and expected future short-term rates) change over the term of the swap, the value of the swap to one of the parties will be positive. The swap position is an asset to that party.

If interest rates increase, the fixed-rate payer in the swap will receive higher than expected floating-rate payments. The swap will have a positive value for the fixed-rate payer. The swap contract value to the other party (receive fixed, pay floating) will be negative, a liability to the pay-floating party.

LOS 54.b: Explain the equivalence of 1) interest rate swaps to a series of off-market forward rate agreements (FRAs) and 2) a plain vanilla swap to a combination of an interest rate call and an interest rate put.

CFA® Program Curriculum, Volume 6, page 254

Equivalence to FRAs

It is common to view swaps as equivalent to a series of forward contracts. While this is approximately true, there are some differences. One difference is that unless the yield curve is flat, there will be a variety of fixed rates on the FRAs expiring on the swap's payment dates. If we view the swap fixed rate as a (complex) average of the fixed rates on an equivalent series of FRAs, some of the FRA rates will be above, and others below, the swap fixed rate.

Viewing the component parts of the swap in this way, we can conclude that they are (individually) off-market forwards. An *off-market forward* is one in which the forward price is different from that which gives the forward a zero value at initiation. That means an interest rate swap is a series of off-market forward rate agreements. Some of them have a positive value to the long, while others have a negative value. When the values of all the off-market FRAs are summed together as a swap, the swap has a value of zero (at initiation).

Now, let's try to show this relationship between the FRAs and swaps visually. The left side of Figure 1 represents the swap, and the diagram on the right portrays the portfolio of FRAs.

Figure 1: Equivalence of a Swap and Portfolio of FRAs

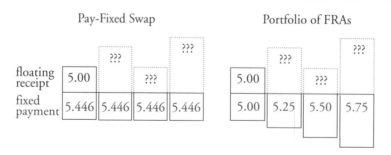

Note in the chart that the only floating-rate payment that is known today is the 5% current LIBOR rate that matures in 90 days; all other floating-rate flows are unknown as of today. However, in both the pay-fixed swap and the portfolio of FRAs, these unknown floating-rate receipts are identical. Also, all fixed-rate payments are known today in both cases. To prevent arbitrage, the present value of both alternatives must be identical. Hence, the (complex) average of the FRA rates must equal the swap fixed rate.

Another difference between a swap and a portfolio of FRAs is that, with a swap, the next payment is always known one period ahead, when the floating rate for the next period becomes known. This is not true for an FRA, because its payment is made at expiration, based on the 1-period rate for the next period.

Although some differences make the equivalence less than exact, it is appropriate to view currency swaps as a series of currency forwards and an equity swap as a series of equity forward contracts.

Equivalence to Options

A fixed-rate payer or receiver swap can be replicated with a series of put/call positions with expiration dates on the payment dates of the swap. For a fixed-rate payer swap, we need an option position that pays when floating rates increase and requires a payment to be made when rates fall. A long interest rate call and a short interest rate put would accomplish this.

A short call and a long put, at the same strike price (equal to the fixed rate on the swap), would replicate the payoffs on a receiver swap. Remember, it takes two options to create the equivalent of a forward agreement—one to mimic the gains and one to mimic the losses.

Just as a swap can be viewed as a series of FRAs, it can also be viewed as a series of long call and short put positions with the strike rates equal to the fixed rate on the swap. While there are some differences with equity and currency options, it is appropriate to view both currency and equity swaps as equivalent to a series of long call/short put combinations, as well.

LOS 54.c: Calculate and interpret the fixed rate on a plain vanilla interest rate swap and the market value of the swap during its life.

CFA® Program Curriculum, Volume 6, page 256

Plain Vanilla Swaps as Combinations of Bonds

There is a simple bond transaction that is equivalent to an interest rate swap. The fixed-payer could gain identical exposure by issuing a fixed-coupon bond and investing the proceeds in a floating-rate bond with the same maturity and payment dates. On each payment date, a fixed coupon payment is paid and the floating-rate payment is received. This is the key insight that we will use to price interest rate swaps.

An equity swap, from the perspective of the fixed-payer, is equivalent to borrowing at a fixed rate and investing in a stock, a portfolio, or an index. The equivalence is not exact, but close enough as an explanation of the capital markets transactions to approximate the exposure of an equity-for-fixed-rate swap. We will look at the issues involved more closely later in this topic review.

The exposure of a currency swap is equivalent to that of issuing a bond in one currency, exchanging the proceeds for another currency at the spot exchange rate, and purchasing a bond denominated in the other currency with the same payment and maturity dates. Either or both of the bonds can have fixed- or floating-rate payments to create equivalent portfolios to the various combinations of fixed and floating rates available in currency swaps. We will use this idea to price and value currency swaps.

Deriving the Formula for Determining the Swap Rate

We can price a plain vanilla (fixed-for-floating) interest rate swap by using the insight that the swap is equivalent to issuing a fixed-rate bond and buying an otherwise identical floating-rate note. The fixed rate must be set so that the values of the floating-rate bond and the fixed-rate bond are the same at swap initiation. By finding this rate, we can price a swap with zero value at the inception of the contract.

At issue, a floating-rate bond has a value equal to its face value. This value can change during the life of the bond, but because the rate is reset to the market rate at each payment date, the value will return to par on each of those dates.

We will use a 4-period floating-rate note with a par value of $1,000 to illustrate this method of pricing a swap. Both the fixed- and floating-rate notes must have the same par value to replicate a swap, so that the principal values match up at maturity. For the swap to have zero value at initiation, the notes must have the same market price at that point in time, as well.

Our fixed-rate note must have periodic payments, C, such that:

$$\$1,000 = \frac{C}{1+R_1} + \frac{C}{1+R_2} + \frac{C}{1+R_3} + \frac{C}{1+R_4} + \frac{\$1,000}{1+R_4}$$

The discount factors $(1 + R_n)$ are the n-period discount factors at the current rates. The present value of $1 to be received n periods from now is:

$$\frac{1}{1+R_n}$$

We can also write:

$$\$1,000 = C\left[\frac{1}{1+R_1} + \frac{1}{1+R_2} + \frac{1}{1+R_3} + \frac{1}{1+R_4}\right] + \frac{\$1,000}{1+R_4}$$

and solve for C as:

$$C = \left(\frac{1 - \left(\frac{1}{1+R_4}\right)}{\frac{1}{1+R_1} + \frac{1}{1+R_2} + \frac{1}{1+R_3} + \frac{1}{1+R_4}}\right)\$1,000$$

The answer is the fixed rate for the swap as a percentage rate, the coupon amount per dollar of principal value.

If we are given the prices of zero-coupon risk-free bonds (per $ of principal) maturing on all our payment dates, the problem is simpler. We could substitute these in the equation as:

$$C = \frac{1 - Z_4}{Z_1 + Z_2 + Z_3 + Z_4}$$

where:

$$Z_n = \frac{1}{1+R_n} = \text{price of n-period zero-coupon bond per \$ of principal}$$

The *Zs* are called discount factors.

For example, the present value of a $100,000 payment 180 days from today at an annual discount rate of 6% (assuming simple interest and a 360-day basis) is:

$$PV = \frac{\$100,000}{1 + 0.06\left(\frac{180}{360}\right)} = \frac{\$100,000}{1.03} = \$97,087$$

That is equivalent to $0.97087 per $ of face value, so the 180-day discount factor is 0.97087.

We can use this 180-day discount factor to calculate the present value of any cash flow occurring in 180 days. For example, the present value of a $15,000 payment in 180 days at 6% is:

$$PV = \$15,000(0.97087) = \$14,563$$

Calculating the Fixed Rate on a Quarterly-Pay, Plain Vanilla Swap

In practice, our payment periods will likely be quarterly and our discount rates expressed as annualized LIBOR (using 360 days), as in the following example.

> **Example: Calculating the fixed rate on a swap with quarterly payments**
>
> Annualized LIBOR spot rates today are:
>
> $R_{90\text{-day}} = 0.030$
>
> $R_{180\text{-day}} = 0.035$
>
> $R_{270\text{-day}} = 0.040$
>
> $R_{360\text{-day}} = 0.045$
>
> You're analyzing a 1-year swap with quarterly payments and a notional principal amount of $5,000,000. Calculate:
>
> - The fixed rate in percentage terms.
> - The quarterly fixed payments in $.

Answer:

First calculate the discount factors. Don't forget to convert from annualized rates to per-period rates.

$$Z_{90\text{-day}} = \frac{1}{1 + \left(0.030 \times \dfrac{90}{360}\right)} = 0.99256$$

$$Z_{180\text{-day}} = \frac{1}{1 + \left(0.035 \times \dfrac{180}{360}\right)} = 0.98280$$

$$Z_{270\text{-day}} = \frac{1}{1 + \left(0.040 \times \dfrac{270}{360}\right)} = 0.97087$$

$$Z_{360\text{-day}} = \frac{1}{1 + \left(0.045 \times \dfrac{360}{360}\right)} = 0.95694$$

 Professor's Note: It's likely that on the exam you will be given a table of discount factors to use in pricing a swap, as in the next example. We've provided the calculations here so you know where the discount factors come from.

The quarterly fixed rate on the swap is:

$$\frac{1 - 0.95694}{0.99256 + 0.98280 + 0.97087 + 0.95694} = 0.011 = 1.1\%$$

The quarterly fixed-rate payments, assuming a notional principal of $5,000,000, are:

$5,000,000 \times 0.011 = $55,000$

The fixed rate on the swap in annual terms is:

$$1.1\% \times \frac{360}{90} = 4.4\%$$

We have priced a swap in which one side pays quarterly LIBOR and the other side pays 4.4% fixed annually (1.1% quarterly).

Calculating the Market Value of a Swap

At any payment date, the market value of a swap (to the fixed-rate payer) is the difference between the value of a floating-rate bond and the value of a fixed-rate bond. Because the fixed-payer is essentially long a floating-rate bond and short a fixed-rate bond, this position will have positive value only when the fixed-rate bond is trading at a discount to par. This follows from the fact that the floating-rate bond will be valued at par at each payment date. Between payment dates, the floating-rate bond may be worth more or less than par.

In the following example, we will subtract the value of the fixed-rate bond from the value of the floating-rate bond to calculate the value of the swap to the fixed-rate payer after initiation and between payment dates.

Professor's Note: Keep in mind that what we are doing is valuing the interest rate swap by valuing an equivalent position in a fixed-rate bond and a floating-rate bond. I don't want you to get confused in the middle of this example and say to yourself, "Why are we worrying about principal payments when the swap doesn't require principal payments?" We calculate the value of the fixed-rate bond as the present value of the expected fixed-rate interest payments and principal payments. We calculate the value of the floating-rate bond the same way. The difference between these two values is the value of the swap. The actual swap, however, doesn't require principal payments, and interest payments are netted.

How Do We Know the Floating Rate Bond Reprices to Par at Each Settlement Date?

One of the most confusing parts of valuing a swap for Level II candidates is understanding how we value a floating-rate bond even though we don't know what all the upcoming coupon payments will be, because the coupon rate changes at every settlement date.

The key is to recognize that at each settlement date, the coupon rate on the floating-rate bond, which determines the coupon payment at the *next* settlement date, is set to the market rate. That means that at every settlement date the coupon rate on the bond is equal to the market rate, and you should remember from Level I that *if the coupon rate on a bond is equal to the market rate, the bond sells at par.*

For example, suppose we have a 2-year floating rate bond with a par value of $100 and annual payments (and annual settlement dates) based on LIBOR. When the bond is issued, the coupon rate is set to 5%, which is the current market 1-year LIBOR rate. That means in one year the bond will make a coupon payment of $5.

After six months, 6-month LIBOR is 6% annually, or 3% for six months, and we want to value the floating-rate bond. Its value will be the present value of the remaining cash flows, but it may seem to you as though we can't solve the problem because we only know the coupon payment will be $5, but we don't know what the bond will be worth at the end of the year. However, we *do* know what the bond will be worth at the end of the year: its par value of $100! Therefore, the bond will be worth ($100 + $5) / 1.03 = $101.94.

Why will the bond trade at par at the end of the year? Think about what will happen at the end of the year: the $5 coupon payment will be made and the next coupon payment (to be made at the end of the second year) will be determined. As long as the second coupon payment (received at the end of the second year) is set equal to 1-year LIBOR at the end of the first year, the bond will be worth $100.

To convince you we are not just making this up, suppose the coupon rate resets to 8% at the end of the first year, which is the 1-year LIBOR rate at the time. Then we know that at the end of the second year, when the bond matures, we will receive a payment of $108 (the $100 principal and the $8 coupon). The present value of that payment, discounted at the current market rate of 8%, is the par value:

$$\text{bond value at end of year 1 (if coupon = 8\%)} = \frac{\$108}{1.08} = \$100$$

Suppose instead that 1-year LIBOR is 15%. Then, the coupon payment will be $15 and the bond will still be valued at par:

$$\text{bond value at end of year 1 (if coupon = 15\%)} = \frac{\$115}{1.15} = \$100$$

What have we shown? A floating-rate bond will always be worth its par value at every settlement date.

Example: Valuing a plain vanilla swap between payment dates

Consider a 1-year LIBOR swap with quarterly payments priced at 6.052% at initiation when 90-day LIBOR was 5.5%. The annualized LIBOR rates and discount factors 30 days later are shown in the following figure. The notional principal amount is $30,000,000. Calculate the value of the swap to the fixed-rate payer after 30 days.

LIBOR and Discount Factors for $30 Million, 1-Year Interest Rate Swap

	Rate	*Present Value Factor*
60-day LIBOR	6.0%	0.99010
150-day LIBOR	6.5%	0.97363
240-day LIBOR	7.0%	0.95541
330-day LIBOR	7.5%	0.93567

Answer:

The quarterly payments per $ of notional principal are:

$$0.06052 \times \frac{90}{360} = \$0.01513$$

The hypothetical fixed-rate bond will pay four coupon payments of $0.01513 in 60, 150, 240, and 330 days. It will also make a final principal payment of $1.0000 in 330 days.

The time line of the cash flows is shown in the following figure. Remember that we're valuing the swap on day 30.

Time Line for Valuing the Fixed-Rate Side of an Interest Rate Swap

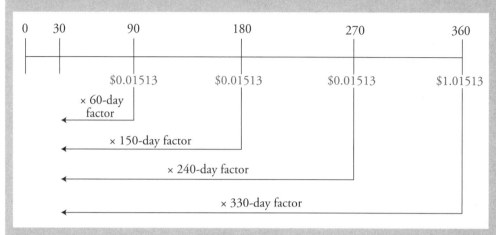

We can calculate the value of the fixed-rate side of the swap as $0.993993, the present value of the expected coupon payments and the face value payment, as shown in the following figure.

Calculation of Value for the Fixed Rate Side of an Interest Rate Swap

Day	Cash Flow	Discount Factor	Present Value
90	$0.01513	0.99010	$0.014980
180	$0.01513	0.97363	$0.014731
270	$0.01513	0.95541	$0.014455
360	$1.01513	0.93567	$0.949827
		Total	$0.993993

To value the floating-rate bond at day 30, we need only note two things. First, at the payment date on day 90, the bond value will be $1.00 because the coupon rate will be reset to the current market rate. Therefore, we don't need to know what the floating-rate bond's cash flows are after day 90. Second, the first payment (per $ of notional principal) is known at inception:

$$0.055 \times \frac{90}{360} = \$0.01375$$

Because the next payment date is 60 days out, we need to discount the first floating-rate payment and the $1.00 bond value immediately after the payment is made by the current 60-day rate of 6%.

The time line is as shown. The 60-day discount factor is 0.99010. The value of the floating-rate bond at day 30 (per $ of notional principal) is therefore $1.01375 × 0.99010 = $1.003714.

Calculation of Value for the Floating Rate Side of an Interest Rate Swap

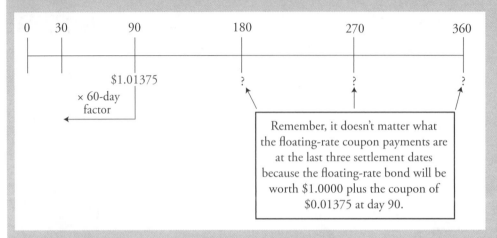

The value of the pay-fixed side of the swap is the difference between the values of the fixed and floating sides (per $ of notional principal):

swap value to fixed-rate payer = $1.003714 – $0.993993 = $0.009721

The total value of the $30,000,000 notional principal swap to the fixed-rate payer is:

swap value to fixed-rate payer = 30,000,000 × $0.009721 = $291,630

Because the relevant portion of the yield curve has shifted up, the fixed-rate liability has decreased in present value terms relative to the floating-rate asset. The reason the floating-rate bond appears to have appreciated above par value is that we have included the accrued interest by valuing the full first coupon.

LOS 54.d: Calculate and interpret the fixed rate, if applicable, and the foreign notional principal for a given domestic notional principal on a currency swap, and estimate the market values of each of the different types of currency swaps during their lives.

CFA® Program Curriculum, Volume 6, page 262

Determining the Fixed Rate and Foreign Notional Principal

Consider two currencies, the U.S. dollar ($) and the British pound (£), where the exchange rate is currently $2 per £ or £0.5 per $. Using the method introduced earlier to price an interest rate swap, we can solve for the fixed rate that will make the present value of the fixed-rate $ payments equal to $1.00, and the fixed rate that will make the present value of the fixed-rate foreign payments equal to £1.00 in Great Britain. The interest rates in a currency swap are simply the swap rates calculated from each country's yield curve or the floating (short-term) rates in the relevant country's currency. Don't forget: With currency swaps, there are two yield curves and two swap rates, one for each currency.

The principal amounts of the fixed-rate obligations must be adjusted for the current exchange rate. We need $2.00 to equal £1.00, so these are the notional amounts, exchanged at the inception of the swap and returned at the termination of the swap. For example, if the notional principal amount of the $ side of the swap is $25 million, the £ notional principal amount will be £12.5 million.

For other than fixed-for-fixed currency swaps, we need only replace the fixed rate on either or both of the currencies with the floating rate *in the country* corresponding to the currency of the payment. A floating-rate loan that pays in £ will have a value of £1.00 at the initiation of the swap, so with our currency adjustment on the principal amounts, the fixed-for-floating currency swap will still have a zero value at initiation.

Given the yield curve information for each country and the exchange rate, we can calculate the notional principal amounts and the fixed-rate for either side of the swap, if necessary.

> **Example: Calculating the fixed rate and notional principal on a currency swap**
>
> In a previous example, we determined that the fixed rate on a 1-year quarterly $5,000,000 interest rate swap, given the following set of spot LIBOR rates, was 1.1% quarterly, or 4.4% on an annual basis.
>
> $$R^{\$}_{90\text{-day}} = 0.030$$
>
> $$R^{\$}_{180\text{-day}} = 0.035$$
>
> $$R^{\$}_{270\text{-day}} = 0.040$$
>
> $$R^{\$}_{360\text{-day}} = 0.045$$
>
> The comparable set of £ rates are:
>
> $$R^{£}_{90\text{-day}} = 0.04$$
>
> $$R^{£}_{180\text{-day}} = 0.05$$
>
> $$R^{£}_{270\text{-day}} = 0.06$$
>
> $$R^{£}_{360\text{-day}} = 0.07$$
>
> The current exchange rate is £0.50 per $. Determine the fixed rate on a 1-year £ interest rate swap. Then determine the notional £ principal amount and the quarterly cash flows on a:
>
> - Pay $ fixed, receive £ fixed currency swap.
> - Pay $ fixed, receive £ floating currency swap.

Answer:

First calculate the £ discount factors. Don't forget to convert from annualized rates to per-period rates.

$$Z^{£}_{90\text{-day}} = \frac{1}{1 + \left(0.04 \times \dfrac{90}{360}\right)} = 0.99010$$

$$Z^{£}_{180\text{-day}} = \frac{1}{1 + \left(0.05 \times \dfrac{180}{360}\right)} = 0.97561$$

$$Z^{£}_{270\text{-day}} = \frac{1}{1 + \left(0.06 \times \dfrac{270}{360}\right)} = 0.95694$$

$$Z^{£}_{360\text{-day}} = \frac{1}{1 + \left(0.07 \times \dfrac{360}{360}\right)} = 0.93458$$

The quarterly fixed rate on the £ swap is:

$$\frac{1 - 0.93458}{0.99010 + 0.97561 + 0.95694 + 0.93458} = 0.017 = 1.7\%$$

The fixed rate on the £ swap in annual terms is:

$$1.7\% \times \frac{360}{90} = 6.8\%$$

Pay $ fixed, receive £ fixed currency swap.

The notional £ principal amount of the swap would be:

$5,000,000 \times 0.50 = £2,500,000$

At the initiation of the swap, we would exchange £2,500,000 for $5,000,000. We would pay 1.1% quarterly on the $5,000,000 notional principal ($55,000) and receive 1.7% on £2,500,000 quarterly (£42,500). At the end of one year, we would exchange the original principal amounts.

Pay $ fixed, receive £ floating currency swap.

The exchange of principal amounts at the initiation and termination of the swap would be the same as in the first example. We would still pay 1.1% quarterly on the $5,000,000. In return, we would receive the floating British rate on the £2,500,000 principal amount.

The value of a currency swap is calculated the same way as an interest rate swap. The value to any party is the present value of the cash flows they expect to receive minus the present value of the cash flows they expect to pay. There are four possible structures for a $ for £ currency swap:

- Receive $ fixed and pay £ fixed.
- Receive $ floating and pay £ fixed.
- Receive $ fixed and pay £ floating.
- Receive $ floating and pay £ floating.

Example: Calculating the value of a currency swap after initiation

Use the data on the $ and £ interest rate swaps in the previous examples to answer this question. After 300 days, the 60-day $ interest rate is 5.4%, the 60-day £ interest rate is 6.6%, and the exchange rate is £0.52 per $. The 90-day $ and £ interest rates on the last settlement date were 5.6% and 6.4%, respectively. Calculate the value of a $5,000,000 swap in which the counterparty receives $ floating and pays £ fixed.

Answer:

After 300 days, the only cash flows remaining are the last interest payments and the principal payments in 60 days. We want to find the present value of those cash flows, so we need the 60-day discount factors based on the current 60-day rates:

$$Z^{\$}_{60\text{-day}} = \frac{1}{1 + \left(0.054 \times \dfrac{60}{360}\right)} = 0.99108$$

$$Z^{£}_{60\text{-day}} = \frac{1}{1 + \left(0.066 \times \dfrac{60}{360}\right)} = 0.98912$$

First calculate the value after 300 days of the $ floating payments. It is equivalent to the value of a $5,000,000 floating-rate bond that matures in 60 days and pays a coupon payment in 60 days of $70,000 ($5,000,000 × 0.056/4). This coupon payment was set at the beginning of the period when the $ interest rate was 5.6%. The value in $ of the $ floating side is the present value of $5,070,000 discounted using the 60-day $ discount factor of 0.99108:

value of $ floating side (in $) = 0.99108 × $5,070,000 = $5,024,776

Next, calculate the value after 300 days of the £ fixed payments. Recall that the fixed £ rate was calculated in the previous example to be 6.8%. Thus, it is equivalent to the value of a 6.8% fixed rate, £2,500,000 bond that matures in 60 days and pays a coupon payment of £42,500 (£2,500,000 × 0.068/4) in 60 days. The value in £ of the £ fixed side is the present value of £2,542,500 discounted using the 60-day £ discount factor of 0.98912:

value of £ fixed side (in £) = 0.98912 × £2,542,500 = £2,514,838

Convert that into $ at the current spot exchange rate of £0.52 per $ to find the value of the £ fixed side in $:

value of £ fixed side (in $) = £2,514,838 / 0.52 = $4,836,227

Finally, the value of the receive $ floating, pay £ fixed side of the swap is equal to the value of the $ floating side minus the £ fixed side, or $5,024,776 – $4,836,227 = $188,549.

 Professor's Note: It is easier to value a currency swap as we have done it here by calculating the total value of both sides (rather than calculating the value per $ of notional principal as we did in the interest rate swap valuation example). However, you should be able to do it either way.

LOS 54.e: Calculate and interpret the fixed rate, if applicable, on an equity swap and the market values of the different types of equity swaps during their lives.

CFA® Program Curriculum, Volume 6, page 267

To price an *N*-period pay-fixed equity swap, we can use the same formula as for a plain vanilla swap:

$$C_N = \frac{1 - Z_N}{Z_1 + Z_2 + \ldots + Z_N}$$

where:
Z_n = the present value of $1 to be received on the nth payment date of *N* dates

To value this swap after time has passed, determine the value of the equity or index portfolio and the value of the fixed-rate payments.

Example: Valuing a pay fixed, receive equity returns swap

A $10 million principal value equity swap has a fixed quarterly rate of 0.01513 and the other side pays the quarterly return on an index. The index is currently trading at 985. After 30 days have passed, the index stands at 996 and the term structure is the same as our earlier example using LIBOR annualized rates of 6%, 6.5%, 7%, and 7.5% for terms of 60, 150, 240, and 330 days. The discount factors are 0.99010, 0.97363, 0.95541, and 0.93567. The value of the pay-fixed side of the swap from that earlier example was $0.993993 per $ of notional principal. Calculate the value of the swap to the fixed-rate payer on day 30.

Answer:

We can calculate the value of the fixed-payer side of the swap by multiplying the value per $ of notional principal by the $10 million notional principal:

value of fixed-pay side = 0.993993 × $10,000,000 = $9,939,930

The value of $10,000,000 invested in the index after 30 days is:

$$\$10,000,000 \times \frac{996}{985} = \$10,111,675$$

The fixed-rate liability has decreased from its original value of $10,000,000. From the standpoint of the fixed-rate payer, the value of the swap after 30 days is:

$10,111,675 – $9,939,930 = $171,745

 Professor's Note: We have not derived this result and have taken some liberties in simplifying the explanation. The LOS asks that you determine the swap rate and value an equity swap at a point in time. The analysis supplied here will accomplish this. It will work at any point during the tenor of the swap because the equity "portfolio" that is implicit in the analysis is set to the notional amount at each payment date.

If the equity swap to be valued is a floating-rate-for-equity swap, the value of the floating-rate side of the swap can be calculated just as before and compared to the value of the equity or index portfolio.

A swap of returns on two different stocks can be viewed as buying one stock (receiving the returns) and shorting an equal value of a different stock (paying the returns). There is no "pricing" at swap initiation, and we can value the swap at any point in time by taking the difference in returns (since the last payment date) times the notional principal.

Example: Valuing a receive equity return and pay different equity return swap

An investor is the Stock A returns payer (and Stock B returns receiver) in a $1 million quarterly-pay swap. After one month, Stock A is up 1.3% and Stock B is down 0.8%. Calculate the value of the swap to the investor.

Answer:

The investor pays the Stock A returns and receives Stock B returns. However, the Stock B returns are negative, so he pays those as well:

value of swap = (–0.013 – 0.008) × $1,000,000 = –$21,000

LOS 54.f: Explain and interpret the characteristics and uses of swaptions, including the difference between payer and receiver swaptions.

CFA® Program Curriculum, Volume 6, page 273

A **swaption** is an option that gives the holder the right to enter into an interest rate swap. The notation for swaptions is similar to FRAs. For example, a swaption that matures in two years and gives the holder the right to enter into a 3-year swap at the end of the second year is a 2x5 swaption.

A **payer swaption** is the right to enter into a specific swap at some date in the future as the fixed-rate payer at a rate specified in the swaption. If swap fixed rates increase (as interest rates increase), the right to enter the pay-fixed side of a swap (a payer swaption) becomes more valuable. The holder of a European payer swaption would exercise if the market rate for fixed-rate swaps is greater than the exercise rate at maturity.

A **receiver swaption** is the right to enter into a specific swap at some date in the future as the fixed-rate receiver (i.e., the floating-rate payer) at a rate specified in the swaption. If swap fixed rates decrease (as interest rates decrease), the right to enter the receive-fixed side of a swap (a receiver swaption) becomes more valuable. The holder of a European receiver swaption would exercise at maturity if market rates are less than the exercise rate.

Swaptions can be American- or European-style options. Like any option, a swaption is purchased for a premium that depends on the strike rate (the fixed rate) specified in the swaption.

There are three primary uses of swaptions:

- *Lock in fixed rate.* If an investor anticipates a floating-rate exposure at some future date (e.g., he will be issuing bonds or getting a loan), a payer swaption would "lock in" a fixed rate and provide floating-rate payments for the loan. It would be exercised if the yield curve shifted up to give the investor (effectively) a loan at the fixed rate on the swaption.
- *Interest rate speculation.* Swaptions can be used to speculate on changes in interest rates. The investor would buy a payer swaption if he expects rate to rise, or buy a receiver swaption if he expects rates to fall.
- *Swap termination.* Swaptions can be used to terminate a swap. A fixed-rate payer on a 5-year swap could buy a 2x5 receiver swaption (at the same fixed rate as the swap). This swaption would give the investor the right to enter into an offsetting 3-year swap at the end of two years, effectively terminating the 5-year swap at the end of the second year.

LOS 54.g: Calculate the payoffs and cash flows of an interest rate swaption.

CFA® Program Curriculum, Volume 6, page 274

Exercising an in-the-money swaption effectively generates an annuity over the term of the underlying swap. The amount of each annuity payment is the interest savings that result from paying a rate lower than the market rate under a payer swaption or the extra interest that results from receiving a higher rate under a receiver swaption.

For example, suppose an investor exercises a receiver swaption on a 1-year quarterly pay LIBOR based $1 million swap with a fixed rate of 5% when the market rate on a current interest rate swap is 4%. The investor has the right to enter into a one-year swap and receive a fixed rate of 5%, while the market fixed rate for one year swaps is 4%. Therefore, the payoff to the swaption each quarter is the interest saved by receiving the higher fixed rate:

$$\text{fixed payment based on exercise rate} = 0.05 \times \frac{90}{360} \times \$1,000,000 = \$12,500$$

$$\text{fixed payment based on market rate} = 0.04 \times \frac{90}{360} \times \$1,000,000 = \$10,000$$

$$\text{extra interest per quarter} = \$12,500 - \$10,000 = \$2,500$$

We can also calculate this directly as: $(0.05 - 0.04) \times \frac{90}{360} \times \$1,000,000 = \$2,500$

LOS 54.h: Calculate and interpret the value of an interest rate swaption at expiration.

CFA® Program Curriculum, Volume 6, page 277

The value of an interest rate swaption at expiration is the present value of the difference between the higher fixed payments received and the lower fixed payments made (i.e., the annuity discussed in the previous LOS), ignoring transactions costs and default risk.

Example: Valuing an interest rate swaption at expiration

An investor exercises at maturity a payer swaption on a 1-year quarterly-pay LIBOR-based $10 million swap with a fixed rate of 5% when the market rate on a current interest rate swap is 6.052%. The (annual) rates and discount factors for 90-, 180-, 270-, and 360-day LIBOR are shown in the following figure. Calculate the value of the swaption at expiration.

LIBOR and Discount Rates for Payer Swaptions

	Rate	Present Value Factor
90-day LIBOR	5.5%	0.98644
180-day LIBOR	6.0%	0.97087
270-day LIBOR	6.5%	0.95352
360-day LIBOR	7.0%	0.93458

Answer:

The swaption allows the investor to take the fixed-rate payer position in the swap at 5%. The investor can also simultaneously enter into a current 1-year swap as the fixed-rate receiver to get 6.052%. The floating-rate payments liability on the second swap will be offset (paid) by the floating-rate payments received on the swaption swap.

The net cash flow to the investor at each payment date will be:

$$(0.06052 - 0.05) \times \frac{90}{360} \times \$10,000,000 = \$26,300$$

The present value of these payments is $101,134, as shown in the figure.

Swaption Value at Expiration

Day	Cash Flow	Present Value Factor	Present Value
90	$26,300	0.98644	$25,943
180	$26,300	0.97087	$25,534
270	$26,300	0.95352	$25,078
360	$26,300	0.93458	$24,579
		Total	$101,134

LOS 54.i: Evaluate swap credit risk for each party and during the life of the swap, distinguish between current credit risk and potential credit risk, and explain how swap credit risk is reduced by both netting and marking to market.

CFA® Program Curriculum, Volume 6, page 279

Credit risk in a swap reflects the probability that a counterparty will default on the required payments. For example, if we are party to an interest rate swap with a positive value to us, we are subject to the credit risk of the counterparty, because if they default, we don't get paid. **Current credit risk** refers to the credit risk associated with the counterparty's default on a payment currently due. **Potential credit risk** reflects the future credit risk over the remaining term of the swap.

The credit quality of institutions in the swaps market is generally very good, so there is low credit risk at the inception of a swap contract. The credit risk is highest in the middle of the swap term because credit quality can have deteriorated and there are significant future payments remaining on the swap. Toward the end of the interest rate swap, few payments are left and credit risk is again low.

In currency swaps, principal is exchanged at termination of the swap, so the period of higher credit risk is a little later in the swap's life.

Interest payments in interest rate swaps are typically netted, so only one party pays the other the net amount due. For example, suppose at the payment date, Party A owes Party B $40,000, and Party B owes Party A $70,000. The payments would be netted and Party B would pay Party A $30,000.

Without netting, credit risk is greater. If B goes bankrupt and defaults on the $70,000 payment, it still has a claim against A of $40,000. A is obligated to pay the $40,000 and gets in line with B's other creditors for payment of A's $70,000 claim.

With netting, B's bankruptcy results in A having a claim of only the net amount, $30,000, as a bankruptcy creditor. A has no obligation to make a payment to B. Netting is usual in single swap contracts but can also be extended to cover all the swaps two parties are in together.

Marking to market involves making a payment equal to the value of the swap at periodic settlement dates and repricing the swap by resetting the swap rate. This reduces credit risk just as it does with futures contracts.

LOS 54.j: Define swap spread and explain its relation to credit risk.

CFA® Program Curriculum, Volume 6, page 281

The **swap spread** is the spread between the swap rate and the comparable maturity Treasury notes. A 2-year swap might have a (swap) spread of 40 basis points over the yield on 2-year Treasury notes.

Remember that we based the swap rate on the LIBOR curve. LIBOR is a rate for large-bank lending and is not a riskless rate. Therefore, the default premium in LIBOR is reflected in the swap rate calculated from it. The swap spread will respond to the same factors as other "quality" spreads.

KEY CONCEPTS

LOS 54.a

The "price" of a swap is the fixed rate of a fixed-for-floating swap and is set so that the swap contract has a zero value at initiation. The value of a swap is the difference between the present values of the fixed- and floating-rate payment streams. Due to shifts in the yield curve, at any point after contract initiation, the swap value may change.

LOS 54.b

A payer swap is equivalent to each of the following:
- Issuing fixed-rate debt and buying a floating-rate note.
- Entering a series of FRAs at the fixed rate.
- A combination of interest rate puts and calls with strike rates equal to the fixed rate on the swap.

A series of interest rate futures is similar to a payer swap, but futures characteristics make it difficult to match the cash flows of a swap with futures.

A swap can be thought of as a strip (or series) of FRAs with successively longer maturity dates. The swap rate is computed as the present-value average of the FRA rates. Imposing a single rate on all the FRAs means that the individual FRAs will be off-market FRAs. An off-market forward is one in which the forward price is different from that which gives the forward a zero value at initiation.

The payoffs on a payer swap are equivalent to those on a series of long call/short put interest rate options with strike prices both equal to the fixed rate on the swap. A series of short call/long put positions will mimic a receiver swap.

LOS 54.c

The fixed periodic-rate on an n-period swap at initiation (as a percentage of the principal value) can be calculated as:

$$C = \frac{1 - Z_4}{Z_1 + Z_2 + Z_3 + Z_4}$$

where:

$$Z_n = \frac{1}{1 + R_n} = \text{price of n-period zero-coupon bond for \$ of principal}$$

The value of a swap to the fixed-rate receiver at a point in time is the difference between the present value of the hypothetical fixed-rate bond and the present value of the hypothetical floating-rate bond at the appropriate rates for each payment. The PV of the floating bond is the discounted value of the next floating payment (which is known) and the notional principal on that date.

Value to pay fixed side = PV (floating) – PV (fixed)
Value to pay floating side = PV (fixed) – PV (floating)

LOS 54.d

When a currency swap includes a fixed rate, this rate is determined using the yield curve for the relevant currency. The notional principal amounts in the two currencies are equated using current exchange rates.

LOS 54.e

The fixed-rate side of an equity swap is priced and valued just like an interest rate swap. The equity side can be valued by multiplying the notional amount of the contract by 1 + the percentage equity appreciation since the last payment date. Use the difference in values to value the swap.

LOS 54.f

A swaption is an option on a swap. A payer swaption gives the holder the right to enter into an interest rate swap as the fixed-rate payer at the exercise of the swaption. A receiver swaption gives the holder the right to enter into an interest rate swap as the fixed-rate receiver.

A swaption can be used to:

*   Hedge an anticipated exposure to fixed or floating interest rate payments.
*   Speculate on the direction of interest rates.
*   Provide a method of exiting an existing swap prior to the normal termination date.

LOS 54.g

A payer-swaption is in-the-money if swap (fixed) rates rise. A receiver swaption is in-the-money if swap rates fall.

LOS 54.h

At expiration, the value of a payer swaption is the maximum of zero and the present value of a stream of payments equal to the fixed-rate payments on a current market rate swap minus the fixed-rate payments on the swaption swap.

LOS 54.i

Credit risk arises because of the possibility that the other party to a swap cannot or will not make the payments required by the swap contract. It is greatest in the middle of the swap term when the creditworthiness of the counterparty may have deteriorated since swap initiation and there are significant payments yet to be made over the remaining term of the swap.

Netting, within a swap or across several swaps with the same counterparty, relieves the party owed the greater amount of a separate claim for the lesser amount. Only the net payment is recognized as a debt. Marking to market can also be used to reduce credit risk.

LOS 54.j

The swap spread is the difference between the current swap (fixed) rate and the yield on a riskless (Treasury) bond of the same term as the swap. It can be interpreted as a quality or default-risk spread between a riskless security and LIBOR.

CONCEPT CHECKERS

1. The current U.S. dollar ($) to Canadian dollar (C$) exchange rate is 0.7. In a $1 million fixed-for-floating currency swap, the party that is entering the swap to hedge existing exposure to a C$-denominated fixed-rate liability will:
    A. receive $1 million at the termination of the swap.
    B. pay a fixed rate based on the yield curve in the United States.
    C. receive a fixed rate based on the yield curve in Canada.

2. A European-style payer swaption gives its holder the:
    A. right to enter a swap by paying the strike price at expiration of the option.
    B. right to enter a swap at expiration of the option as the fixed-rate payer.
    C. option to take either side of a swap at a certain date in the future, by making a current payment.

3. At what point in a swap's life is the credit risk in an interest rate swap the greatest?
    A. In the middle.
    B. At the end, when the largest payments are due.
    C. At the beginning, because all the payments remain.

4. Consider a 6-year currency swap in which we will receive LIBOR semiannually and pay 9% fixed semiannually in British pounds (£). The notional value of the swap is £50 million. The current spot rate is $1.50 per £. Which of the following transactions would replicate the payoffs to the pay-fixed side of the swap?

	Bond to issue	Bond to purchase
A.	9% fixed, £50 million	LIBOR, $33 million
B.	9% fixed, £50 million	LIBOR, $75 million
C.	LIBOR, £112 million	9% fixed, $33 million

5. Annualized LIBOR spot rates and the present value factors today are:

	Rate	Present value factor
90-day LIBOR	4.2%	0.98961
180-day LIBOR	4.8%	0.97656
270-day LIBOR	5.0%	0.96386
360-day LIBOR	5.2%	0.95057
Total		3.88060

    Based on a notional principal of $40,000,000, the annualized swap rate is *closest* to:
    A. 1.27%.
    B. 2.54%.
    C. 5.08%.

Use the following information to answer Questions 6 and 7.

Raul Hernandez, CFA, purchased a 1-year European receiver swaption with an exercise rate of 6% that is about to expire. The underlying is a 2-year swap with semiannual payments, and the notional principal is $10,000,000. Annualized LIBOR rates and present value factors are:

	Rate	Present value factor
180-day LIBOR	4.0%	0.9804
360-day LIBOR	4.5%	0.9569
540-day LIBOR	5.0%	0.9302
720-day LIBOR	5.5%	0.9009

6.   The receiver swaption is:
    A. out-of-the-money.
    B. at-the-money.
    C. in-the-money.

7.   The value of the receiver swaption at maturity is *closest* to:
    A. $139,431.
    B. $143,360.
    C. $148,000.

Use the following information to answer Questions 8 and 9.

Two parties enter into a 2-year fixed-for-floating interest rate swap with semiannual payments. The floating-rate payments are based on LIBOR. The 180-, 360-, 540-, and 720-day annualized LIBOR rates and present value factors are:

	Rate	Present value factor
180-day LIBOR	5.0%	0.9756
360-day LIBOR	6.0%	0.9434
540-day LIBOR	6.5%	0.9112
720-day LIBOR	7.0%	0.8772

8.   The swap rate is *closest* to:
    A. 6.62%.
    B. 6.87%.
    C. 7.03%.

9.   After 180 days, the swap is marked-to-market when the 180-, 360-, and 540-day annualized LIBOR rates are 4.5%, 5%, and 6%, respectively. The present value factors, respectively, are 0.9780, 0.9524, and 0.9174. What is the market value of the swap per $1 notional principal, and which of the two counterparties (the fixed-rate payer or the fixed-rate receiver) would make the payment to mark the swap to market?

	Market value	Payment made by
A.	$0.01166	Fixed-rate payer
B.	$0.04290	Fixed-rate payer
C.	$0.01166	Fixed-rate receiver

10. A bank entered into a $5,000,000, 1-year equity swap with quarterly payments 300 days ago. The bank agreed to pay an annual fixed rate of 4% and receive the return on an international equity index. The index was trading at 3,000 at the end of the third quarter, 30 days ago. The current 60-day LIBOR rate is 3.6%, the discount factor is 0.9940, and the index is now at 3,150. The value of the swap to the bank is *closest* to:
    A. –$257,795.
    B. –$114,676.
    C. $230,300.

CHALLENGE PROBLEMS

11. The equity return receiver in an equity return-for-fixed-rate equity swap receives payments that are equivalent to which of the following strategies?
    A. Buy and hold the index stocks and issue a fixed-rate bond.
    B. Issue a bond, short the index stocks, and adjust the short position value to the principal amount at each payment date.
    C. Buy the index stocks, adjust the portfolio value to the notional amount of the swap at each payment date, and issue a fixed-rate bond.

12. Consider a receiver and payer swaption on a $1 million, 1-year swap on quarterly LIBOR with a fixed rate of 6% (1.5% quarterly). The annual swap market rate at expiration of the swaption is 6.8%.

    LIBOR rates:

	Annual Rate	Discount Factor
90-day LIBOR	5.5%	0.98644
180-day LIBOR	6.0%	0.97087
270-day LIBOR	6.5%	0.95352
360-day LIBOR	7.0%	0.93458

    The difference between the payoffs at expiration to a payer swaption and a receiver swaption is *closest* to:
    A. $0.
    B. $6,000.
    C. $7,690.

13. Consider a 2-year interest rate swap in which we pay LIBOR quarterly and receive 8% fixed semiannually. The notional value is $10 million. Assume the yield curve is flat. The receive-fixed side of this swap can be replicated with which of the following portfolios of interest rate options?

	Long position	Short position
A.	Puts at 8%	Calls at 8%
B.	Puts at 8%	Puts at 8%
C.	Calls at 8%	Puts at 8%

14.   A bank entered into a 1-year currency swap with quarterly payments 200 days
      ago by agreeing to swap $1,000,000 for €800,000. The bank agreed to pay
      an annual fixed rate of 5% on the €800,000 and receive a floating rate tied to
      LIBOR on the $1,000,000. Current LIBOR and Euribor rates and present value
      factors are shown in the following table.

	Rate	Present Value Factor
70-day LIBOR	4.0%	0.9923
90-day LIBOR	4.4%	0.9891
160-day LIBOR	4.8%	0.9791
180-day LIBOR	5.2%	0.9747
70-day Euribor	5.2%	0.9900
90-day Euribor	5.6%	0.9862
160-day Euribor	6.1%	0.9736
180-day Euribor	6.3%	0.9695

The current spot exchange rate is €0.75 per $. 90-day LIBOR at the last
payment date was 4.2%. The value of the swap to the bank today is *closest* to:
A.   −$61,969.
B.   −$42,049.
C. $42,049.

15.   If interest rates increase, the value of a receiver swaption will:
A.   increase, and the value of a payer swaption will decrease.
B.   decrease, and the value of a payer swaption will increase.
C.   decrease, and the value of a payer swaption will decrease.

ANSWERS – CONCEPT CHECKERS

1. **C** A receive-fixed C$ position will hedge the liability risk. That party would receive $1 million at swap inception (in exchange for $\frac{1,000,000}{0.7}$ = C$1,428,571) and pay it back at termination. The fixed-rate received will be calculated using the yield curve in Canada at the initiation of the swap. Because this is a fixed-for-floating currency swap, the receive-fixed position will pay a floating rate based on the U.S. yield curve.

2. **B** A payer swaption gives the holder the right to enter a swap as the fixed-rate payer at the strike rate. The strike price on the swap is the fixed rate, so there is no exercise price per se. The payment for the swaption is the premium paid for purchase, just like any other options.

3. **A** In the middle of the swap, credit quality of one or both parties can have deteriorated over time and there are still significant payments remaining.

4. **B** This swap can be viewed as the following set of capital market transactions:
   - We issue a £50 million, 6-year, 9% semiannual bond denominated in pounds.
   - Exchange our pounds proceeds from the bond issue for U.S. dollars at the current spot rate: £50 million × $1.50 per pound = $75 million.
   - We purchase a $75 million, 6-year, FRN at LIBOR denominated in $.

5. **C** The quarterly fixed rate on the swap is:

$$\frac{1 - 0.95057}{3.88060} = 0.0127 = 1.27\%$$

   The fixed rate on the swap in annual terms is:

$$1.27\% \times \frac{360}{90} = 5.08\%$$

6. **C** Calculate the swap rate:

$$\text{semi-annual swap rate} = \frac{1 - 0.9009}{0.9804 + 0.9569 + 0.9302 + 0.9009} = 0.0263$$

$$\text{annualized swap rate} = 0.0263 \times \frac{360}{180} = 0.0526 = 5.26\%$$

   The receiver swaption is in-the-money because the exercise rate on the swaption (6%) is greater than the current swap rate (5.26%).

7. **A** The net cash flow to Hernandez at each payment date would be:

$$\left(0.06 - 0.0526\right) \times \frac{180}{360} \times \$10,000,000 = \$37,000$$

   The value of the swaption is the present value of these payments:

   $37,000 × (0.9804 + 0.9569 + 0.9302 + 0.9009) = $139,431

8. **A**   Calculate the swap rate:

$$\text{semi-annual swap rate} = \frac{1 - 0.8772}{0.9756 + 0.9434 + 0.9112 + 0.8772} = 0.0331$$

$$\text{swap rate} = 0.0331 \times \frac{360}{180} = 0.0662 = 6.62\%$$

9. **A** $$\text{value of fixed-rate side (per \$ of notional principal)} = \big[\$0.0331 \times (0.9780 + 0.9524 + 0.9174)\big] \\ + (\$1.00 \times 0.9174) = \$1.01166$$

The market value of the floating-rate side is $1.0000 because we're at a payment date. The market value of the swap per $ of notional principal to the receive-fixed (and pay-floating) side is $1.01166 – $1.0000 = $0.01166. As the swap is marked to market, the pay-fixed swap holder makes a payment of $0.01166 to the receive-fixed holder for each $1 of notional principal.

10. **C** $$\text{value of fixed-rate side} = 0.9940 \times \$5,050,000 = \$5,019,700$$

$$\text{value of index return side} = \$5,000,000 \times \frac{3,150}{3,000} = \$5,250,000$$

$$\text{value of swap to bank} = \$5,250,000 - \$5,019,700 = \$230,300$$

ANSWERS – CHALLENGE PROBLEMS

11. **C**   The amount by which the portfolio value exceeds the notional principal amount is sold at each payment date to make the equity return payment. If the value has declined, the equity return receiver must make a payment in that amount, equivalent to adding funds to bring the portfolio value back up to the notional principal amount. Issuing or shorting a bond will mimic the fixed-rate liability in the swap.

12. **C**   The current market rate is 0.068 / 4 = 0.017. The swaption swap has a fixed rate of 0.015. Because rates have increased, the payer swaption will be in-the-money. The net cash flow to the investor at each payment date will be:

$$(0.068 - 0.060) \times \frac{90}{360} \times \$1,000,000 = \$2,000$$

The present value of these payments is:

$2,000 × (0.98644 + 0.97087 + 0.95352 + 0.93458) = $7,690

A receiver swaption is out-of-the-money and no payments would be made. The difference between the two is $7,690.

13. **A**   To replicate the receive-fixed side of this swap, we would go long a series of interest rate puts with a strike rate of 8%, and short a series of interest rate calls with a strike rate of 8%. The expiration dates of the options should be the payment dates of the swap.

As interest rates rise above the swap-fixed rate of 8%, the receive-fixed party to the swap loses because he is receiving a below-market rate. This loss would be mimicked by the payoff required on the short calls. The puts would be out-of-the-money.

As interest rates fall below the swap-fixed rate of 8%, the receive-fixed party to the swap gains because she is receiving an above-market rate. This gain is mimicked by the payoff on the long interest rate puts. The calls would be out-of-the-money.

14. **A**   coupon on $ floating side = $1,000,000 × (0.042 / 4) = $10,500

value of the $ floating side = 0.9923 × $1,010,500 = $1,002,719

coupon on € fixed side = €800,000 × (0.05 / 4) = €10,000

value of € fixed side (in €) = (0.9900 × €10,000) + (0.9736 × €810,000) = €798,516

value of € fixed side (in $) = $\dfrac{798,516}{0.75}$ = $1,064,688

value of swap to bank = $1,002,719 – $1,064,688 = –$61,969

15. **B**   A receiver swaption is the right to enter into a specific swap at some date in the future as the fixed-rate receiver (i.e., the floating-rate payer) at a rate specified in the swaption. If swap fixed rates increase (as interest rates increase), the right to enter the pay-floating side of a swap (a receiver swaption) becomes less valuable.

A payer swaption is the right to enter into a specific swap at some date in the future as the fixed-rate payer at a rate specified in the swaption. If swap fixed rates increase (as interest rates increase), the right to enter the pay-fixed side of a swap (a payer swaption) becomes more valuable.

The following is a review of the Derivative Investments: Options, Swaps, and Interest Rate Credit Derivatives principles designed to address the learning outcome statements set forth by CFA Institute. This topic is also covered in:

INTEREST RATE DERIVATIVE INSTRUMENTS

Study Session 17

EXAM FOCUS

This topic review fills a few "holes" in the curriculum related to caps and floors that were not covered in prior topic reviews. Make sure you can calculate the payoff to a cap and a floor and explain how caps and floors are equivalent to packages of other securities.

LOS 55.a: Demonstrate how both a cap and a floor are packages of 1) options on interest rates and 2) options on fixed-income instruments.

CFA® Program Curriculum, Volume 6, page 334

An **interest rate cap** is an agreement in which one party agrees to pay the other at regular intervals over a certain period of time when the benchmark interest rate (e.g., LIBOR) exceeds the strike rate specified in the contract. This strike rate is called the **cap rate**. For example, the seller of a cap might agree to pay the buyer at the end of any quarter over the next two years if LIBOR is greater than a cap rate of 6%. We'll discuss the calculation of the payoff to a cap in the next LOS.

The buyer of a cap has a position similar to that of a buyer of a call on LIBOR, both of whom benefit when interest rates rise. Because an interest rate cap is a multi-period agreement, a cap is actually a portfolio of call options on LIBOR called **caplets**. For example, the 2-year cap discussed above is actually a portfolio of eight interest rate options with different maturity dates.

The cap buyer pays a premium to the seller and exercises the cap if the market rate of interest rises above the cap strike. The diagram in Figure 1 illustrates the profits of an interest rate cap at the end of one particular settlement period. It has the familiar shape of a long position in a call option.

Figure 1: Profit to a Long Cap

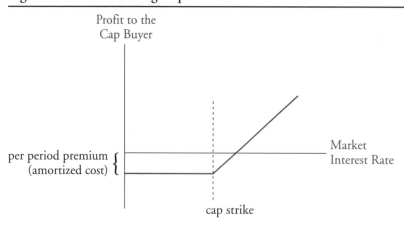

An **interest rate floor** is an agreement in which one party agrees to pay the other at regular intervals over a certain time period when the benchmark interest rate (e.g., LIBOR) falls below the strike rate specified in the contract. This strike rate is called the **floor rate**. For example, the seller of a floor might agree to pay the buyer at the end of any quarter over the next two years if LIBOR is less than a floor rate of 4%. We'll discuss the calculation of the payoff to a floor in the next LOS.

The buyer of a floor benefits from an interest rate decrease and, therefore, has a position that is similar to that of a buyer of a put on LIBOR, who benefits when interest rates fall and the price of the instrument rises. Once again, because a floor is a multi-period agreement, a floor is actually a portfolio of put options on LIBOR called **floorlets**.

The floor buyer pays a premium and exercises the floor if the market rate of interest falls below the floor strike. The diagram in Figure 2 illustrates the profits of an interest rate floor at the end of one particular settlement period. It has the same shape as a long put option.

Figure 2: Profit to a Long Floor

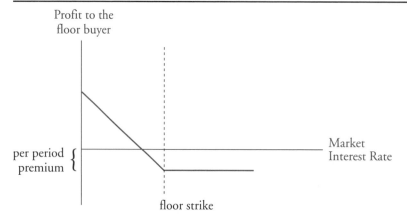

Options are traded both on *interest rates* and on *prices* of fixed-income securities. So far, we've talked about options on interest rates. The values of comparable options on rates and prices respond differently to changes in interest rates because of the inverse relationship between bond yields and bond prices. Figure 3 outlines how each type of option responds to changes in yields and bond prices.

Figure 3: Options on Rate vs. Options on Prices

Option	If Rates Increase and Bond Prices Decrease	If Rates Decrease and Bond Prices Increase
Value of call on LIBOR	Increases	Decreases
Value of call on bond price	Decreases	Increases
Value of put on LIBOR	Decreases	Increases
Value of put on bond price	Increases	Decreases

We can also interpret caps and floors in terms of options on the prices of fixed-income securities:

- A long cap is equivalent to a portfolio of long put options on fixed-income security prices.
- A long floor is equivalent to a portfolio of long call options on fixed-income security prices.

LOS 55.b: Calculate the payoff for a cap and a floor, and explain how a collar is created.

CFA® Program Curriculum, Volume 6, page 335

A floating-rate borrower can use a cap to limit interest expense during the life of the cap. The payoff to the cap buyer is:

$$\text{periodic payment} = \max\left[0, (\text{notional principal}) \times (\text{index rate} - \text{cap strike}) \times \left(\frac{\text{actual days}}{360}\right)\right]$$

A floating-rate investor can use a floor to limit reductions in interest income during the life of the floor. The payment to the floor buyer is:

$$\text{periodic payment} = \max\left[0, (\text{notional principal}) \times (\text{floor strike} - \text{index rate}) \times \left(\frac{\text{actual days}}{360}\right)\right]$$

Example: Calculating the payoff for an interest rate cap

Suppose that a 1-year cap has a cap rate of 8% and a notional amount of $100 million. The frequency of settlement is quarterly, and the reference rate is 3-month LIBOR. Assume that 3-month LIBOR for the next four quarters is as shown in the following figure. Calculate the payoff for each quarter.

Payoff to 8% Interest Rate Cap

Quarter	3-month LIBOR	Payoff
1	7.7%	?
2	8.0%	?
3	8.4%	?
4	8.6%	?

Answer:

The cap will have a payoff each quarter equal to:

$$\max\left[0,\ \$100{,}000{,}000 \times \left(\frac{\text{LIBOR} - 0.08}{4}\right)\right]$$

 Professor's Note: The division by 4 comes from the settlement frequency, assuming exactly 90 days per quarter.

$$\text{quarter 1 payoff} = \max\left[0,\ \$100{,}000{,}000 \times \left(\frac{0.077 - 0.08}{4}\right)\right] = \$0$$

$$\text{quarter 2 payoff} = \max\left[0,\ \$100{,}000{,}000 \times \left(\frac{0.08 - 0.08}{4}\right)\right] = \$0$$

$$\text{quarter 3 payoff} = \max\left[0,\ \$100{,}000{,}000 \times \left(\frac{0.084 - 0.08}{4}\right)\right] = \$100{,}000$$

$$\text{quarter 4 payoff} = \max\left[0,\ \$100{,}000{,}000 \times \left(\frac{0.086 - 0.08}{4}\right)\right] = \$150{,}000$$

Example: Calculating the payoff for an interest rate floor

Let's change the cap to a *floor*, keeping the other information the same. Calculate the payoff for a floor with a floor rate of 8%.

Answer:

$$\text{quarter 1 payoff} = \max\left[0, \$100,000,000 \times \left(\frac{0.08 - 0.077}{4}\right)\right] = \$75,000$$

$$\text{quarter 2 payoff} = \max\left[0, \$100,000,000 \times \left(\frac{0.08 - 0.08}{4}\right)\right] = \$0$$

$$\text{quarter 3 payoff} = \max\left[0, \$100,000,000 \times \left(\frac{0.08 - 0.084}{4}\right)\right] = \$0$$

$$\text{quarter 4 payoff} = \max\left[0, \$100,000,000 \times \left(\frac{0.08 - 0.086}{4}\right)\right] = \$0$$

An **interest rate collar** is a simultaneous position in a floor and a cap on the same benchmark rate over the same period with the same settlement dates. There are two types of collars:

- The first type of collar is to purchase a cap and sell a floor. For example, an investor with a LIBOR-based liability could purchase a cap on LIBOR at 8% and simultaneously sell a floor on LIBOR at 4% over the next year. The investor has now hedged the liability so that the borrowing costs will stay within the "collar" of 4% to 8%. If the cap and floor rates are set so that the premium paid from buying the cap is exactly offset by the premium received from selling the floor, the collar is called a "zero-cost" collar.
- The second type of collar is to purchase a floor and sell a cap. For example, an investor with a LIBOR-based asset could purchase a floor on LIBOR at 3% and simultaneously sell a cap at 7% over the next year. The investor has now hedged the asset so the returns will stay within the collar of 3% to 7%. The investor can create a zero-cost collar by choosing the cap and floor rates so that the premium paid on the floor offsets the premium received on the cap.

KEY CONCEPTS

LOS 55.a

An interest rate cap is an agreement in which one party agrees to pay the other at regular intervals over a certain period of time when the benchmark interest rate (e.g., LIBOR) exceeds the strike rate specified in the contract. The buyer of a cap has a position similar to that of a buyer of a call on LIBOR, both of whom benefit when interest rates rise. Because an interest rate cap is a multi-period agreement, a cap is actually a portfolio of call options on LIBOR called caplets.

An interest rate floor is an agreement in which one party agrees to pay the other at regular intervals over a certain period of time when the benchmark interest rate (e.g., LIBOR) falls below the strike rate specified in the contract. The buyer of a floor benefits from an interest rate decrease and, therefore, has a position that is similar to that of a buyer of a put on LIBOR. Because a floor is a multi-period agreement, a floor is actually a portfolio of put options on LIBOR called floorlets.

LOS 55.b

A floating-rate borrower can use a cap to limit interest expense during the life of the cap. The payoff to the cap buyer is:

$$\text{periodic payment} = \max\left[0, (\text{notional principal}) \times (\text{index rate} - \text{cap strike}) \times \left(\frac{\text{actual days}}{360}\right)\right]$$

A floating-rate investor can use a floor to limit reductions in interest income during the life of the floor. The payment to the floor buyer is:

$$\text{periodic payment} = \max\left[0, (\text{notional principal}) \times (\text{floor strike} - \text{index rate}) \times \left(\frac{\text{actual days}}{360}\right)\right]$$

An interest rate collar is a simultaneous position in a floor and a cap on the same benchmark rate over the same period with the same settlement dates. The collar investor can either buy a cap and sell a floor or buy a floor and sell a cap. If the cap and floor rates are set so that the premium paid for the long position is equal to the premium received for the short position, it is called a zero-cost collar.

CONCEPT CHECKERS

1. A 1-year cap has a cap rate of 8% and a notional amount of $10 million. The frequency of settlement is quarterly, and the reference rate is 3-month LIBOR. Assume that 3-month LIBOR for the next four quarters is as shown in the following figure.

Quarter	3-month LIBOR
1	8.7%
2	8.0%
3	7.8%
4	8.2%

    The payoff for the cap for the third quarter is *closest* to:
    A. $0.
    B. $5,000.
    C. $17,500.

2. A portfolio of put options on a benchmark interest rate like LIBOR is called an interest rate:
    A. cap.
    B. floor.
    C. collar.

3. If interest rates increase, what will *most likely* happen to the value of a long position in a:

	Call option on LIBOR?	Put option on a bond price?
A.	Increase	Increase
B.	Increase	Decrease
C.	Decrease	Increase

CHALLENGE PROBLEM

4. An interest rate floor at 7% is available from a dealer. To create an interest rate collar, an investor is *most likely* to:
    A. buy the floor and sell a 12% interest rate cap.
    B. buy the floor and sell a 7% interest rate cap.
    C. sell the floor and buy a 3% interest rate cap.

ANSWERS – CONCEPT CHECKERS

1. **A** $\text{period 1 payoff} = \max\left[0, \ \$10,000,000 \times \left(\frac{0.087 - 0.08}{4}\right)\right] = \$17,500$

    $\text{period 2 payoff} = \max\left[0, \ \$10,000,000 \times \left(\frac{0.08 - 0.08}{4}\right)\right] = \$0$

    $\text{period 3 payoff} = \max\left[0, \ \$10,000,000 \times \left(\frac{0.078 - 0.08}{4}\right)\right] = \$0$

    $\text{period 4 payoff} = \max\left[0, \ \$10,000,000 \times \left(\frac{0.082 - 0.08}{4}\right)\right] = \$5,000$

2. **B** An interest rate floor is an agreement in which one party agrees to pay the other party at regular intervals over a certain period of time when the benchmark interest rate (e.g., LIBOR) falls below the strike rate, or floor rate, specified in the contract. It is equivalent to a portfolio of put options on LIBOR. Each individual put option is called a floorlet.

3. **A** If interest rates increase, a long position in a call option on LIBOR will increase in value. An increase in interest rates will cause bond prices to fall, which will also increase the value of a long position in a put option on a bond price.

ANSWER – CHALLENGE PROBLEM

4. **A** An interest rate collar is a simultaneous position in a floor and a cap on the same benchmark rate over the same period with the same settlement dates. The strike rate on the floor must be less than the strike rate on the cap. The investor either (1) buys the floor and sells the cap, or (2) sells the floor and buys the cap. The only way to create an interest collar from the choices is to buy the floor at 7% and sell the cap at 12%.

    Buying the floor at 7% and selling the cap at 7% will result in a position similar to a short position in a forward contract on LIBOR (i.e., a forward rate agreement, or FRA). Selling the floor and buying the cap at the same rate will result in a position similar to a long position in an FRA.

CREDIT DEFAULT SWAPS

EXAM FOCUS

A credit default swap (CDS) is a contract between two parties in which one party purchases protection from another party against losses from the default of a borrower. For the exam, you should be able to describe CDS, as well as related securities like index CDS. You should know what a credit event is and how the different protocols for settlement work. You should be familiar with the principles and factors that drive market pricing of CDS. Be able to describe how CDS are used to manage credit exposure, and how they can be used to profit from anticipated changes in the credit curve. You should understand how CDS are used for arbitrage to take advantage of relative mispricings of different risky securities.

CREDIT DEFAULT SWAPS

A **credit default swap** (CDS) is essentially an insurance contract. If a credit event occurs, the *credit protection buyer* gets compensated by the *credit protection seller*. To obtain this coverage, the protection buyer pays the seller a premium called the **CDS spread**. The protection seller is assuming (i.e., long) credit risk, while the protection buyer is short credit risk. Note that the CDS does not provide protection against market-wide interest rate risk, only against credit risk. The contract is written on a face value of protection called the **notional principal** (or "notional").

Even though the CDS spread should be based on the underlying credit risk of the reference obligation, standardization in the market has led to a fixed **coupon** on CDS products: 1% for investment-grade securities and 5% for high-yield securities. Hence, the coupon rate on the CDS and the actual credit spread may be different. The present value of the difference between the standardized coupon rate and the credit spread on the reference obligation is paid upfront by one of the parties to the contract. For example, a CDS on an investment-grade bond with a credit spread of 75 basis points (bps) would require a premium payment of 100bps (CDS coupon rate) by the protection buyer. To compensate the protection buyer (who pays a higher-than-market premium), the protection seller would then pay upfront to the buyer the present value of 25bps of the notional principal.

For a protection buyer, a CDS has some of the characteristics of a put option—when the underlying performs poorly, the holder of the put option has a right to exercise the option.

The **International Swaps and Derivatives Association** (ISDA), the unofficial governing body of the industry, publishes standardized contract terms and conventions to facilitate smooth functioning of the CDS market.

LOS 56.a: Describe credit default swaps (CDS), single-name and index CDS, and the parameters that define a given CDS product.

CFA® Program Curriculum, Volume 6, page 345

SINGLE-NAME CDS

In the case of a single-name CDS, the **reference obligation** is the fixed-income security on which the swap is written, usually a senior unsecured obligation (in the case of a **senior CDS**). The issuer of the reference obligation is called the **reference entity**. The CDS pays off not only when the reference entity defaults on the reference obligation but also when the reference entity defaults on any other issue that is ranked pari passu (i.e., same rank) or higher. The CDS payoff is based on the market value of the **cheapest-to-deliver** (CTD) bond that has the same seniority as the reference obligation.

Example: Cheapest-to-deliver

Party X is a protection buyer in a $10 million notional principal senior CDS of Alpha, Inc. There is a credit event (i.e., Alpha defaults) and the market prices of Alpha's bonds after the credit event are as follows:

- Bond P, a subordinated unsecured debenture, trading at 15% of par.
- Bond Q, a five-year senior unsecured debenture, trading at 25% of par.
- Bond R, a three-year senior unsecured debenture, trading at 30% of par.

What will be the payoff on the CDS?

Answer:

The cheapest-to-deliver senior unsecured debenture (i.e., same seniority as the senior CDS) is bond Q. The payoff will be the difference between the notional principal and market value of the CTD.

$$\text{payoff} = \$10 \text{ million} - (0.25)(\$10 \text{ million}) = \$7.5 \text{ million}.$$

INDEX CDS

An *index CDS* covers multiple issuers, allowing market participants to take on an exposure to the credit risk of several companies simultaneously in the same way that stock indexes allow investors to take on an equity exposure to several companies at once. In this case, the protection for each issuer is equal (i.e., equally weighted) and the total notional principal is the sum of the protection on all the issuers.

Example: Index CDS

Party X is a protection buyer in a five-year, $100 million notional principal CDS for CDX-IG, which contains 125 entities. One of the index constituents, company A, defaults and its bonds trade at 30% of par after default.

1. What will be the payoff on the CDS?

2. What will be the notional principal of the CDS after default?

Answer:

1. The notional principal attributable to entity A is $100 million / 125 = $0.8 million. Party X should receive payment of $0.8 million – (0.3)(0.8) = $560,000.

2. Post the default event, the remainder of the CDS continues with a notional principal of $99.2 million.

The pricing of an index CDS is dependent on the correlation of default (credit correlation) among the entities in the index. The higher the correlation of default among index constituents, the higher the spread on the index CDS.

LOS 56.b: Describe credit events and settlement protocols with respect to CDS.

CFA® Program Curriculum, Volume 6, page 348

A default is defined as the occurrence of a credit event. Common types of credit events specified in CDS agreements include bankruptcy, failure to pay, and restructuring.

- Bankruptcy: A bankruptcy protection filing allows the defaulting party to work with creditors under the supervision of the court so as to avoid full liquidation.
- Failure to pay: Occurs when the issuer misses a scheduled coupon or principal payment without filing for formal bankruptcy.
- Restructuring: Occurs when the issuer forces its creditors to accept terms that are different than those specified in the original issue. Restructuring is less common in the United States as issuers prefer to go the bankruptcy protection route.

A 15-member group of the ISDA called the **Determinations Committee** (DC) declares when a credit event has occurred. A supermajority vote (at least 12 members) is required for a credit event to be declared.

When there is a credit event, the swap will be settled in cash or by physical delivery. With physical delivery, the protection seller receives the reference obligation (i.e., the bond or loan) and pays the protection buyer the notional amount, as shown in Figure 1.

Figure 1: Physical Settlement on Credit Default Swap after a Credit Event

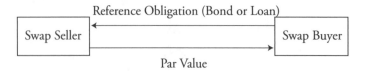

In the case of a cash settlement, the payout amount is the payout ratio times the notional principal. The payout ratio depends on the recovery rate (i.e., the proportion of par that the bond trades at after default) as shown in Figure 2.

payout amount = payout ratio × notional principal

where:
payout ratio = 1 – recovery rate (%)

Figure 2: Cash Settlement on Credit Default Swap after a Credit Event

LOS 56.c: Explain the principles underlying, and factors that influence, the market's pricing of CDS.

CFA® Program Curriculum, Volume 6, page 354

The factors that influence the pricing of CDS (i.e., CDS spread) include the probability of default, the loss given default, and the coupon rate on the swap. The CDS spread is higher for higher probability of default and for higher loss given default. For this discussion, we will focus on single-name CDS. However, the principles apply to index CDS as well.

 Professor's Note: Candidates are not expected to precisely estimate the credit spread on a CDS. You should understand the factors that influence the spread and the spread's relation to the upfront payment.

Probability of default is the likelihood of default by the reference entity in a given year. However, because the CDS typically covers a multi-year horizon, the probability of default is not constant; the probability of default usually increases over time. For a single-name CDS, when a default occurs, a payment is made by the protection seller to the protection buyer and the CDS ceases to exist. Hence, in the context of a CDS, the probability of default in any given year assumes that no default has occurred in the preceding years. We call the probability of default *given that it has not already occurred*

the **conditional probability of default** or **hazard rate**. The credit risk of a reference obligation and hence the cost of protection is proportional to the hazard rate.

Example: Hazard rate

Consider a five-year senior CDS on Xeon Corp. Xeon's hazard rate is 2% and increases by 1% per year.

Compute the survival rate in five years.

Answer:

The hazard rates for the five years are: 2%, 3%, 4%, 5%, and 6%.

$$\text{Survival rate in five years} = (1 - 0.02)(1 - 0.03)(1 - 0.04)(1 - 0.05)(1 - 0.06) = 0.815 \text{ or } 81.5\%$$

Loss given default is the expected amount of loss in the event that a default occurs. Loss given default is inversely related to the recovery rate. The expected loss for any given period is the hazard rate for that period times the loss given default for that period.

$$(\text{expected loss})_t = (\text{hazard rate})_t \times (\text{loss given default})_t$$

The cash payments made by the protection buyer on the CDS (i.e., the coupon payments) cease when there is a default (i.e., the CDS terminates). Hence, the expected value of the coupon payments also depends on the hazard rate.

The payments made by the protection buyer to the seller are the **premium leg**. On the other side of the contract, the protection seller must make a payment to the protection buyer in case of a default; these contingent payments make up the **protection leg**.

The difference between the present value of the premium leg and the present value of the protection leg determines the upfront payment.

$$\text{upfront payment (paid by protection buyer)} = PV(\text{protection leg}) - PV(\text{premium leg})$$

We can approximate the upfront premium as the difference between the CDS spread and the CDS coupon rate, multiplied by the duration of the CDS. Again, the CDS spread is the compensation for bearing the credit risk of the reference obligation.

 Professor's Note: Be careful here! The formula uses duration of the CDS and not the duration of the reference obligation.

$$\text{upfront premium \% (paid by protection buyer)} \approx (\text{CDS spread} - \text{CDS coupon}) \times \text{duration}$$

We can also quote the **CDS price** as:

price of CDS (per $100 notional) $\approx$ $100 – upfront premium (%)

Example: Upfront premium and price of CDS

Aki Mutaro, bond portfolio manager for a regional bank, is considering buying protection on one of the bank's high-yield holdings: Alpha Inc. bonds. Ten-year CDS on Alpha bonds have a coupon rate of 5% while the 10-year Alpha CDS spread is 3.5%. The duration of the CDS is 7.

Calculate the approximate upfront premium and price of a 10-year Alpha Inc., CDS.

Answer:

upfront premium % $\approx$ (CDS spread – CDS coupon) $\times$ duration
= (3.5% – 5.0%) $\times$ 7 = –10.5%

Hence, the protection seller would pay (approximately) 10.5% of the notional to the protection buyer upfront because the CDS coupon is higher than the credit spread.

CDS price = 100 – (–10.5) = $110.50 per $100 notional

VALUATION AFTER INCEPTION OF CDS

At inception of a CDS, the CDS spread (and the upfront premium) is computed based on the credit quality of the reference entity. After inception, the credit quality of the reference entity (or the credit risk premium in the overall market) may change. This will lead to the underlying CDS having a nonzero value. For example, if the credit spread declines, the protection seller, having locked in a higher credit spread at initiation, would gain.

The change in value of a CDS after inception can be approximated by the change in spread multiplied by the duration of the CDS:

profit for protection buyer $\approx$ change in spread $\times$ duration $\times$ notional principal

or

profit for protection buyer (%) $\approx$ change in spread (%) $\times$ duration

Note that the protection buyer is short credit risk and hence benefits (i.e., profit is positive) when credit spreads widen.

The protection buyer (or seller) can unwind an existing CDS exposure (prior to expiration or default) by entering into an offsetting transaction. For example, a protection seller can remove his exposure to the CDS by buying protection with the same terms as the original CDS and maturity equal to the remaining maturity. The difference between the upfront premium paid and received should be (approximately) equal to the profit for the protection buyer estimated using the earlier equation. This process of capturing value from an in-the-money (out-of-money) CDS exposure is called **monetizing** the gain (or loss).

LOS 56.d: Describe the use of CDS to manage credit exposures and to express views regarding changes in shape and/or level of the credit curve.

CFA® Program Curriculum, Volume 6, page 363

CREDIT CURVE

The **credit curve** is the relationship between credit spreads for different bonds issued by an entity, and the bonds' maturities. The credit curve is similar to the term structure of interest rates. If the longer maturity bonds have a higher credit spread compared to shorter maturity bonds, the credit curve will be upward sloping. However, if the hazard rate is constant, the credit curve will be flat.

CDS can be used to manage credit exposures of a bond portfolio. For example, in anticipation of declining (increasing) credit spreads, a portfolio manager may increase (decrease) credit exposure in the portfolio by being a protection seller (buyer).

In a **naked CDS**, an investor with no underlying exposure purchases protection in the CDS market. In a **long/short trade**, an investor purchases protection on one reference entity while simultaneously selling protection on another (often related) reference entity. The investor is betting that the difference in credit spreads between the two reference entities will change to the investor's advantage. This is similar to going long (protection seller exposure) in one reference entity bond and simultaneously going short (protection buyer exposure) in the other reference entity bond.

A **curve trade** is a type of long/short trade where the investor is buying and selling protection on the *same* reference entity but with a different maturity. If the investor expects that an upward-sloping credit curve on a specific corporate issuer will flatten, she may take the position of protection buyer in a short maturity CDS and the position of protection seller in a long maturity CDS.

An investor concerned about the credit risk of an issuer in the near term while being more confident of the long-term prospects of the issuer might buy protection in the short-term CDS and offset the premium cost by selling protection in the long-term CDS. An investor who believes that the short-term outlook for the reference entity is better than the long-term outlook can use a curve-steepening trade; buying protection in a long-term CDS and selling protection in a short-term CDS. The investor will profit if the credit curve steepens; that is, if long-term credit risk increases relative to short-term credit risk. Conversely, an investor who is bearish about the reference entity's prospects in the short term will enter into a curve-flattening trade.

LOS 56.e: Describe the use of CDS to take advantage of valuation differences among separate markets, such as bonds, loans, and equities.

CFA® Program Curriculum, Volume 6, page 365

Uses of CDS

Earning arbitrage profits is another motivation for trading in the CDS market. Differences in pricing between asset and derivative markets, or differences in pricing of different products in the market, may offer potential arbitrage profits.

A **basis trade** is an attempt to exploit the difference in credit spreads between bond markets and the CDS market. Basis trades rely on the idea that such mispricing will be temporary and that disparity should eventually disappear after it is recognized. For example, if a specific bond is trading at a credit spread of 4% over LIBOR in the bond market but the CDS spread on the same bond is 3%, a trader can profit by buying the bond and taking the protection buyer position in the CDS market. If the expected convergence occurs, the trader will make a profit.

Another arbitrage transaction involves buying and selling debt instruments issued by the same entity based on which instruments the CDS market suggests to be undervalued or overvalued.

In the case of a leveraged buyout (LBO), the firm will issue a great amount of debt in order to repurchase all of the company's publicly traded equity. This additional debt will increase the CDS spread because default is now more likely. An investor who anticipates an LBO might purchase both the stock and CDS protection, both of which will increase in value when the LBO happens.

In the case of an index CDS, the value of the index should be equal to the sum of the values of the index components. An arbitrage transaction is possible if the credit risk of the index constituents is priced differently than the index CDS spread.

Collateralized debt obligations (CDO) are claims against a portfolio of debt securities. A synthetic CDO has similar credit risk exposure to that of a cash CDO but is assembled using CDS rather than debt securities. If the synthetic CDO can be created at a cost lower than that of the cash CDO, investors can buy the synthetic CDO and sell the cash CDO, engaging in a profitable arbitrage.

KEY CONCEPTS

LOS 56.a

A credit default swap (CDS) is essentially an insurance contract wherein upon occurrence of a credit event, the credit protection buyer gets compensated by the credit protection seller. To obtain this coverage, the protection buyer pays the seller a premium called the CDS spread. In the case of a single-name CDS, the reference obligation is the fixed income security on which the swap is written. An index CDS covers an equally-weighted combination of borrowers.

LOS 56.b

A default is defined as occurrence of a credit event. Common types of credit events specified in CDS agreements include bankruptcy, failure to pay, and restructuring.

When there is a credit event, the swap will be settled in cash or by physical delivery.

LOS 56.c

The factors that influence the pricing of CDS (i.e., CDS spread) include the probability of default, the loss given default, and the coupon rate on the swap. The CDS spread is higher for a higher probability of default and for a higher loss given default. The conditional probability of default (i.e., the probability of default given that default has not already occurred) is called the hazard rate.

$$(\text{expected loss})_t = (\text{hazard rate})_t \times (\text{loss given default})_t$$

The upfront premium on a CDS can be computed as:

$$\text{upfront payment (paid by protection buyer)} = \text{PV(protection leg)} - \text{PV(premium leg)}$$

Or approximately:

$$\text{upfront premium (paid by protection buyer)} \approx (\text{CDS spread} - \text{CDS coupon}) \times \text{duration}$$

The change in value for a CDS after inception can be approximated by the change in spread multiplied by the duration of the CDS.

$$\text{profit for protection buyer} \approx \text{change in spread} \times \text{duration} \times \text{notional principal}$$

Or

$$\text{profit for protection buyer (\%)} \approx \text{change in spread (\%)} \times \text{duration}$$

LOS 56.d

In a naked CDS, an investor with no exposure to the underlying purchases protection in the CDS market.

In a long/short trade, an investor purchases protection on one reference entity while selling protection on another reference entity.

A curve trade is a type of long/short trade where the investor is buying and selling protection on the same reference entity but with different maturities. An investor who believes the short-term outlook for the reference entity is better than the long-term outlook can use a curve-steepening trade (buying protection in a long-term CDS and selling protection in a short-term CDS) to profit if the credit curve steepens. Conversely, an investor who is bearish about the reference entity's prospects in the short term will enter into a curve-flattening trade.

LOS 56.e

A **basis trade** is an attempt to exploit the difference in credit spreads between bond markets and the CDS market. Basis trades rely on the idea that such mispricings will be temporary and that disparity should eventually disappear after it is recognized.

If a synthetic CDO can be created at a cost lower than that of the equivalent cash CDO, investors can buy the synthetic CDO and sell the cash CDO, producing a profitable arbitrage.

CONCEPT CHECKERS

Use the following information to answer questions 1 through 6.

Jamshed Banaji, CFA, manages a $400 million bond portfolio for a large public pension fund. Banaji is concerned about volatility in the credit markets and expects credit spreads to widen in the short-term but revert back to current levels over the long-term.

Banaji has flagged two of his holdings for further scrutiny: IDG Corp. and Zeta Corp.

The portfolio currently has $10 million par value of 6% 10-year senior unsecured IDG Corp. bonds. Because he is concerned about IDG's credit risk, Banaji enters into a credit default swap as a protection buyer. Banaji selects a five-year senior CDS for IDG with a coupon rate of 5% and a duration of 4. IDG bonds have a yield-to-maturity of 6.5%. The LIBOR yield curve is flat at 2%.

Banaji is also concerned about the Zeta Corp. bonds that he holds. Zeta's management is planning to pursue a recapitalization plan that involves a large stock buyback program financed by new debt.

1. The *most* appropriate strategy for Banaji, given his expectation about changing credit spreads, is a:
    A. credit curve trade; selling protection in the short-term and purchasing protection in the long-term.
    B. credit curve trade; buying protection in the short-term and selling protection in the long-term.
    C. CDS trade; buying protection in the short-term only.

2. At inception of the CDS for IDG bonds, Banaji is *most likely* to:
    A. receive a premium of $200,000.
    B. pay a premium of $300,000.
    C. receive a premium of $400,000.

3. For this question only, suppose that six months after the inception of the swap, IDG declares bankruptcy. Exhibit 1 shows the market prices of IDG bonds after the company files for bankruptcy.

    Exhibit 1: Market Price of IDG Bonds Post Bankruptcy Filing

Description	Market Price (%) of Par
9.5-year 6% senior unsecured	45% of par
5-year 5% senior unsecured	40% of par
5-year 6% subordinated unsecured	30% of par

    If Banaji has a choice of settlement procedure, he is *most likely* to choose:
    A. physical settlement.
    B. cash settlement and the payoff would be $6 million.
    C. cash settlement and the payoff would be $7 million.

4. Which of the following statements about hazard rate is *most* accurate? Hazard rate:
    A. is the probability of default given that default has already occurred in a previous period.
    B. affects both the premium leg as well as the protection leg in a CDS.
    C. is higher for higher loss given default.

5. The most appropriate strategy for Banaji to follow in regard to Zeta Corp. would be to buy Zeta Corp.:
    A. stock and buy CDS protection on Zeta Corp. bonds.
    B. bonds and sell CDS protection on Zeta Corp. bonds
    C. stock and sell CDS protection on Zeta Corp. bonds.

6. The statement "credit spreads are positively related to loss given default and to hazard rate" is *most accurately* described as:
    A. correct.
    B. correct regarding loss given default but incorrect regarding hazard rate.
    C. correct regarding hazard rate but incorrect regarding loss given default.

ANSWERS – CONCEPT CHECKERS

1. **B** Banaji expects credit spreads to widen in the short-term; therefore, the appropriate strategy is to buy short-term CDS protection. Similarly, long-term credit spreads are expected to revert back to current levels (narrow) and hence Banaji can sell protection in the long-term CDS. Buying protection only would cost more money (the protection buyer premium is not offset by premium income from selling protection) and does not use Banaji's entire information set and, therefore, is not most appropriate.

2. **A** Credit spread on IDG bonds = yield – LIBOR = 6.5% – 2% = 4.5%

    upfront premium (paid by protection buyer) ≈ (CDS spread – CDS coupon) × duration × notional principal

    = (0.045 – 0.05) × 4 × $10 million = –$200,000

    Because the computed value is negative, $200,000 would be received by Banaji as the protection buyer.

3. **B** The CDS in the question is a senior CDS, hence the reference obligation is a senior unsecured bond. The payoff on the CDS is based on the CTD with same seniority as reference obligation. From the three choices given, the five-year 5% senior unsecured is the cheapest to deliver. Hence, the payoff will be notional principal – market value of the CTD = $10 million – $ 4 million = $6 million.

    Note that physical settlement would not be advantageous to Banaji; the bonds to be surrendered have a market value of $4.5 million so the implied payoff would be only $5.5 million ($10 million – $4.5 million).

4. **B** Hazard rate is the conditional probability of default given that default has not occurred in previous periods. The hazard rate affects the protection leg: the higher the hazard rate, the higher the expected value of payoffs made by the protection seller upon default. Hazard rate also affects the premium leg because once default occurs, the CDS ceases to exist and premium income would also cease. Loss given default depends on the recovery rate and not on hazard rate (probability of default).

5. **A** Due to leveraged recapitalization of Zeta Corp., it can be expected that the credit spread on Zeta bonds would widen leading to increased value for CDS protection buyer. Additionally, the increase in stock buyback would be expected to increase the value of Zeta stock. Banaji should purchase both the stock and CDS protection, both of which will increase in value when the LBO occurs.

6. **A** Credit spreads are positively related to hazard rates and loss given default, and negatively related to recovery rates.

18 minutes

Use the following information to answer Questions 1 through 6.

Derrick Honny, CFA, has operated his own portfolio management business for many years. Several of his clients have fixed income positions, and one of Honny's analysts has advised him that the firm can improve the performance of these portfolios through swaps. Honny has begun investigating the properties of swaps. His plan is first to establish some minor positions to gain some experience before actively using swaps on behalf of his clients.

Honny knows that the most basic type of swap is the plain vanilla swap where one counterparty pays LIBOR as the floating rate, and the other counterparty pays a fixed rate determined by the swap market. He feels this would be a good place to begin and plans to engage in a 2-year, annual-pay plain vanilla swap where he pays LIBOR and receives the fixed swap rate from the other counterparty. To get an idea regarding the swap rate he can expect on the 2-year swap, he collects market data on LIBOR. Details are shown in Figure 1.

Figure 1: Market Data on Term Structure of Interest Rates

Year	LIBOR	Discount Factor
1	5.00%	0.9524
2	4.60%	0.9158

He finds that when taking a swap position that there are other types of risks to consider. Honny thinks he should try to hedge some of these other types of risk the contract might have. He first focuses on credit risk. He finds it interesting that the credit risk of a swap typically varies over the time between inception and maturity. Also, there is something called potential credit risk, which also varies over the life of the swap. Sometimes current credit risk is more of a concern than potential credit risk, sometimes potential credit risk is more of a concern than current credit risk, and sometimes they are of equal concern.

As he learns more, Honny considers other possible swap positions that he might take. He is considering entering into a 4-year swap instead of a 2-year swap, but he knows this can be more risky. Instead of a 4-year swap, he investigates taking the 2-year swap position, which he first considered, and then taking a position in a derivative that will allow him to extend the horizon two more years when the 2-year swap expires. He finds that there are two appropriate varieties of derivatives that can be used to achieve this goal: (1) swaptions and (2) forward swaps.

One of Honny's clients, George Rosen, is aware of Honny's plans to use swaps and other derivatives in the management of his clients' portfolios. Rosen has a position for which he thinks a swap strategy will be appropriate. Rosen asks Honny to arrange for him a payer swaption that matures in three years. Honny is uncertain of the level of Rosen's familiarity with swaps and swaptions, so he wants to make sure that the derivative is

©2013 Kaplan, Inc.

appropriate for the client. He asks Rosen exactly what he intends to accomplish by entering into the swaption.

Honny realizes that more of his clients may approach him about using swaptions. He wants to be able to advise his clients about how to use them, how to close positions early, and how to settle positions at maturity. He finds that there are several ways to close a swaption position and to settle a swaption at maturity.

1. Which of the following would be the *least appropriate* alternative investments to replicate the exposure Honny will get from the 2-year, plain vanilla swap position that he plans to take?
    A. Long a series of interest rate puts and short a series of interest rate calls.
    B. Short a series of bond futures.
    C. Short a series of forward rate agreements.

2. Given the 1- and 2-year rates, the 2-year swap fixed rate would be *closest* to:
    A. 4.20%.
    B. 4.51%.
    C. 4.80%.

3. At the inception of a swap, the:
    A. potential credit risk is greater than the current credit risk.
    B. current credit risk is greater than the potential credit risk.
    C. current credit risk is equal to the potential credit risk, and both are equal to zero.

4. To have the right to extend the 2-year swap position when the swap expires, the *most appropriate* position for Honny would be to long a:
    A. payer swaption.
    B. receiver swaption.
    C. forward swap.

5. Which of the following is *least likely* a reason that Rosen might want to enter into a swaption with a maturity of three years? To:
    A. close an existing swaption position.
    B. hedge a floating rate bond that he owns with three years to maturity.
    C. have the right to terminate a 5-year swap early.

6. Which of the following is the *least likely* way the market value of a swaption at expiration can be received?
    A. As an annuity settlement.
    B. By receiving the swap spread.
    C. By entering into the underlying swap.

SELF-TEST ANSWERS: DERIVATIVES

1. **B** Since Honny will pay the floating rate in the 2-year swap, he gains when the floating rate goes down and loses when it goes up (relative to expectations at inception). This exposure could be replicated with either a short position in a series of FRAs or with a series of short interest rate calls and long interest rate puts. Since short bond futures gain when floating rates increase and lose when floating rates decrease, such a position would give him an exposure opposite to the floating rate payer position in a fixed-for-floating interest rate swap.

2. **B** Given the discount factors, the swap-fixed rate can be calculated as:

$$\text{swap fixed rate} = \frac{1 - Z_{2\text{-year}}}{Z_{1\text{-year}} + Z_{2\text{-year}}} = \frac{1 - 0.9158}{0.9524 + 0.9158} = 0.0451$$

Since the rates are already in annual terms, no further adjustment is necessary.

3. **A** At the inception of a swap the expected value of the swap is zero, and there is no current credit risk. Potential credit risk always exists. Potential credit risk is typically assumed to be low at inception because of the high credit worthiness of the swap market participants. Yet, even at the beginning of a swap, there is some potential credit risk, because the counterparty may experience a change in credit worthiness during the life of the swap.

4. **B** To have the "right" to extend the swap, a swaption is the more appropriate choice. Forward swaps require both counterparties to engage in the swap (i.e., an obligation is created). A payer swaption gives the owner the right to pay the fixed rate, and a receiver swaption gives the owner the right to receive the fixed rate.

5. **B** The swaption can be used to hedge the planned issuance of a floating rate bond in the future, but the instrument would not be an effective means of hedging an existing floating rate bond that expires on or before the maturity date of the swaption. It is possible to use swaptions to achieve all of the other objectives listed.

6. **B** The swap spread refers to the difference between the fixed rate of a swap and the comparable Treasury notes and would not play a direct role in the settlement of a swaption. There are three possible ways to exercise a swaption: (1) the holder can exercise the swaption, thereby entering into a swap, as in choice C; (2) the holder can arrange to receive a net payment stream (i.e., an annuity), as in choice A; and (3) the holder can receive an up-front cash payment.

PORTFOLIO CONCEPTS

EXAM FOCUS

This is a very long, intensive topic review of a very important Level II topic, so expect it to be tested extensively on the exam. It will require a significant amount of time for you to master the concepts addressed in the LOS. You should focus on both the broad concepts and the particular details. Although everything in this topic review is fair game for the exam, you must have a firm grasp of the key differences among (and applications to portfolio management of) mean-variance analysis, the capital asset pricing model, the single-factor market model, the arbitrage pricing theory, macroeconomic multifactor models, and fundamental multifactor models.

LOS 57.a: Explain mean–variance analysis and its assumptions, and calculate the expected return and the standard deviation of return for a portfolio of two or three assets.

CFA® Program Curriculum, Volume 6, page 376

Mean-variance analysis refers to the use of expected returns, variances, and covariances of individual investments to analyze the risk-return tradeoff of combinations (i.e., portfolios) of these assets.

Over a half century has passed since Professor Harry Markowitz established the tenets of mean-variance analysis, or capital market theory, the focal point of which is the efficient frontier. Several assumptions underlie mean-variance analysis. The assumptions establish a uniformity of investors, which greatly simplifies the analysis.

The main assumptions of mean-variance analysis can be summarized as follows:

- All investors are **risk averse**. Investors minimize risk for any given level of expected return, or, stated differently, investors demand additional compensation in exchange for additional risk. Investors may differ in their degree of risk aversion, but the key is that all investors are assumed to be risk averse to some degree.
- Expected returns, variances, and covariances are known for all assets. Investors know the future values of these parameters.
- Investors create optimal portfolios by relying solely on expected returns, variances, and covariances. No other distributional parameter is used. For example, returns are often assumed to follow a normal distribution in which skewness and kurtosis can be ignored.
- Investors face no taxes or transaction costs. Therefore, there is no difference between before-tax gross returns and after-tax net returns, placing all investors on equal footing.

Mean-variance analysis is used to identify optimal or efficient portfolios. Before we can discuss the implications of efficient portfolios, however, we must first be able to understand and calculate portfolio expected returns and standard deviations.

EXPECTED RETURN AND STANDARD DEVIATION FOR A TWO-ASSET PORTFOLIO

The **expected return** on a portfolio is a weighted average of the expected returns on the individual assets that are included in the portfolio. For example, for a two-asset portfolio:

$$E(R_p) = w_1 E(R_1) + w_2 E(R_2)$$

where:
$E(R_p)$ = expected return on Portfolio P
w_i = proportion ("weight") of the portfolio allocated to Asset i
$E(R_i)$ = expected return on Asset i

The weights (w_1 and w_2) must sum to 100% for a two-asset portfolio.

The variance of a two-asset portfolio equals:

$$\sigma_P^2 = w_1^2 \sigma_1^2 + w_2^2 \sigma_2^2 + 2w_1 w_2 Cov_{1,2}$$

where:
σ_P^2 = variance of the returns for Portfolio P
σ_1^2 = variance of the returns for Asset 1
σ_2^2 = variance of the returns for Asset 2
w_i = proportion (weight) of the portfolio allocated to Asset i
$Cov_{1,2}$ = covariance between the returns of the two assets

The covariance, $Cov_{1,2}$, measures the strength of the relationship between the returns earned on assets 1 and 2. The covariance is unbounded (ranges from negative infinity to positive infinity), and, therefore, is not a very useful measure of the strength of the relationship between two asset's returns. Instead, we often scale the covariance by the standard deviations of the two assets to derive the **correlation**, $\rho_{1,2}$:

$$\rho_{1,2} = \frac{Cov_{1,2}}{\sigma_1 \sigma_2}$$

From the previous equation, notice that the covariance equals $\rho_{1,2} \sigma_1 \sigma_2$, where $\rho_{1,2}$ is the correlation of returns between the two assets. Therefore, the variance of the two-asset portfolio can be written:

$$\sigma_P^2 = w_1^2 \sigma_1^2 + w_2^2 \sigma_2^2 + 2w_1 w_2 \rho_{1,2} \sigma_1 \sigma_2$$

Example: Expected return and standard deviation for a two-asset portfolio

Using the information in the following figure, calculate the expected return and standard deviation of the two-asset portfolio.

Characteristics for a Two-Stock Portfolio

	Caffeine Plus	*Sparklin'*
Amount invested	$40,000	$60,000
Expected return	11%	25%
Standard deviation	15%	20%
Correlation	0.30	

Answer:

First, determine the **weight** of each stock relative to the entire portfolio. Since the investments are $40,000 and $60,000, we know the total value of the portfolio is $100,000:

$$w_c = \text{investment / portfolio value} = \$40,000 / \$100,000 = 0.40$$

$$w_s = \text{investment / portfolio value} = \$60,000 / \$100,000 = 0.60$$

Next, we determine the **expected return** on the portfolio:

$$E(R_p) = w_c E(R_c) + w_s E(R_s)$$

$$E(R_p) = (0.40)(0.11) + (0.60)(0.25) = 0.1940 = 19.40\%$$

Then, we calculate the **variance** of the portfolio:

$$\sigma_p^2 = w_c^2 \sigma_c^2 + w_s^2 \sigma_s^2 + 2 w_c w_s \rho_{cs} \sigma_c \sigma_s$$
$$= (0.40)^2 (0.15)^2 + (0.60)^2 (0.20)^2 + 2(0.40)(0.60)(0.30)(0.15)(0.20)$$
$$= 0.02232$$

And, finally, the **standard deviation** of the portfolio:

$$\sigma_p = \sqrt{\sigma_p^2} = \sqrt{0.02232} = 0.1494 = 14.94\%$$

In the Caffeine Plus and Sparklin' example, we calculated the expected return and standard deviation of one possible combination: 40% in Caffeine Plus and 60% in Sparklin'. An infinite number of combinations of the two stocks are possible, however. We can plot these combinations on a graph with expected return on the *y*-axis and standard deviation on the *x*-axis, commonly referred to as plotting in risk/return "space." Figure 1 shows some of these combinations.

Figure 1: Portfolio Returns for Various Weights of Two Assets

$w_{\text{Caffeine Plus}}$	100%	80%	60%	40%	20%	0%
$w_{\text{Sparklin'}}$	0%	20%	40%	60%	80%	100%
$\hat{R}_p$	11.00%	13.80%	16.60%	19.40%	22.20%	25.00%
σ_p	15.00%	13.74%	13.72%	14.94%	17.10%	20.00%

The plot in Figure 2 represents all possible expected return and standard deviation combinations attainable by investing in varying amounts of Caffeine Plus and Sparklin'.

Figure 2: Expected Return and Standard Deviation Combinations

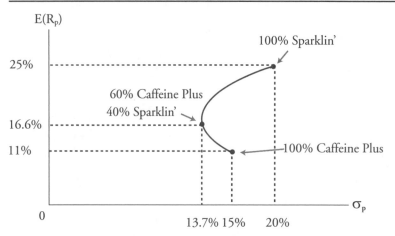

There are several things to notice about Figure 2:

- If 100% of the portfolio is allocated to Caffeine Plus, the portfolio will have the expected return and standard deviation of Caffeine Plus (i.e., Caffeine Plus *is* the portfolio), and the investment return and risk combination is at the lower end of the curve.
- As the investment in Caffeine Plus is decreased and the investment in Sparklin' is increased, the investment moves up the curve to the point where the portfolio's expected return is 16.6% and its standard deviation is 13.72% (labeled 60% Caffeine Plus/40% Sparklin').
- Finally, if 100% of the portfolio is allocated to Sparklin', the portfolio will have the expected return and standard deviation of Sparklin', and the investment return and risk combination is at the upper end of the curve (i.e., higher risk and higher expected return).

Three-Asset Portfolio

Just as in the two-asset case, the **expected return** on a portfolio of *three* assets is the weighted average of the returns on the individual assets:

$$E(R_P) = w_1 E(R_1) + w_2 E(R_2) + w_3 E(R_3)$$

where:
$$w_1 + w_2 + w_3 = 100\%$$

The standard deviation of a portfolio of three assets is calculated similarly to that for the two-asset portfolio, except that there are three new terms: a weighted variance term (for the third asset) and two more covariance terms (for assets 1 and 3 and assets 2 and 3).

$$\sigma_P^2 = w_1^2\sigma_1^2 + w_2^2\sigma_2^2 + \left[w_3^2\sigma_3^2\right] + 2w_1w_2\,cov_{1,2} + \left[2w_1w_3\,cov_{1,3} + 2w_2w_3\,cov_{2,3}\right]$$

$$\sigma_P^2 = w_1^2\sigma_1^2 + w_2^2\sigma_2^2 + w_3^2\sigma_3^2 + 2w_1w_2\rho_{1,2}\sigma_1\sigma_2 + 2w_1w_3\rho_{1,3}\sigma_1\sigma_3 + 2w_2w_3\rho_{2,3}\sigma_2\sigma_3$$

$$\sigma_P = \sqrt{\sigma_P^2}$$

Example: Three-asset portfolio

Calculate the expected return and standard deviation of the three-asset portfolio shown in the following figure.

Expected Returns and Standard Deviations for Three Stocks

	Caffeine Plus	Sparklin'	Golo
Amount invested	$40,000	$25,000	$35,000
Expected return	11%	25%	30%
Standard deviation	15%	20%	25%
	Correlations		
Caffeine Plus and Sparklin'	0.30		
Caffeine Plus and Golo	0.10		
Sparklin' and Golo	0.50		

Answer:

First, determine the **weight** of each stock in the portfolio:

$$w_c = \$40,000\, /\, \$100,000 = 0.40$$

$$w_s = \$25,000\, /\, \$100,000 = 0.25$$

$$w_g = \$35,000\, /\, `\$100,000 = 0.35$$

Next, calculate the **expected return** of the portfolio:

$$E(R_p) = w_c E(R_c) + w_s E(R_s) + w_g E(R_g)$$
$$= (0.40)(0.11) + (0.25)(0.25) + (0.35)(0.30) = 0.2115 = 21.15\%$$

Now, calculate the **variance** and **standard deviation** of the portfolio:

Portfolio variance:

$$= (0.40)^2 (0.15)^2 + (0.25)^2 (0.20)^2 + (0.35)^2 (0.25)^2$$
$$+ 2(0.40)(0.25)(0.30)(0.15)(0.20) + 2(0.40)(0.35)(0.10)(0.15)(0.25)$$
$$+ 2(0.25)(0.35)(0.50)(0.20)(0.25)$$
$$= 0.02098$$

Porfolio standard deviation $= \sqrt{0.020981} = 0.14485 = 14.485\%$

LOS 57.b: Describe the minimum-variance and efficient frontiers, and explain the steps to solve for the minimum-variance frontier.

CFA® Program Curriculum, Volume 6, page 377

The Minimum-Variance Frontier

A **minimum-variance portfolio** is one that has the smallest variance among all portfolios with identical expected return. For instance, assume we wish to earn a return equal to 25% on a portfolio comprising Caffeine Plus, Sparklin', and Golo from the three-asset example above. Many different portfolio combinations of the three stocks provide an expected return of 25%. One possibility is simply to invest 100% of the portfolio in Sparklin' stock. The expected return on the portfolio will equal 25% and the variance will equal $(0.20)^2 = 0.04 = 4\%$. But, we can achieve a 25% expected return on our portfolio with smaller variance by forming a portfolio of the three stocks. In this example, the minimum-variance portfolio is the one that provides a 25% expected return with the smallest possible variance among all portfolios that provide a 25% expected return.

Figure 3 illustrates the portfolio possibilities all of which are constrained to have a 25% expected return. All portfolios with an expected return of 25% lie on the horizontal line, but the portfolios have different variances (risk). All the portfolios comprise the identical set of three assets, but with different weightings. Portfolios to the left on the horizontal line have smaller variance (lower risk). If faced with these portfolio possibilities, any risk-averse investor will prefer the portfolio lying farthest to the left (the minimum-variance Portfolio E).

Figure 3: Minimum-Variance Portfolio

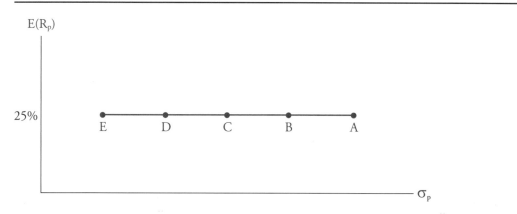

 Professor's Note: The mathematical solution for the minimum-variance portfolio is beyond the scope of analysis here. Instead, be sure to understand the general steps that are followed when deriving each minimum-variance portfolio.

The **minimum-variance frontier** is a graph of the expected return/variance combinations for all minimum-variance portfolios. The shape of the minimum-variance frontier for many assets (stocks) will look similar to that for two assets (e.g., Figure 2), but constructing it is considerably more complicated. Here are the steps in the process:

1. *Estimation step*: Estimate the expected return and variance for each individual asset and the correlation of each pair of assets. Historical standard deviations and correlations provide unbiased estimates of their future measures, but we need good forecasts of the future.

2. *Optimization step*: Solve for the weights that minimize the portfolio variance subject to the following constraints:
    *   The portfolio expected return equals a pre-specified target return, τ:

$$\sum_{i=1}^{n} w_i E(R_i) = \tau$$

    *   The portfolio weights sum to 100%: $\displaystyle\sum_{i=1}^{n} w_i = 100\% = 1$

Repeat Step 2 for many different values of τ. We would not want to solve this problem by hand! Fortunately, Step 2 usually is accomplished with the aid of a computer.

The optimization step solves for the weights, w_i^*, that minimize the portfolio variance subject to the two constraints (the asterisk signifies that the values determined for the weights are the ones that guarantee that the portfolio variance has been minimized).

3. *Calculation step*: Calculate the expected returns and variances for all the minimum-variance portfolios determined in Step 2. The graph of the expected return and variance combinations from Step 2 is the minimum-variance frontier.

    For instance, for one of the portfolio expected return choices in Step 2, assume we select a target portfolio expected return of 10% ($t = 10\%$). After the weights have been determined in Step 2, we then let the computer calculate the variance for the portfolio, using the minimum-variance weights. The optimized portfolio, P^*, will have the smallest possible variance among all portfolios that have an expected return equal to 10%.

For example, suppose the results in Figure 4 have been derived from the estimation, optimization, and calculation steps discussed previously.

Figure 4: Expected Return/Variance Combinations

Portfolio	Expected Return	Variance
A	0.02	0.05
B	0.04	0.02
C	0.06	0.01
D	0.08	0.02
E	0.10	0.05
F	0.12	0.10
G	0.14	0.17

Portfolio A has the smallest possible variance among all portfolios with an expected return of 2%, Portfolio B has the smallest possible variance among all portfolios with an expected return of 4%, and so on. All seven portfolios are *minimum-variance portfolios* (i.e., derived from the estimation, optimization, and calculations steps described previously).

Portfolio C, in the previous example, is the **global minimum-variance portfolio**—the portfolio with the smallest variance among all possible portfolios.

The graph of the minimum-variance frontier using the data in Figure 4 is provided in Figure 5 (the minimum-variance frontier is the curve from Point A to Point G).

Figure 5: Minimum-Variance Frontier: Expected Return vs. Variance

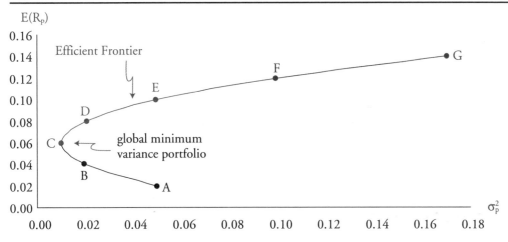

In practice, the minimum-variance frontier is plotted in expected return, standard deviation space. The standard deviation is easier to work with than variance because it is measured in the same units (single percentage units, rather than squared percentage units provided by the variance) as expected return.

Notice that the minimum-variance frontier in Figure 5 includes some portfolios that no rational investor would select. All portfolios lying on the convex portion (negatively sloped portion, from A to C) of the minimum-variance frontier are inferior to portfolios lying on the concave portion (positively sloped portion, from C to G) of the minimum-variance frontier. For example, portfolios A and E have identical risk, but Portfolio E has a much higher expected return, and a similar contrast exists for Portfolio D versus Portfolio B. All rational investors would prefer Portfolio D over Portfolio B and Portfolio E over Portfolio A.

The Efficient Frontier

Portfolios such as D and E in Figure 5 are called **efficient portfolios**, which are portfolios that have:

- Minimum risk of all portfolios with the same expected return.
- Maximum expected return for all portfolios with the same risk.

 Professor's Note: Another way to say this is that Portfolio D "dominates" Portfolio B and Portfolio E "dominates" Portfolio A.

This brings us to one of the most important concepts in portfolio theory—the **efficient frontier**, developed by Professor Harry Markowitz in 1952 (for which he was awarded the 1990 Nobel Prize in Economics). The *efficient frontier* is a plot of the expected return and risk combinations of all efficient portfolios, all of which lie along the upper portion of the minimum-variance frontier (from Point C to Point G in Figure 5).

The efficient frontier is an extremely useful portfolio management tool. Once the investor's risk tolerance is determined and quantified in terms of variance or standard deviation, the optimal portfolio for the investor can be easily identified. For example, the best portfolio for an investor willing to accept variance equal to 0.02 is Portfolio D. The best portfolio for an investor willing to accept variance equal to 0.17 is Portfolio G. Note that the investor choosing Portfolio D is more risk averse than the investor choosing Portfolio G.

LOS 57.c: Explain the benefits of diversification and how the correlation in a two-asset portfolio and the number of assets in a multi-asset portfolio affect the diversification benefits.

CFA® Program Curriculum, Volume 6, page 378

Portfolio diversification refers to the strategy of reducing risk by combining many different types of assets into a portfolio. Portfolio variance falls as more assets are added to the portfolio because not all asset prices move in the same direction at the same time. Therefore, portfolio diversification is affected by the:

- *Correlations between assets*: lower correlation means greater diversification benefits.
- *Number of assets included in the portfolio*: more assets mean greater diversification benefits.

Effect of Correlation on Portfolio Diversification

As the correlation between two assets *decreases*, the benefits of diversification *increase*. As the correlation decreases, there is less tendency for stock returns to move together. The separate movements of each stock serve to reduce the volatility of a portfolio to a level that is less than the weighted sum of its individual components (e.g., less than $w_1\sigma_1 + w_2\sigma_2$). No diversification is achieved if the correlation between assets equals +1. The greatest diversification is achieved if the correlation between assets equals −1.

To illustrate the effects of correlation on diversification, consider the expected return and standard deviation data derived for domestic stocks (DS) and domestic bonds (DB) as shown in Figure 6.

Figure 6: Diversification Example

	Expected Return	Standard Deviation
Domestic Stocks (DS)	0.20	0.30
Domestic Bonds (DB)	0.10	0.15

The expected return, standard deviation combinations for various portfolio percentage allocations to domestic stocks and domestic bonds for each of the following correlations +1, 0, and −1 is shown in Figure 7.

Figure 7: Expected Return/Standard Deviation Combinations for Various Allocations

Correlation	DS % Allocation	DB % Allocation	$E(R_p)$	σ_P
+1	100.00	0.00	0.200	0.300
	66.67	33.33	0.167	0.250
	50.00	50.00	0.150	0.225
	33.33	66.67	0.133	0.200
	0.00	100.00	0.100	0.150
0	100.00	0.00	0.200	0.300
	66.67	33.33	0.167	0.206
	50.00	50.00	0.150	0.168
	33.33	66.67	0.133	0.141
	0.00	100.00	0.100	0.150
−1	100.00	0.00	0.200	0.300
	66.67	33.33	0.167	0.150
	50.00	50.00	0.150	0.075
	33.33	66.67	0.133	0.000
	0.00	100.00	0.100	0.150

The plot of the expected returns and standard deviations for each of the three correlations is provided in Figure 8.

Figure 8: Effects of Correlation on Portfolio Risk

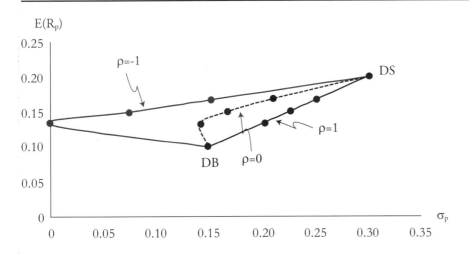

The lower and upper endpoints of the minimum-variance frontier in Figure 8 denote the risk and return of assets DB and DS, respectively. Starting at the point representing 100% invested in DB, as we increase the weight of DS and decrease the weight of DB, the frontier bulges to the left. The amount of bulge (i.e., the diversification effect) is a function of the correlation between the two assets.

As indicated in Figure 8, the lower the correlation between the returns of the stocks in the portfolio, the greater the diversification benefits. If the correlation equals +1 (the solid black line), the minimum-variance frontier is a straight line between the two points (DB and DS), and there is no benefit to diversification. If the correlation equals −1 (the blue line), the minimum-variance frontier is two straight-line segments, and there exists a portfolio combination of stocks and bonds with a standard deviation of *zero* (the allocation of 66.67% to domestic bonds and 33.33% to domestic stocks).

Effect of Number of Assets on Portfolio Diversification

While the previous example shows how diversification benefits increase as correlation among assets decreases, also note that diversification benefits increase as the number of assets increases. For instance, assume we add international bonds to the asset mix. Because international bonds are not perfectly positively correlated with domestic stocks or bonds, diversification benefits will increase (portfolio risk will fall) as illustrated in Figure 9. The graph assumes that the risk on international bonds is higher than the risk of domestic bonds, the expected return on international bonds is less than the expected return on domestic stocks, and the correlation of international bonds with domestic stocks and/or bonds is less than +1.

Figure 9: Effect of Number of Assets on Diversification

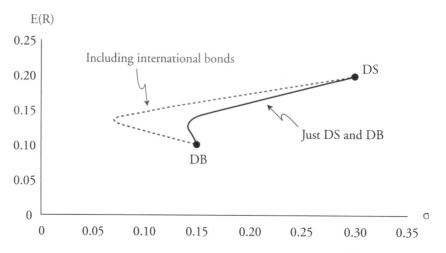

Note that portfolio risk will fall at a decreasing rate, as the number of assets included in the portfolio rises. The standard deviation of a large, well-diversified portfolio will get closer and closer to the broad market standard deviation as the number of assets in the portfolio increases.

LOS 57.d: Calculate the variance of an equally weighted portfolio of n stocks, explain the capital allocation and capital market lines (CAL and CML) and the relation between them, and calculate the value of one of the variables given values of the remaining variables.

CFA® Program Curriculum, Volume 6, page 393

Equally-Weighted Portfolio Risk

The formula for the variance of an *n*-asset portfolio is very complex, but the formula is simplified dramatically for equally-weighted portfolios (i.e., each w = 1/n):

$$\sigma_P^2 = \frac{1}{n}\overline{\sigma_i^2} + \frac{n-1}{n}\overline{\text{Cov}}$$

where:

$\overline{\sigma_i^2}$ = average variance of all assets in the portfolio
$\overline{\text{Cov}}$ = average covariance of all pairings of assets in the portfolio

Note that the equally-weighted portfolio variance equals the sum of two components, each of which is affected by the size of the portfolio:

- $(1/n)\times\overline{\sigma_i^2}$ gets closer to zero as *n* gets large because 1/n approaches zero.

- $[(n-1)/n]\times\overline{\text{Cov}}$ gets closer to the average covariance as *n* gets large because (n – 1) / n approaches 1.

Therefore, the following important result emerges:

The variance of an equally-weighted portfolio approaches the average covariance as *n* gets large.

Example: Calculating the variance of an equally-weighted portfolio

Consider two equally-weighted portfolios, A and B, in which the average asset variance equals 0.15 and the average covariance equals 0.09. Portfolio A comprises three assets, and Portfolio B comprises 100 assets. Calculate the variance of each portfolio.

Answer:

Variance for Portfolio A = [(1 / 3) × 0.15] + [(2 / 3) × 0.09]

= 0.05 + 0.06 = 0.11

Variance for Portfolio B = [(1 / 100) × 0.15] + [(99 / 100) × 0.09]

= 0.0015 + 0.0891 = 0.0906

Notice that for Portfolio B (the large portfolio), the first component is very close to zero and that the second component is very close to the average covariance.

With a little bit of algebraic manipulation, we can also calculate the variance of an equally-weighted portfolio as a function of the average correlation between all pairs of two stocks (ρ):

$$\sigma_P^2 = \overline{\sigma_i^2}\left(\frac{1-\rho}{n} + \rho\right)$$

The main point to take away from this equation is to notice that the maximum amount of risk reduction occurs when the number of stocks is very large, so that:

$$\text{maximum risk reduction} \Rightarrow \sigma_P^2 \approx \overline{\sigma_i^2}(\rho)$$

Thus, we have a convenient means of estimating the risk of the minimum-variance portfolio. If the average correlation is 0.3 ($\rho = 0.3$), then the maximum risk reduction possible corresponds to a portfolio variance that is 30% of individual stock variance.

Second, note how changes in the level of the average correlation affect the portfolio variance. The lower the level of correlation, the greater the potential diversification benefits, but the greater the number of securities required to realize them. For example, if the average correlation is 0.5, a portfolio of only 10 stocks gets us to within 10% of that for the minimum-variance portfolio. If the average correlation is 0.1, it takes 90 stocks to get within 10% of the minimum-variance portfolio.

Figure 10 shows the risk reduction benefits at three levels of the average correlation as the number of stocks in the portfolio changes. The numbers in the figure are the values that would be multiplied by the average stock variance to obtain the portfolio variance. For example, if the average correlation is 0.1, and a 10 stock portfolio is formed, the value 0.19 would be multiplied by the average stock variance to estimate the portfolio variance. The portfolio variance is estimated to be 19% of the average stock variance. The theoretical minimum-variance portfolio would have variance of only 10% of the average stock variance.

Figure 10: Risk Reduction Benefits of Adding Stocks to a Portfolio

Number of stocks in portfolio (n)	Average Correlation		
	$\rho = 0.1$	$\rho = 0.3$	$\rho = 0.5$
10	0.19	0.37	**0.55**
23	0.14	**0.33**	0.52
90	**0.11**	0.31	0.51
Maximum risk reduction benefit (minimum portfolio variance)	0.10	0.30	0.50

Professor's Note: This is a long topic review with a great deal of information. Let's not lose sight of the big picture. What we've learned so far is that (1) we can improve our risk/return prospects by increasing the number of assets in our portfolio and (2) the minimum-variance frontier depends on the expected returns, variances and correlations of returns, and the number of assets held.

The Capital Allocation Line and the Capital Market Line

 Professor's Note: Up to this point, we have discussed risky assets. Now, we add the risk-free asset to the set of asset choices and examine the effect that has on investment choices.

Warm-Up: Investment Combinations that Include the Risk-Free Asset

Until now, our portfolios have consisted of risky assets only. But, in reality, investors usually allocate their wealth across both risky and risk-free assets. The following discussion illustrates the effects of the inclusion of the risk-free asset. A risk-free asset is the security that has a return known ahead of time, so the variance of the return is zero. Key concepts that will be discussed are the **capital allocation line** and the **capital market line**.

Consider the task of creating portfolios comprising the risk-free asset, F, and a risky portfolio, P. Assume that Portfolio P lies on the efficient frontier of risky assets. Various combinations (weightings) of Portfolio P and the risk-free asset can be created. By adding the risk-free asset to the investment mix, a very important property emerges:

> The shape of the efficient frontier changes from a curve to a line after the inclusion of the risk-free asset.

Recall that the expected return for a portfolio of two assets equals the weighted average of the asset expected returns. Therefore, the expected return on Investment C that combines the risk-free asset and risky Portfolio P equals:

$$E(R_C) = w_F R_F + w_P E(R_P)$$

where:
w_F = percentage allocated to the risk-free asset
w_P = percentage allocated to Portfolio P

Also, recall that the variance of the portfolio of two assets (F and P) equals:

$$\sigma_C^2 = w_F^2\sigma_F^2 + w_P^2\sigma_P^2 + 2w_Fw_PCov_{FP}$$

where:

σ_C^2 = variance for Investment C

σ_F^2 = variance for the risk-free asset

σ_P^2 = variance for Portfolio P

Cov_{FP} = covariance between F and P

Observe that since we know that the variance and the standard deviation of the risk-free asset both equal zero, and that the covariance of the risk-free asset with any risky asset also equals zero, the equations for the variance and standard deviation for Investment C simplify to:

$$\sigma_C^2 = w_P^2\sigma_P^2$$

$$\sigma_C = w_P\sigma_P$$

That is, by including the risk-free asset, we have caused the efficient frontier to become linear.

The Capital Allocation Line

The following example illustrates this important property, and leads us into our discussion of the capital allocation line. Assume that the expected return for Portfolio P equals 12% and that its standard deviation equals 24%. Also, assume that the risk-free rate equals 6%.

The expected returns and standard deviations for various combinations of the risk-free asset and portfolio are shown in the Figure 11. Notice that a weight less than zero means we've sold the asset short. For example, suppose we have $100,000 to invest in a portfolio, and we borrow an additional $25,000 at the risk-free rate. The weight on the risk-free asset is –0.25 (–$25,000 / $100,000) and the weight on the risky portfolio is 1.25 ($125,000 / $100,000). Notice that the weights still add up to 1, however.

Figure 11: Combining the Risk-Free Asset With a Risky Portfolio

Portfolio Possibility (C)	w_F	w_P	$E(R_C)$	σ_C
1	1	0	0.06	0
2	0.75	0.25	0.075	0.06
3	0.50	0.50	0.09	0.12
4	0.25	0.75	0.105	0.18
5	0	1	0.12	0.24
6	–0.25	1.25	0.135	0.30
7	–0.50	1.50	0.15	0.36

Notice that the relationship shown in the example between the investment combination's (C) risk and return is linear. For example, each time the expected return changes by 1.50%, the risk changes by 6%.

Figure 12 illustrates the linear relationship between expected return and risk for the investment combinations of P and F.

Figure 12: Linear Relationship Between Risk and Return When Investing in the Risk-Free Asset

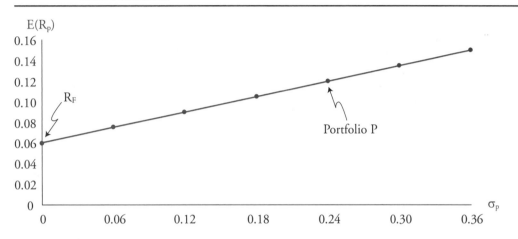

This linear relationship is a key result and is instrumental in the investor's asset allocation decisions. We will use the capital allocation line to answer several important questions. For example:

Question 1: How should the investor choose which risky portfolio among the many possible risky portfolios to combine with the risk-free asset?

Question 2: Given the investor's risk tolerance (i.e., target standard deviation), what rate of return should be expected?

Question 3: Given the investor's risk-return objectives, what percentage allocation should be given to the risk-free asset and the risky portfolio?

All of these questions are answered by employing the linear risk-return relationship that results from the opportunity to invest in the risk-free asset. The discussion will highlight the key role that the capital allocation line plays in determining optimal asset allocations for the investor.

Question 1: How should the investor choose among the many possible risky portfolios to combine with the risk-free asset? The linear risk-return relationship helps the investor make this very important decision, which can be summarized as follows: when combined with the risk-free asset, the investor should choose the risky portfolio that maximizes the reward-to-risk tradeoff.

This leads us to the *Capital Allocation Line*, which is the risk-return line that lies tangent to the efficient frontier. Figure 13 provides an example.

Figure 13: Capital Allocation Line

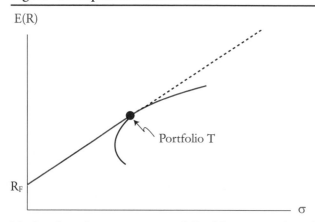

Notice that the tangency portfolio, T, is optimal in the sense that it has the highest possible reward-to-risk ratio, defined as:

$$\text{reward-to-risk ratio} = \frac{E(R_T) - R_F}{\sigma_T}$$

The reward-to-risk ratio also can be viewed as the expected risk premium, $E(R_T) - R_F$, for each unit of risk, σ_T, and is also known as the **Sharpe ratio** for Portfolio T.

Note that no other portfolio along the efficient frontier of risky assets (the curve in Figure 13) provides a higher expected reward-to-risk ratio than the tangency portfolio when combined with the risk-free asset. Stated in terms of the CAL, all risk-return lines connecting the risk-free rate and portfolios *other than* the tangency portfolio on the efficient frontier will have a flatter slope (lower reward-to-risk ratio) than the CAL. Therefore, the tangency portfolio is the *optimal risky portfolio* along the efficient frontier. The slope of the CAL represents the best possible risk-return tradeoff attainable given the investor's expectations.

Professor's Note: Under the standard CAL assumptions, investors can have different expectations about returns, variances, and covariances. Therefore, the efficient frontiers and CALs faced by investors will differ depending on the asset expectations of investors. For example, the efficient frontier derived by a highly optimistic investor might lie above the efficient frontier derived by a less optimistic investor. The CAL derived by the highly optimistic investor will have a steeper slope than the CAL derived by the less optimistic investor.

So, back to our original question—which risky portfolio should be combined with the risk-free asset? The tangency portfolio (at the point where the risk-return line touches the efficient frontier) is the optimal risky portfolio because it maximizes the investor's reward-to-risk ratio, when combined with the risk-free asset.

Question 2: Given the investor's risk tolerance, what rate of return should be expected? To answer this question, note that investors can hold any portfolio along the CAL by changing their allocation between Treasury bills (the risk-free asset, *F*) and the optimal risky Portfolio T. If the client invests 100% in Treasury bills, then the expected return and standard deviation on the investment equals 6% and zero, respectively. As the investor reallocates money from Treasury bills to Portfolio T, the investment combination moves up the line, increasing both expected return and risk.

All points on the line up to optimal Portfolio T represent "lending" portfolios, indicating that some money is invested in the risk-free asset (i.e., "lending" to the government treasury). All points on the line beyond optimal risky Portfolio T represent "leveraged" portfolios (i.e., borrowing money at the risk-free rate, and investing more than 100% of the original wealth in Portfolio T).

If risk-free borrowing is not available, then the CAL ends at the tangency point. Investors desiring a higher return will need to select portfolios along the original (curved) efficient frontier beyond the tangency point of the CAL. The efficient frontier without risk-free borrowing will therefore not be a straight line, but instead will consist of two segments: a straight line between the risk-free asset and Portfolio T, and the upper part of the curved portion of the original efficient frontier beyond T (shown in blue in Figure 13).

The CAL Equation

To determine the rate of return commensurate with the investor's risk tolerance, we can use the mathematical equation for the CAL.

For the CAL:

- The intercept equals the risk-free rate.
- The slope equals the reward-to-risk ratio for the optimal risky portfolio.

Because the CAL is a straight line, we can express it as a linear equation:

Y = a + bX

where:
Y = dependent variable [$E(R_C)$, the expected return on the investment combination]
X = independent variable (σ_C, the standard deviation on the investment combination)
a = intercept (R_F, the risk-free rate)
b = slope (the reward-to-risk ratio for the optimal risky portfolio)

Therefore, the equation for the CAL is:

$$E(R_C) = R_F + \left(\frac{E(R_T) - R_F}{\sigma_T} \right) \sigma_C$$

The intercept and slope of the CAL in Figure 13 are:

- Intercept equals the risk-free rate of 0.06.
- Slope equals the reward-to-risk ratio for optimal risky portfolio, T, which is (0.12 − 0.06) / 0.24 = 0.25.

Therefore, the equation for the CAL in Figure 13 is:

$$E(R_C) = 0.06 + 0.25\sigma_C$$

The slope coefficient (the reward-to-risk ratio) of the CAL indicates that the expected return on the investor's portfolio, $E(R_C)$, will change by 0.25 units for every 1-unit change in the investor's portfolio risk (σ_C).

Example: Calculating expected return from the CAL

Your firm manages a portfolio with an expected return equal to 12% and standard deviation equal to 24%. The risk-free rate equals 6%. One of your clients desires a portfolio standard deviation equal to 12%. Use the CAL to calculate the highest expected return for your client.

Answer:

Your client has a target standard deviation equal to 12% ($\sigma_C = 0.12$). Using the CAL, the expected return on an investment that combines the optimal risky portfolio, T, and the risk-free asset, F, is:

$$E(R_C) = 0.06 + 0.25(0.12) = 0.09 = 9\%$$

Therefore, the expected rate of return commensurate with your client's risk tolerance equals 9%.

Example: Calculating standard deviation from the CAL

The CAL can be used to calculate the standard deviation associated with a target expected return. For example, imagine that your client has a target expected return equal to 9%. Use the CAL to calculate the standard deviation associated with her optimal investment combination.

Answer:

Expected return in the CAL equation must equal the target return of 9%, $E(R_C) = 0.09$:

$$E(R_C) = 0.09 = 0.06 + 0.25\sigma_C$$

Then, solve the CAL for the standard deviation:

$$\sigma_C = (0.09 - 0.06) / 0.25 = 0.12 = 12\%$$

Therefore, the client's investment (that combines T and F) has an expected return of 9% (as stipulated by the client) and a standard deviation of 12%.

Study Session 18

Question 3: Given the investor's risk-return objectives, what percentage allocation should be given to the risk-free asset and the risky portfolio? The following example addresses this important question.

> **Example: Determining the appropriate allocation to the risk-free asset and to the optimal risky portfolio**
>
> Your client has a target standard deviation equal to 12%. Use the data above to determine the appropriate allocation to Treasury bills and to the optimal risky portfolio that will satisfy your client's risk tolerance.
>
> **Answer:**
>
> Using the equation derived in the Warm-Up, recall that the client's portfolio standard deviation (for the investment combination of Treasury bills and risky Portfolio T) equals:
>
> $$\sigma_C = w_T \sigma_T$$
>
> Therefore, if the client has a target standard deviation equal to 12%:
>
> $$0.12 = w_T(0.24)$$
>
> $$w_T = 0.12 / 0.24 = 0.50$$
>
> Your client should invest 50% in Treasury bills and 50% in the optimal risky Portfolio T. We already know that the expected return commensurate with a 12% standard deviation equals 9%. Therefore, the investor who allocates 50/50 to Treasury bills and risky Portfolio T should expect a standard deviation equal to 12% and a rate of return equal to 9%.

Here's what you need to remember about the CAL:

- If a risk-free investment is available, investors can combine it with a risky portfolio to increase their return at all levels of risk.
- The CAL is the straight line that intersects the *y*-axis at the risk-free rate and lies tangent to the efficient frontier.
- The intercept of the CAL equals the risk-free rate and the slope equals the maximum portfolio reward-to-risk ratio, defined as $[E(R_T) - R_F] / \sigma_T$.
- The tangency portfolio is the optimal risky portfolio because it has the highest possible expected reward-to-risk tradeoff.
- The CAL can be used to determine the risk associated with any desired target return, or the expected return associated with any desired target standard deviation.
- The slope of the CAL depends on the asset expectations of the investor. Therefore, investors with different asset expectations will face different CALs.

The Capital Market Line

The **Capital Market Line (CML)** is the capital allocation line in a world in which all investors agree on the expected returns, standard deviations, and correlations of all assets (also known as the "homogeneous expectations" assumption). Assuming identical expectations, there will be only one capital allocation line, and it is called the capital market line.

Under the assumptions of the CML, all investors agree on the exact composition of the optimal risky portfolio. This universally agreed upon optimal risky portfolio is called the *market portfolio*, *M*, defined as the portfolio of all marketable assets, weighted in proportion to their relative market values. For instance, if the market value of Asset X is $1 billion, and the market value of all traded assets is $100 billion, then the weight allocated to Asset X in the market portfolio equals 1%.

The key conclusion of the CML can be summarized as follows:

> All investors will make optimal investment decisions by allocating between the risk-free asset and the market portfolio.

A graph of the CML is provided in Figure 14.

Figure 14: The Capital Market Line

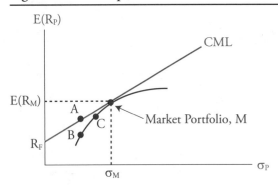

The equation for the CML is:

$$E(R_A) = R_F + \left[\frac{E(R_M) - R_F}{\sigma_M}\right]\sigma_A$$

The slope of the CML is often called the *market price of risk*, and equals the reward-to-risk ratio (or Sharpe ratio) for the market portfolio. This is calculated as:

$$\frac{E(R_M) - R_F}{\sigma_M}$$

Because the CML is just a special case of the CAL, the CML also can be used to calculate the expected return commensurate with the investor's risk tolerance. All prior examples hold for the CML if we make one simple assumption—that investors have identical expectations. Under this assumption, the tangency portfolio discussed earlier for the specific investor (Portfolio T) is the market Portfolio M.

As illustrated in the previous discussion, the addition of the risk-free asset has profound implications for the efficient frontier. Most importantly, all investors can maximize their reward-to-risk ratio by investing in a combination of the risk-free asset and the market portfolio. So, with the introduction of the risk-free asset, the shape of the efficient frontier changes from a curve (the Markowitz frontier) to a line (the Capital Market Line). Stated more emphatically, the Capital Market Line dominates the Markowitz frontier.

For example, all investors would prefer Portfolio A over Portfolio B in Figure 14. Portfolio A has the same risk but higher expected return than Portfolio B. Moreover, all investors would prefer Portfolio A over Portfolio C. Portfolio A has the same expected return but lower risk than Portfolio C. Similar contrasts can be found all along the Capital Market Line and Markowitz frontier. Because optimal portfolios are now found on the Capital Market Line, the Capital Market Line becomes the new efficient frontier.

Investors with high risk aversion will invest a larger percentage in the risk-free asset and a smaller percentage in the market portfolio (for an investment combination lying on the lower end of the Capital Market Line). The reverse is true for investors with low risk aversion.

Differences Between the CAL and the CML

Although the CAL and CML are generated using exactly the same mean-variance calculations, there are a few important differences:

- There is only one CML because it is developed assuming all investors agree on the expected return, standard deviation, and correlations for all assets.
- There is an unlimited number of CALs because each is developed uniquely for each investor.
- The tangency portfolio for the CML is the *market* portfolio, and there is only one market portfolio. The market portfolio uses market value weights.
- The tangency portfolio for the CAL can differ across investors depending on differences in investor expectations.
- The CML is a special case of the CAL.

LOS 57.e: Explain the capital asset pricing model (CAPM), including its underlying assumptions and the resulting conclusions.

CFA® Program Curriculum, Volume 6, page 406

The Capital Asset Pricing Model (CAPM) is one of the most celebrated models in all of finance. The model describes the relationship we should expect to see between risk and return for individual assets. Specifically, the CAPM provides a way to calculate an asset's expected return (or "required" return) based on its level of systematic (or market-related) risk, as measured by the asset's beta.

CAPM has a number of underlying assumptions, which are very similar to those of the CML:

- Investors only need to know expected returns, variances, and covariances in order to create optimal portfolios.
- All investors have the same forecasts of risky assets' expected returns, variances, and covariances.

- All assets are marketable, and the market for assets is perfectly competitive.
- Investors are price takers whose individual buy and sell decisions have no effect on asset prices.
- Investors can borrow and lend at the risk-free rate, and unlimited short-selling is allowed.
- There are no frictions to trading, such as taxes or transaction costs.

Implications of the CAPM Assumptions

Given these assumptions, there are *four* important implications of the CAPM:

1. Because all investors have the same expectations and all use mean-variance analysis, they all identify the same risky tangency portfolio (the "market portfolio") and combine that risky portfolio with the risk-free asset when creating their portfolios.

2. Because all investors hold the same risky portfolio, the weight on each asset must be equal to the proportion of its market value to the market value of the entire portfolio. In other words, if a stock represents 1% of the total market value of all traded assets, and every investor holds the same portfolio, that stock must also represent 1% of each investor's portfolio before combination with the risk-free asset.

3. The security market line (SML), which is the graph of the CAPM, describes the relationship between the expected return and systematic risk for all assets, both individual securities and portfolios.

4. Systematic risk, measured by beta, is the only risk priced by the market.

LOS 57.f: Explain the security market line (SML), the beta coefficient, the market risk premium, and the Sharpe ratio, and calculate the value of one of these variables given the values of the remaining variables.

CFA® Program Curriculum, Volume 6, page 406

The **Security Market Line (SML)** is the graph of the CAPM, representing the cross-sectional relationship between an asset's expected return and its systematic risk. Systematic risk for any asset is measured by the asset's beta, which estimates the sensitivity of the asset's rate of return to changes in the broad market's returns.

The intercept and slope for the SML are determined as follows:

- Intercept equals the risk-free rate, R_F.
- Slope equals the market risk premium, $E(R_M) - R_F$.

The **market risk premium** equals the expected difference in returns between the market portfolio and the risk-free asset. Using the CAPM, the market risk premium equals the additional return that investors require as compensation for additional units of systematic risk.

The SML equation is:

$$E(R_i) = R_F + \beta_i[E(R_M - R_F)]$$

Example: Use the CAPM to calculate the expected return on a stock

Assume you are assigned the task of evaluating the stock of Sky-Air, Inc. To evaluate the stock, you calculate its required return using the CAPM. The following information is available:

expected market risk premium	5%
risk-free rate	4%
Sky-Air beta	1.5

Calculate and interpret the CAPM expected return for Sky-Air.

Answer:

Using the CAPM, the expected return for Sky-Air is:

$$E(R_{SA}) = 0.04 + 1.5(0.05) = 0.115 = 11.5\%$$

The CAPM return can be viewed as the minimum return that investors should be willing to accept, commensurate with the risk associated with the asset. For example, if investors predict that the return will exceed 11.5%, then they should buy Sky-Air stock. However, if investors predict that the return will be less than 11.5%, then they should sell Sky-Air stock (or short sell the stock).

The graph of the SML and the location of the Sky-Air stock are illustrated in Figure 15.

Figure 15: The Security Market Line

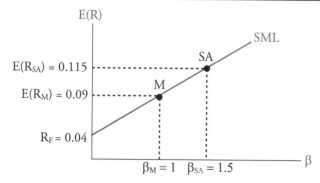

The graph illustrates the positive relationship that exists between risk (as measured by beta) and expected return. The positive relationship is a reflection of the risk aversion of investors. The SML will become steeper (i.e., the market risk premium will increase) as investors, on average, become more risk averse.

Calculating the Beta Coefficient

Systematic risk is estimated by the asset's beta, which is a standardized measure of an asset's systematic risk. The formula for the beta (systematic risk) for security i is:

$$\beta_i = \frac{\text{Cov}_{i,M}}{\sigma_M^2} = \frac{\rho_{i,M}\sigma_i\sigma_M}{\sigma_M^2} = \rho_{i,M}\left(\frac{\sigma_i}{\sigma_M}\right)$$

where:

σ_i = standard deviation of returns for stock i

σ_M = standard deviation of returns for the market portfolio

$\text{Cov}_{i,M}$ = covariance between the returns for stock i and the market portfolio

$\rho_{i,M}$ = correlation between the returns for stock i and the market portfolio

σ_M^2 = variance of the returns on the market portfolio

 Professor's Note: The equation for beta is the equation for the slope coefficient in a simple linear regression equation, specifically the market model, which is used to estimate betas.

Since beta measures the stock's reactions to movements in the market, the beta for the market as a whole must be 1.0. A stock's systematic risk can be assessed relative to the market in the following manner:

- A stock with a beta of 1 has an average level of market sensitivity. If beta is set equal to 1 in the SML, the expected return on the stock equals the expected return on the market portfolio. Stocks of large, diversified conglomerates tend to have betas close to 1.
- A stock with a beta greater than 1 has more-than-average systematic risk and will have an expected return greater than the market's expected return. Stocks of companies in industries that are more sensitive to the level of economic activity tend to have betas greater than 1 and are sometimes referred to as cyclical stocks.
- A stock with a beta less than 1 has less-than-average systematic risk and will have an expected return smaller than the market's expected return. Stocks of companies in industries not very sensitive to the economy (e.g., oil companies and grocery store chains) tend to have betas less than 1 and are referred to as defensive stocks.

Example: Calculate and interpret the beta of a stock

Assume the correlation of returns between Transport Co. and the market portfolio equals 0.80, the standard deviation of Transport Co. equals 0.60, and the standard deviation for the market portfolio equals 0.30. Calculate the beta for Transport Co.

Answer:

The beta equals the product of the correlation and the ratio of the standard deviation of the stock to the market standard deviation. Therefore, the beta for Transport Co. is:

$$\beta_{TC} = 0.80 \left(\frac{0.60}{0.30} \right) = 1.60$$

Therefore, Transport Co. is a relatively high (systematic) risk stock. The average stock beta equals 1, so TC is 60% riskier than the average stock, using systematic risk as our measure of risk.

Beta Summary

The beta for a stock is the ratio of its standard deviation to the standard deviation of the market multiplied by its correlation with the market:

$$\beta_i = \rho_{iM} \left(\frac{\sigma_i}{\sigma_M} \right)$$

It might be useful to think of beta as a measure of a stock's variability that is caused by market factors. Figure 16 summarizes the beta relationships.

Figure 16: Beta Interpretation

Beta	Risk Relative to the Market	Example Beta	Interpretation
< 1.0	Less systematic risk	0.5	Half as much systematic risk as the average stock
= 1.0	Same systematic risk	1.0	Same systematic risk as the average stock
> 1.0	More systematic risk	1.2	20% more systematic risk than the average stock

Financial Market Equilibrium

Financial market equilibrium exists when demand and supply forces cause market prices to stay at levels corresponding to expected/required returns. The CAPM is an example of an *equilibrium model*—its predictions result from market forces acting whenever prices get out of equilibrium to force them back into equilibrium.

For example, if based on its beta, the required return on an asset is too low, this indicates that the market price is too high. Under these circumstances, the SML predicts that investors will sell the stock until the price falls to the point where the forecast return is again equal to its required return (i.e., equilibrium) level.

Because the CAPM assumes investors hold the market portfolio, unsystematic risk (risk that is unrelated to the market) is irrelevant. The risk related to movements in the market portfolio is all that really matters, so investors *price* only systematic risk. That's why the independent variable in the SML is beta, not standard deviation.

 Professor's Note: Standard deviation measures standalone risk, which is the asset's total risk. For an individual stock, standalone risk is total systematic and unsystematic risk. For a well-diversified portfolio, however, standalone risk is only systematic risk, because unsystematic risk has been eliminated. For concentrated portfolios (i.e., partially diversified portfolios), there is systematic risk plus the unsystematic risk that has not been diversified away.

Differences Between the CML and the SML

As discussed earlier, the CML is the efficient frontier, plotting expected returns and standard deviations (total risk) for portfolios comprising a combination of the risk-free asset and the market portfolio. If markets are in equilibrium, risk and return combinations for individual securities will lie along the SML, but not along the CML. Risk and return combinations for individual securities will lie below the CML because their standard deviations include unsystematic risk that is diversified away in the market portfolio.

Figure 17: Key Differences Between the SML and the CML

	SML	CML
Measure of risk	Uses systematic risk (non-diversifiable risk).	Uses standard deviation (total risk).
Application	Tool used to determine the appropriate expected (benchmark) returns for securities.	Tool used to determine the appropriate asset allocation (percentages allocated to the risk-free asset and to the market portfolio) for the investor.
Definition	Graph of the capital asset pricing model.	Graph of the efficient frontier.
Slope	Market risk premium.	Market portfolio Sharpe ratio.

 Professor's Note: The last part of the LOS says "calculate the values of one of these variables given the values of the remaining variables." Presumably, that means using the formula for the SML, beta, the market risk premium, and the Sharpe ratio. The possibilities are almost endless here, so we'll just give you a few examples of the types of problems you might see on the exam.

Example: Using the SML

A stock has a beta of 0.75 and an expected return of 13%. The risk-free rate is 4%. Calculate the market risk premium and the expected return on the market portfolio.

Answer:

According to the SML: $0.13 = 0.04 + 0.75[E(R_M) - R_F]$.

Therefore, the market risk premium is equal to: $[E(R_M) - R_F] = 0.12 = 12\%$.

The expected return on the market is calculated as: $[E(R_M) - 0.04] = 0.12$, or $E(R_M) = 0.16 = 16\%$.

Example: Using the beta formula

A stock has a beta of 2.0. The correlation of the stock's returns with the market is 0.5 and the variance of the returns on the market portfolio is 0.04. Calculate the variance of returns on the stock.

Answer:

The variance of the market portfolio returns is 0.04, so the standard deviation of market returns is the square root of 0.04, or 0.20. Plugging that into the beta formula gives us:

$$2.0 = 0.5\left(\frac{\sigma_i}{0.2}\right) \Rightarrow \sigma_i = 0.8$$

The variance of the stock's returns is the $0.8^2 = 0.64$.

Example: Using the Sharpe ratio

Given a Sharpe ratio for the market portfolio of 0.40, calculate the expected return on a stock with a standard deviation of returns of 0.50 and a correlation with the market portfolio returns of 0.6. The risk-free rate is 5% and the standard deviation of the market portfolio returns is 0.25.

Answer:

First calculate the stock's beta:

$$\beta = 0.6\left(\frac{0.50}{0.25}\right) = 1.2$$

Then, use the market Sharpe ratio to calculate the market risk premium:

$$\left[\frac{E(R_M) - R_F}{0.25}\right] = 0.40 \Rightarrow E(R_M) - R_F = 0.10$$

Finally, use the SML to calculate the expected return on the stock:

$$E(R) = 0.05 + 1.2(0.10) = 0.17 = 17\%$$

DERIVING INPUTS TO THE MEAN-VARIANCE MODEL

There are three methods of obtaining the inputs to the mean-variance framework:

1. Using historical means, variances, and correlations.

2. Estimating betas using the market model.

3. Calculating adjusted betas.

We will discuss each in turn.

Historical Estimates

The efficient frontier is derived by creating optimal portfolios that consider all assets in the market. However, the forecast process needed to derive the efficient frontier is daunting and arduous.

The first problem with using historical estimates is that we have to estimate a very large number of inputs. For portfolios of n assets, we will need the following number of forecasts:

> n individual asset expected returns
>
> $+ \ n$ individual asset standard deviations
>
> $+ \ \dfrac{n(n-1)}{2}$ covariances

For example, even if we limit ourselves to stocks in the S&P 500, the inputs required to conduct a mean-variance analysis would include 500 expected returns, 500 variances, and 124,750 covariances.

The second problem with using historical estimates is that there is typically a large amount of estimation error, particularly for estimates of expected returns and covariances.

Obviously, we need more practical methods for computing inputs to mean-variance analysis.

LOS 57.g: Explain the market model, and state and interpret the market model's predictions with respect to asset returns, variances, and covariances.

CFA® Program Curriculum, Volume 6, page 413

The Market Model

A more practical and useful method is the **market model**. The premise of the market model is that there are just two sources of risk:

1. Unanticipated macroeconomic events (systematic risk).

2. Firm-specific events (unsystematic risk).

In the market model, the market portfolio is the macroeconomic factor and stocks are assumed to have varying degrees of sensitivity to this one factor. In addition, each stock's returns are uniquely affected by firm-specific events uncorrelated across stocks and with the macro events.

The market model is the regression model often used to estimate betas for common stocks:

$$R_i = \alpha_i + \beta_i R_M + \varepsilon_i$$

where:
R_i = return on Asset i
R_M = return on the market Portfolio M
α_i = intercept (the value of R_i when R_M equals zero)
β_i = slope (estimate of the systematic risk for Asset i)
ε_i = regression error with expected value equal to zero (firm-specific surprises)

The market model makes three assumptions:

1. The expected value of the error term is zero.

2. The errors are uncorrelated with the market return.

3. The firm-specific surprises are uncorrelated across assets.

Based on these assumptions, the market model greatly simplifies the estimation procedures needed to conduct the mean-variance analysis, as illustrated next.

Market Model Predictions of Expected Returns, Variances, and Covariances

The market model offers a simple way to derive forecasts of expected returns, variances, and covariances for individual assets. In particular, after making a few simplifying assumptions, it can be shown that:

expected return for Asset i:
$$E(R_i) = \alpha_i + \beta_i E(R_M)$$

variance of Asset i:
$$\sigma_i^2 = \beta_i^2 \sigma_M^2 + \sigma_\varepsilon^2$$

covariance between assets i and j:
$$Cov_{ij} = \beta_i \beta_j \sigma_M^2$$

In general, the n expected returns, n variances, and $n(n-1)/2$ covariance forecasts can be derived from just $3n + 2$ parameters using the market model, which greatly simplifies the estimation procedure.

The market model makes three predictions:

1. The expected return on Asset i depends only on the expected return on the market portfolio, $E(R_M)$, the sensitivity of the returns on Asset i to movements in the market, β_i, and the average return to Asset i when the market return is zero, α_i.

2. The variance of the returns on Asset i consists of two components: a systematic component related to the asset's beta, $\beta_i^2 \sigma_M^2$, and an unsystematic component related to firm-specific events, σ_ε^2.

3. The covariance between any two stocks is calculated as the product of their betas and the variance of the market portfolio.

Example: Calculating the market model forecasts

Assume the betas for assets i and j equal 0.80 and 1.5, respectively, and that the expected return and variance for the market portfolio returns equal 0.12 and 0.04, respectively. Also assume the intercept and error variance (unsystematic risk) for Asset i equals 0.02 and 0.10, respectively. Determine the market model forecasts for expected return for Asset i, its variance, and its covariance with Asset j.

Answer:

The following forecasts can be made using the market model:

expected return for Asset i: $0.02 + 0.80(0.12) = 0.116 = 11.6\%$

variance for Asset i: $0.8^2(0.04) + 0.10 = 0.1256$

covariance between assets: $(0.80)(1.5)(0.04) = 0.048$

To generate values for the market model (i.e., to estimate alpha, beta, and the error variance), historical returns for a stock are regressed against corresponding returns for a market index. The following example illustrates how the market model simplifies the forecasting process.

 Professor's Note: The market model is simply an application of simple linear regression to portfolio management. Recall from Study Session 3 that when we ran a regression with individual stock returns as the dependent variable and market returns as the independent variable, the estimated slope coefficient was the stock's beta.

Example: The number of statistical inputs needed to derive the efficient frontier using the market model

Determine the number of statistical inputs needed to derive the efficient frontier comprising 500 assets, using the market model.

Answer:

The efficient frontier is derived after forecasting the following:

- 500 expected returns
- 500 variances

- $\dfrac{500 \times 499}{2} = 124{,}750$ covariances

This equals a total of 125,750 forecasts. However, by running 500 market model regressions, we will obtain 500 α estimates, 500 β estimates, and 500 regression error variance estimates. All we need now is one estimate of the expected market return, and one estimate of the market variance. From these 1,502 statistical inputs, we can generate forecasts for all of the 125,750 asset parameters.

LOS 57.h: Calculate an adjusted beta, and explain the use of adjusted and historical betas as predictors of future betas.

CFA® Program Curriculum, Volume 6, page 416

To implement the market model estimates of expected returns, variances, and covariances, we must have regression estimates of the beta for each asset. As discussed above, one method of estimating beta is simply to use the historical regression estimate derived from the market model. There is a slight problem, however. To conduct mean-variance analysis for optimal portfolio selection, we need forecasts, not historical estimates, of expected returns, variances, and covariances.

The beta derived from the market model is a good estimate of *historical* relationships but not necessarily a good predictor of *future* relationships. This is called the *beta instability problem.* If the historical beta inaccurately predicts the future beta, then inaccurate forecasts will be used when attempting to derive the efficient frontier and to make optimal portfolio decisions. Therefore, in practice, we often apply some adjustments to the historical beta to improve its ability to forecast the future beta.

For example, if we assume that beta follows a first-order autoregressive process, then we can formulate the beta forecast as:

$$\beta_{i,t} = \alpha_0 + \alpha_1 \beta_{i,t-1} + \upsilon_{i,t}$$

where:
$\upsilon_{i,t}$ = a random error with expected value equal zero

If $\alpha_1 = 1$, then we would conclude that beta follows a random walk (the changes in beta are random over time). $\beta_{i,t}$ is the beta forecast and $\beta_{i,t-1}$ is the historical beta derived from the market model:

forecast $\beta_{i,t} = \beta_{i,t-1}$ from a market model

Professor's Note: Remember from Study Session 3 that in a first-order autoregressive process, the dependent variable is regressed against its first lagged value. In the application here, the dependent variable is beta.

More often, though, the beta instability problem is addressed by adjusting the beta to account for its tendency to gravitate to a value of 1 over time. The general form of the "adjusted beta" equation can be presented as:

forecast $\beta_{i,t} = \alpha_0 + \alpha_1 \beta_{i,t-1}$

where:
the sum $\alpha_0 + \alpha_1$ is set equal to 1

The most popular values of α_0 and α_1 are: $\alpha_0 = 1/3$ and $\alpha_1 = 2/3$.

From our understanding of first order autoregressive processes, we know that the mean reverting value for any time series variable equals the intercept divided by 1 minus the slope, $\alpha_0 / (1 - \alpha_1)$. Therefore, by assuming α_0 and α_1 sum to 1, then $\alpha_0 = 1 - \alpha_1$, and:

$$\frac{\alpha_0}{1-\alpha_1} = \frac{1-\alpha_1}{1-\alpha_1} = 1$$

The mean-reverting level of the beta is 1. If the historical beta is greater than 1, then the adjusted beta will be less than the historical beta and closer to 1. If the historical beta is less than 1, then the adjusted beta will be greater than the historical beta and closer to 1. The adjusted beta forecast will move toward 1 more quickly for larger values of α_0 (i.e., as α_0 approaches a value of 1).

Example: Calculate an adjusted beta

The historical beta for the Compware Company equals 2. Calculate the adjusted beta for Compware Company using the adjusted beta formula: $(1/3) + (2/3) \times \beta_{t-1}$.

Answer:

The adjusted beta for Compware Company equals:

$(1/3) + (2/3) \times 2 = 1.67$

Notice how the adjusted beta calculation used the historical beta estimate of 2.0 to derive a forecast beta that moved closer to a value of 1.

LOS 57.i: Explain reasons for and problems related to instability in the minimum-variance frontier.

CFA® Program Curriculum, Volume 6, page 417

The risk-return characteristics of the minimum-variance frontier are determined by the expected returns, variances, and covariances among individual assets. Therefore, the shape and location of the minimum-variance frontier (in risk-return space) changes as the risk and return attributes of individual assets change over time. More optimistic expected return forecasts will cause the curve to shift up, and lowered variance and covariance forecasts will cause the curve to shift to the left (also with larger curvature or bulge to the left). Small changes in risk-return attributes of individual assets can cause large changes in the composition of the portfolios that form the minimum-variance frontier.

The instability in the minimum-variance frontier and, therefore, the efficient frontier, is a concern for a number of reasons:

- The statistical inputs (means, variances, covariances) are unknown, and must be forecast; greater uncertainty in the inputs leads to less reliability in the efficient frontier.
- Statistical input forecasts derived from historical sample estimates often change over time, causing the estimated efficient frontier to change over time (this is called time instability).
- Small changes in the statistical inputs can cause large changes in the efficient frontier (called the "overfitting" problem), resulting in unreasonably large short positions, and overly frequent rebalancing.

To address the instability problem, the analyst might consider constraining the portfolio weights (e.g., prohibiting short sales so that all portfolio weights are positive), employing forecasting models that provide better forecasts than historical estimates, and avoiding rebalancing until significant changes occur in the efficient frontier.

MULTIFACTOR MODELS

LOS 57.j: Describe and compare macroeconomic factor models, fundamental factor models, and statistical factor models.

CFA® Program Curriculum, Volume 6, page 421

The market model could be described as a single factor model, because it assumes asset returns are explained by a single factor: the return on the market portfolio. A *multifactor model* assumes asset returns are driven by more than one factor. There are three general classifications of multifactor models: (1) macroeconomic factor models, (2) fundamental factor models, and (3) statistical factor models.

1. *Macroeconomic factor models* assume that asset returns are explained by surprises (or "shocks") in macroeconomic risk factors (e.g., GDP, interest rates, and inflation). Factor surprises are defined as the difference between the realized value of the factor and its consensus predicted value.

> *Professor's Note: The key to macroeconomic factor models is that the variables that explain returns are not the value of the macroeconomic variable itself, but rather the unexpected part (i.e., the surprise), because we assume that the expected value has already been reflected in stock prices. For example, if the government announces that GDP grew at an annual rate of 1.5% and the consensus prediction was 2.5%, the surprise was a negative 1%. The 2.5% consensus forecast was already reflected in market prices, so the negative surprise, which was bad news to the market, should cause stock prices to fall.*

2. *Fundamental factor models* assume asset returns are explained by the returns from multiple firm-specific factors (e.g., P/E ratio, market cap, leverage ratio, and earnings growth rate).

3. *Statistical factor models* use statistical methods to explain asset returns. Two primary types of statistical factor models are used: factor analysis and principal component models. In factor analysis, factors are portfolios that explain covariance in asset returns. In principal component models, factors are portfolios that explain the variance in asset returns. The major weakness is that the statistical factors do not lend themselves well to economic interpretation. Therefore, *statistical* factors are *mystery* factors.

Because most investment firms employ macroeconomic factor or fundamental factor models (or mixtures of the two), we will provide a more expanded discussion of these models.

MACROECONOMIC FACTOR MODELS

The following model is an example of a two-factor macroeconomic model in which stock returns are explained by surprises in GDP growth rates and credit quality spreads:

$$R_i = E(R_i) + b_{i1}F_{GDP} + b_{i2}F_{QS} + \varepsilon_i$$

where:

R_i = return for Asset i

$E(R_i)$ = expected return for Asset i using APT (in the absence of any surprises)

F_{GDP} = surprise in the GDP rate

F_{QS} = surprise in the credit quality spread (BB-rated bond yield – Treasury bond yield)

b_{i1} = GDP surprise sensitivity of Asset i

b_{i2} = credit quality spread surprise sensitivity of Asset i

ε_i = firm-specific surprise (unrelated to the two macro factors)

Let's take a closer look at each of the components:

- The stock's expected return comes from an asset pricing model.
- The "F's" are the factor surprises, the difference between the predicted value of the factor and the realized value.
- The "b's" are the sensitivities of the stock to the surprises. They are very similar to betas in the market model. The higher the sensitivity, the larger the change in return for a given factor surprise.
- The error term is the part of the return that can't be explained by the model. It represents unsystematic risk related to firm-specific events like a strike or a warehouse fire.

Example: Compute a stock return using a macroeconomic factor model

The following two-factor model is used to explain the returns for Media Tech (MT):

$$R_{MT} = E(R_{MT}) + b_{MT,1}F_{GDP} + b_{MT,2}F_{QS} + \varepsilon_{MT}$$

The expected return for Media Tech equals 10%. Over the past year, GDP grew at a rate that was 2 percentage points higher than originally expected, and the quality spread was 1 percentage point lower than originally expected. Media Tech's sensitivity to the GDP rate factor equaled 2 and its sensitivity to the quality spread factor equaled –0.5. Over the past year, Media Tech also experienced a 2% company-unique surprise return (i.e., unrelated to the two macrofactors). Construct the macroeconomic factor model for Media Tech, and calculate its return for the year.

Answer:

The two-factor model for Media Tech is:

$$R_{MT} = 0.10 + 2(0.02) - 0.50(-0.01) + 0.02 =$$

   0.100 (the expected return)
+ 0.040 (the return from the positive GDP surprise)
+ 0.005 (the return from the positive quality spread surprise)
+ 0.020 (the return from unexpected firm specific events)
= 0.165, or 16.5%

The Media Tech return was higher than originally expected because MT was positively affected by higher than expected economic growth (GDP), lower than expected credit quality risk spreads (QS), and by positive company specific surprise events.

 Professor's Note: Be careful to interpret the signs properly: a decrease in the quality spread (a surprise less than zero) is good news for stock MT, because it has a negative sensitivity to the factor. When credit quality spreads increase, MT's return goes down, and when credit quality spreads decrease, MT's return goes up.

The main features of the macroeconomic factor model include the systematic or "priced risk" factors and the factor sensitivities.

Priced Risk Factors

A risk that does not affect many assets (i.e., an *unsystematic risk*) can usually be diversified away in a portfolio and will not be priced by the market. By "not priced," we mean investors cannot expect to be rewarded for being exposed to that type of risk. The factors in our example model, GDP and credit quality spread shocks, are *systematic* risk factors. That means they can affect even well-diversified portfolios. Since they cannot be avoided, systematic factors represent priced risk; risk for which investors can expect compensation.

Factor Sensitivities

In a macroeconomic multifactor model, asset returns are a function of unexpected surprises to systematic factors, and different assets have different *factor sensitivities*. For example, retail stocks are very sensitive to GDP growth and, hence, have a large sensitivity to the GDP factor. Small, unexpected changes in GDP growth cause large changes in retail stock prices, because changes in income affect retail spending. Other stocks are less sensitive to GDP and have smaller GDP factor sensitivities. Retail grocer stocks, for example, do not react as much to changes in GDP, because spending on food items is less sensitive to changes in national income. The factor sensitivities of the model can be estimated by regressing historical asset returns on the corresponding historical macroeconomic factors.

FUNDAMENTAL FACTOR MODELS

Consider the following fundamental factor model:

$$R_i = a_i + b_{i1}F_{P/E} + b_{i2}F_{SIZE} + \varepsilon_i$$

where:
R_i = return for stock i
$F_{P/E}$ = return associated with the P/E factor
F_{SIZE} = return associated with the SIZE (market capitalization) factor
a_i = intercept
b_{i1} = standardized sensitivity of stock i to the P/E factor
b_{i2} = standardized sensitivity of stock i to the SIZE factor

Let's take a closer look at each of the components of a fundamental factor model.

Standardized sensitivities (b_{i1} and b_{i2}). Sensitivities in most fundamental factor models are not regression slopes. Instead, the fundamental factor sensitivities are standardized attributes (similar to z-statistics from the standard normal distribution). For example, the standardized P/E sensitivity in a fundamental factor model is calculated as:

$$b_{i1} = \frac{(P/E)_i - \overline{P/E}}{\sigma_{P/E}}$$

where:
$(P/E)_i$ = P/E ratio for stock i
$\overline{P/E}$ = average P/E calculated across all stocks
$\sigma_{P/E}$ = standard deviation of P/E ratios across all stocks

Also note that by standardizing the factor sensitivity, we measure the number of standard deviations each sensitivity is from the average. For example, a stock with a standardized P/E sensitivity of 2.0 has a P/E that is 2 standard deviations above the mean; a stock with a sensitivity of −1.5 has a P/E that is one and a half standard deviations below the mean. This standardization process allows us to use different fundamental factors measured in different units in the same factor model. For example, P/E ratios are usually greater than 1.00 while dividend yields are in percentages (i.e., less than 1.00).

> **Example: Calculating a standardized sensitivity in a fundamental factor model**
>
> The P/E for Stock i is 15.20, the average P/E for all stocks is 11.90, and the standard deviation of P/E ratios is 6.30. Calculate the standardized sensitivity of Stock i to the P/E factor.

Answer:

The sensitivity of Stock i to the P/E factor is:

$$\beta_{i,\frac{P}{E}} = \frac{15.20 - 11.90}{6.30} = 0.52$$

Therefore, the P/E ratio for the stock is 0.52 standard deviations higher than the average stock P/E.

Factor returns ($F_{P/E}$ *and* F_{SIZE}). The fundamental factors are rates of return associated with each factor (e.g., rate of return difference between low and high P/E stocks). The return difference between low and high P/E stocks is commonly referred to as the return on a "factor mimicking portfolio." In practice, the values of the fundamental factors are estimated as slopes of cross-sectional regressions in which the dependent variable is the set of returns for all stocks and the independent variables are the standardized sensitivities.

Intercept term (a_i). In fundamental factor models, the factors are not return "surprises." Hence, the expected factor values are not zero, and the intercept term is no longer interpreted as the expected return.

The Macroeconomic Factor Model vs. the Fundamental Factor Model

The key differences between the macroeconomic factor model and the fundamental factor model can be summarized as follows:

- *Sensitivities.* The standardized sensitivities in the fundamental factor model (b_{i1} and b_{i2}) are calculated directly from the attribute (e.g., P/E) data—they are not estimated. This contrasts with the macroeconomic factor model, in which the sensitivities are regression slope estimates.
- *Interpretation of factors.* The macroeconomic factors (F_{GDP} and F_{QS}) are surprises in the macroeconomic variables (e.g., inflation shock and interest rate shock). In contrast, the fundamental factors ($F_{P/E}$ and F_{SIZE}) are rates of return associated with each factor and are estimated using multiple regression.
- *Number of factors.* Macroeconomic factors are intended to represent systematic risk factors, and are usually small in number (i.e., a parsimonious model). Fundamental factors often are large in number, providing a more cumbersome, yet more detailed, model of the risk-return relationship for assets.
- *Intercept term.* The intercept in the macroeconomic factor model equals the stock's expected return (based on market consensus expectations of the macro factors) from an equilibrium pricing model like the APT. In contrast, the intercept of a fundamental factor model with standardized sensitivities has no economic interpretation; it is simply the regression intercept necessary to make the unsystematic risk of the asset equal to zero.

LOS 57.k: Calculate the expected return on a portfolio of two stocks, given the estimated macroeconomic factor model for each stock.

CFA® Program Curriculum, Volume 6, page 422

As explained in the previous LOS, the macroeconomic model intercept equals the stock's expected return. Using the macroeconomic model, we can describe the returns for stocks i and j as follows:

$$R_i = E(R_i) + b_{i1}F_{IP} + b_{i2}F_{QS} + \varepsilon_i$$

$$R_j = E(R_j) + b_{j1}F_{IP} + b_{j2}F_{QS} + \varepsilon_j$$

The expected values of the factors and random error in a macroeconomic factor model equal zero. Therefore, using the macroeconomic factor model, the expected return for a stock equals the intercept. Using the two-factor macroeconomic factor model, the expected return on the portfolio is:

$$E(R_p) = w_i E(R_i) + w_j E(R_j)$$

Example: Calculate the expected return for a portfolio

Consider a portfolio allocated 75% to Rent Shop and 25% to Carpets Plus. Calculate the expected return for the portfolio, given the following macroeconomic model results:

$$R_{RENT} = 0.14 + 1.5F_1 + 0.8F_2 + \varepsilon_{RENT}$$

$$R_{CARPETS} = 0.08 + 1.2F_1 + 0.2F_2 + \varepsilon_{CARPETS}$$

Answer:

The portfolio expected return simply equals the weighted average of the two intercepts.

$$E(R_p) = 0.75(0.14) + 0.25(0.08) = 0.125 = 12.5\%$$

Also, note that the portfolio sensitivity to each factor equals the weighted average of the two stock sensitivities:

$$b_{p1} = 0.75(1.5) + 0.25(1.2) = 1.425$$

$$b_{p2} = 0.75(0.8) + 0.25(0.2) = 0.65$$

Professor's Note: If the macroeconomic model is used to derive the actual portfolio return (rather than the portfolio expected return), then we simply use the weighted average of the macroeconomic models for the two stocks. From the previous example, the portfolio return equals:

$$R_p = 0.125 + 1.425F_1 + 0.65F_2 + 0.75(\varepsilon_{RENT}) + 0.25(\varepsilon_{CARPETS})$$

LOS 57.l: Describe the arbitrage pricing theory (APT), including its underlying assumptions and its relation to the multifactor models, calculate the expected return on an asset given an asset's factor sensitivities and the factor risk premiums, and determine whether an arbitrage opportunity exists, including how to exploit the opportunity.

CFA® Program Curriculum, Volume 6, page 425

The **Arbitrage Pricing Theory** (APT) refers to an asset pricing theory that assumes:

- *Returns are derived from a multifactor model.* Unfortunately, the APT provides little practical guidance for the identification of the risk factors. The lack of clarity for the risk factors is a major weakness of the APT.
- *Unsystematic risk can be completely diversified away.* This implies that unsystematic risk is not priced (has zero risk premium).
- No arbitrage opportunities exist. An arbitrage opportunity is defined as an investment opportunity that bears no risk, no cost, and yet provides a profit. This assumption implies that investors will undertake infinitely large positions (long and short) to exploit any perceived mispricing, causing asset prices to adjust immediately to their equilibrium values.

The asset pricing model developed by the arbitrage pricing theory is called the *arbitrage pricing model.*

The APT Equation

The APT describes the equilibrium relationship between expected returns for well-diversified portfolios and their multiple sources of systematic risk.

$$E(R_p) = R_F + \beta_{P,1}(\lambda_1) + \beta_{P,2}(\lambda_2) + \ldots + \beta_{P,k}(\lambda_k)$$

Each λ stands for the expected risk premium associated with each risk factor. Each λ_j equals the risk premium for a portfolio (called a *pure factor portfolio*, which is discussed later) with factor sensitivity equal to 1 to factor j and factor sensitivities equal to zero for the remaining factors. Remember that a risk premium is the difference between the expected return and the risk-free rate. It is the extra expected return from taking on more risk.

Each β represents the sensitivity (also called factor "loading") of Portfolio P to each risk factor. Each factor in the arbitrage pricing model is "priced," meaning that each risk premium is statistically and economically significant. Unlike the CAPM, the APT does *not* require that one of the risk factors is the market portfolio. This is a major advantage of the arbitrage pricing model.

 Professor's Note: The CAPM can be considered a special restrictive case of the APT in which there is only one risk factor, and that one factor is restricted to be the market risk factor.

Example: Calculating expected returns from the arbitrage pricing model

An investment firm employs a two-factor APT model. The risk-free rate equals 5%. Determine the expected return for the Invest Fund using the following data:

	Factor 1	Factor 2
Invest Fund factor betas	1.50	2.00
Factor risk premiums	0.0300	0.0125

Answer:

Using the two-factor APT model, the expected return for the Invest Fund (IF) equals:

$$E(R_{IF}) = 0.05 + 1.5(0.03) + 2(0.0125) = 0.12 = 12\%$$

The method for exploiting arbitrage opportunities in the APT framework is detailed in the following example.

Example: Exploiting an arbitrage opportunity

Assume your investment firm uses a single factor model to evaluate assets. Consider the following data for portfolios, A, B, and C:

Portfolio	Expected Return	Beta
A	10%	1.0
B	20%	2.0
C	13%	1.5

Calculate the arbitrage opportunity from the data provided. *Hint: Create a portfolio with 50% in A and 50% in B, and then compare the expected return and beta of that portfolio to Portfolio C.*

Answer:

By allocating 50% to portfolios A and B, we can obtain a portfolio (D) with beta equal to the Portfolio C beta (1.50):

beta for Portfolio D = 0.50(1) + 0.50(2) = 1.50

While the betas for portfolios D and C are identical, the expected returns are different:

expected return for Portfolio D = 0.50(0.10) + 0.50(0.20) = 0.15 = 15%

Therefore, we have created Portfolio D that has the same risk as Portfolio C (beta = 1.50), but has higher expected return than Portfolio C (15% versus 13%). By purchasing Portfolio D and short-selling Portfolio C, we expect to earn a 2% return (15% minus 13%).

Professor's Note: Recall that a portfolio beta equals the weighted average of the individual asset betas, and, likewise, the portfolio expected return equals the weighted average of the individual asset expected returns.

The portfolio that is long Portfolio D and short Portfolio C is called the *arbitrage portfolio*. We have invested nothing upfront because we merely use the proceeds of the short sale on Portfolio C to purchase Portfolio D, and we have undertaken no systematic risk. The beta on our investment equals the difference in betas between our long and short positions: 1.5 – 1.5 = 0. As investors exploit the arbitrage opportunity, prices of assets in Portfolio C will drop and the (future) expected return for Portfolio C will rise to its equilibrium value.

The APT assumes there are no market imperfections preventing investors from exploiting arbitrage opportunities. As a result, extreme long and short positions are permitted and mispricing will disappear immediately. Therefore, all arbitrage opportunities such as the one described in the previous example would be exploited and eliminated immediately.

Differences Between the APT and Multifactor Models

It's important to understand the differences between the APT and the macroeconomic and fundamental multifactor models we discussed in the previous LOS.

- The APT is a cross-sectional equilibrium pricing model that explains the variation *across assets'* expected returns during a single time period. The multifactor model is a time-series regression that explains the variation *over time* in returns for one asset.
- The APT is an equilibrium-pricing model that assumes no arbitrage opportunities. The macroeconomic multifactor models are *ad hoc* (i.e., rather than being derived directly from an equilibrium theory, the factors are identified empirically by looking for macroeconomic variables that best fit the data).
- The intercept term in a macroeconomic factor model is the asset's expected return, and is derived from the APT equation. The APT intercept is the risk-free rate.

LOS 57.m: Explain sources of active risk, interpret tracking error, tracking risk, and the information ratio, and explain factor portfolio and tracking portfolio.

CFA® Program Curriculum, Volume 6, page 443

Active return equals the differences in returns between a managed portfolio and its benchmark:

active return = $R_P - R_B$

Active risk (also known as *tracking error* or *tracking risk*) is defined as the standard deviation of the active return:

$$\text{active risk} = s_{(R_P - R_B)} = \sqrt{\frac{\sum(R_{Pt} - R_{Bt})^2}{n-1}}$$

The active risk of a portfolio can be separated into two components:

1. *Active factor risk*: Risk from active factor tilts attributable to deviations of the portfolio's factor sensitivities versus the benchmark's sensitivities to the same set of factors.

2. *Active specific risk*: Risk from active asset selection attributable to deviations of the portfolio's individual asset weightings versus the benchmark's individual asset weightings, after controlling for differences in factor sensitivities of the portfolio versus the benchmark.

The sum of active factor risk and active specific risk is equal to active risk squared (which is the variance of active returns):

active risk squared = active factor risk + active specific risk

Both components contribute to deviations of the portfolio's returns from the benchmark's returns. For example, consider a fundamental factor model that includes industry risk factors. In this case, active risk can be described as follows:

- *Active factor risk example*: An active portfolio manager may decide to under or overweight particular industries relative to the portfolio's benchmark. Therefore, the portfolio's industry factor sensitivities will not coincide with those of the benchmark, and, consequently, the portfolio returns may deviate from the benchmark.
- *Active specific risk example*: The active portfolio manager may decide to overweight or underweight individual stocks within specific industries. For example, a stock's market capitalization may comprise 1% of the industry, but the portfolio manager may allocate 2% of industry allocation to the stock, causing the portfolio returns to deviate from the benchmark returns.

Example: Active risk comparisons

Consider two funds: Management Fund and Steady Fund. The benchmark for both funds is the Wilshire 5000, a well-diversified stock index. The active factor risk for Management Fund equals 20 and for Steady Fund equals 5. The active specific risk for Management Fund equals 30 and for Steady Fund equals 2. Contrast the two styles of portfolio management for the two funds.

Answer:

Management Fund is more actively managed, exhibiting both higher active factor risk and higher active specific risk. Management Fund more actively manages its factor exposures, leading to high active factor risk. Also, Management Fund is characterized by asset selection that differs substantially from the benchmark, as indicated by its high active specific risk.

In contrast, Steady Fund is much more passively managed. Note that a passively managed index fund should have zero active risk (when examining gross returns only). Also, note that a tracking fund (discussed in detail later), with active asset selection but with factor sensitivities that match those of the benchmark, will have no active factor risk, but will still have some degree of exposure to active specific risk.

The Information Ratio

Active return alone is insufficient in measuring the manager's performance over a series of measurement periods. For example, assume Manager A earned a constant 0.5% (50 bps) active return over each of the last four quarters. On the other hand, assume Manager B earned active returns of 8%, 5%, –3%, and –8% over the same four quarters. The average active returns for managers A and B are both 0.5%, but Manager B experienced far more volatility (i.e., less consistency) than Manager A.

To demonstrate a manager's consistency in generating active return, we utilize the *information ratio* in which we standardize average active return by dividing it by its standard deviation. In other words, the information ratio equals the portfolio's average active return divided by the portfolio's tracking risk:

$$IR = \frac{\bar{R}_P - \bar{R}_B}{s_{(R_P - R_B)}}$$

Example: Calculating the information ratio

Assume the portfolio and benchmark returns over the past 12 months have been as shown in the following table.

Portfolio and Benchmark Returns for Twelve Months

Month	R_p	R_B	$R_p - R_B$
1	0.0101	0.0091	0.0010
2	−0.0013	0.0062	−0.0075
3	0.0110	0.0069	0.0041
4	0.0135	0.0071	0.0064
5	0.0103	0.0067	0.0036
6	0.0093	0.0051	0.0042
7	−0.0011	0.0007	−0.0018
8	0.0085	0.0105	−0.0020
9	0.0091	0.0101	−0.0010
10	−0.0073	−0.0030	−0.0043
11	0.0186	0.0012	0.0174
12	0.0103	0.0097	0.0006
Average	0.0076	0.0059	0.0017
		Sample Std. Dev.	0.0063

Given the data in the table, calculate and interpret the manager's information ratio.

Answer:

$$IR = \frac{(\bar{R}_P - \bar{R}_B)}{s_{(R_P - R_B)}} = \frac{0.0076 - 0.0059}{0.0063} \approx 0.27$$

The higher the IR, the more active return the manager earned per unit of active risk. An information ratio of 0.27 indicates the manager earned about 27 basis points of active return per unit of active risk.

Professor's Note: The information ratio is very similar to the Sharpe ratio. First, their numerators are similar in that they both compare the average portfolio return to a benchmark. The difference is that the Sharpe ratio uses the risk-free rate as the benchmark and the IR uses a portfolio benchmark return (one that best matches the investment style of the managed portfolio). In the denominator, both use standard deviation to measure dispersion, so both measure return per unit of total variability. The Sharpe ratio uses the standard deviation of portfolio returns over the measurement period and the information ratio uses the standard deviation of the active return over the measurement period.

Uses of Factor and Tracking Portfolios

A *pure factor portfolio* (or simply a *factor portfolio*) is a portfolio that has been constructed to have sensitivity equal to 1.0 to only one risk factor, and sensitivities of zero to the remaining factors. Factor portfolios are particularly useful for speculation or hedging purposes. For example, assume a portfolio manager believes GDP growth will be stronger than expected, but wishes to hedge against all other factor risks. The manager can take a long position in the GDP "factor portfolio." The factor portfolio is exposed to the GDP risk factor, but is hedged (zero sensitivity) to all other risk factors. This manager is speculating that GDP will rise above market expectations.

Alternatively, consider a manager who wishes to hedge his portfolio against GDP factor risk. Assume the portfolio's GDP factor sensitivity equals 0.80, and the portfolio's sensitivities to the remaining risk factors are different from zero. Suppose the portfolio manager wishes to hedge against GDP risk, but remain exposed to the remaining factors. The manager can hedge against GDP risk by taking an 80% short position in the GDP factor portfolio. The 0.80 GDP sensitivity of the managed portfolio will be offset by the −0.80 GDP sensitivity from the short position in the GDP factor portfolio.

The important point is that a factor portfolio is assumed to be hedged against all but one source of risk (i.e., has zero sensitivities for all but one risk factor), and has unit sensitivity to the remaining factor.

In contrast, *tracking portfolios* have a deliberately designed *set* of factor exposures. That is, a tracking portfolio is deliberately constructed to have the same set of factor exposures to match ("track") a predetermined benchmark. The strategy involved in constructing a tracking portfolio is usually an active bet on asset selection. The manager constructs the portfolio to have the same factor exposures as the benchmark, but then selects what they believe to be superior securities (subject to the factor sensitivities constraint), thus hopefully outperforming the benchmark without taking on more systematic risk than the benchmark.

For example, suppose a portfolio manager is evaluated relative to the S&P 500 benchmark, but believes she can beat the index with superior stock selection. One strategy would be to create a tracking portfolio with the same set of factor exposures as the S&P 500, but with a different set of securities. Any differences in performance between her portfolio and the S&P 500 benchmark should be the result of her stock selection ability and not from different exposures to macroeconomic risk factors.

LOS 57.n: Compare underlying assumptions and conclusions of the CAPM and APT model, and explain why an investor can possibly earn a substantial premium for exposure to dimensions of risk unrelated to market movements.

CFA® Program Curriculum, Volume 6, page 453

Both the arbitrage pricing model and the capital asset pricing model discussed earlier are models describing equilibrium expected returns for assets, but there are some very important differences between the two models.

The CAPM suggests that all investors should hold some combination of the market portfolio and the risk-free asset. To adjust risk, less risk-averse investors simply hold more of the market portfolio, and less of the risk-free asset. More risk-averse investors hold more of the risk-free asset, and less of the market portfolio. The risk of the investor's portfolio is determined solely by the resulting portfolio beta (market risk), so the CAPM assumes there is only one source of systematic ("priced") risk.

In contrast, the APT gives no special role to the market portfolio (i.e., the APT does not require the existence of the "market portfolio"), and is, therefore, a far more flexible model than the CAPM. Also, in contrast to the CAPM, the APT states that asset returns follow a multifactor process, thereby allowing investors to manage several risk factors, rather than just one. This more targeted approach to portfolio management may help improve portfolio performance. The investor can identify and earn returns or hedge risks associated with factors such as recession risk, interest rate risk, or inflation risk. Thus, the investor's unique circumstances (different from the average investor) may drive the investor to hold portfolios tilted away from the market portfolio in order to hedge or speculate on multiple risk factors.

For example, the typical investor, who has a job and depends on a salary for income, is sensitive to recessions (which occur when GDP declines). Therefore, the typical investor faces a systematic risk of recessions and will tend to avoid cyclical stocks (depressing their prices, which leads to a higher risk premium) and pursue countercyclical stocks (bidding up their prices, which leads to a lower risk premium).

The result of the behavior of the typical investor is that the business cycle actually becomes a priced risk factor (which is why GDP surprise is often used as a factor in macroeconomic models). Investors who are independently wealthy and don't depend on their salary as a source of income may be able to earn a substantial risk premium by increasing their portfolio allocation to cyclical stocks, because they are exposed to less than average systematic recession risk by virtue of not being dependent upon salary income.

KEY CONCEPTS

LOS 57.a

In mean-variance analysis, we use the expected returns, variances, and covariances of individual investment returns to analyze the risk-return tradeoff of combinations (portfolios) of individual investments.

Key assumptions made in mean-variance analysis include: investors are risk averse; statistical inputs (means, variances, covariances) are known; investors make all portfolio decisions based solely on means, variances, and covariances; and investors face no taxes or transactions costs.

The expected return on a portfolio of two assets is the weighted average of the returns on the individual assets:

$$E(R_p) = w_1 E(R_1) + w_2 E(R_2)$$

Similarly, the expected return for a three-asset portfolio equals:

$$E(R_p) = w_1 E(R_1) + w_2 E(R_2) + w_3 E(R_3)$$

The variance of a portfolio of two assets equals:

$$\sigma_p^2 = w_1^2 \sigma_1^2 + w_2^2 \sigma_2^2 + 2 w_1 w_2 \rho_{12} \sigma_1 \sigma_2$$

And, the variance of a portfolio of three assets equals:

$$\sigma_p^2 = w_1^2 \sigma_1^2 + w_2^2 \sigma_2^2 + w_3^2 \sigma_3^2 + 2 w_1 w_2 \rho_{12} \sigma_1 \sigma_2 + 2 w_1 w_3 \rho_{13} \sigma_1 \sigma_3 + 2 w_2 w_3 \rho_{23} \sigma_2 \sigma_3$$

The standard deviation equals the square root of the variance.

LOS 57.b

The minimum-variance frontier is a graph drawn in risk-return space of the set of portfolios that have the lowest variance at each level of expected return. To derive the minimum-variance frontier, we must estimate the risk-return attributes of all assets, run an optimizer that selects portfolio weightings that minimize portfolio variance subject to expected return constraints, and calculate and graph the risk and return for the minimum-variance portfolios.

The efficient frontier is the positively sloped portion of the minimum-variance frontier. Portfolios on the efficient frontier have the highest expected return at each given level of risk.

The minimum-variance frontier and efficient frontier are unstable because expected returns, variances, and covariances change over time. This is problematic and may lead to large portfolio weighting errors.

LOS 57.c

Portfolio diversification refers to the strategy of reducing risk by combining different types of assets into a portfolio. Diversification benefits increase as the correlations among assets decrease, and as the number of assets included in the portfolio increase (but portfolio risk falls at a decreasing rate as the number of assets in the portfolio increases).

LOS 57.d

The variance of an equally-weighted portfolio is:

$$\sigma_P^2 = \frac{1}{n}\overline{\sigma_i^2} + \frac{n-1}{n}\overline{Cov} = \overline{\sigma_i^2}\left[\frac{1-\rho}{n} + \rho\right]$$

If a risk-free investment is part of the investment opportunity set, the efficient frontier is a straight line called the CAL.

The CAL is developed using the investor's unique set of expectations.

The *y*-intercept of the CAL is the risk-free rate and the slope is the Sharpe ratio for the optimal risky portfolio. The CAL lies tangent to the efficient frontier of risky assets. The CAL equation is:

$$E(R_C) = R_F + \left[\frac{E(R_T) - R_F}{\sigma_T}\right]\sigma_C$$

where $E(R_C)$ = expected return on the portfolio combination of the risk-free asset and the optimal risky Portfolio T (the tangency portfolio), and σ_C is the standard deviation on the portfolio combination.

The CML is the CAL developed assuming all investors have identical expectations. All investors agree on the composition of the optimal risky portfolio, now called the market portfolio, which uses market-value weights. The equation of the CML is:

$$E(R_C) = R_F + \left[\frac{E(R_M) - R_F}{\sigma_M}\right]\sigma_C$$

LOS 57.e

The capital asset pricing model (CAPM) describes the relationship we should expect to see between risk and return for individual assets. Specifically, the CAPM provides a way to calculate an asset's expected return (or "required" return) based on its level of systematic (or market-related) risk, as measured by the asset's beta. The CAPM equation is:

$$E(R_i) = R_F + \beta_i[E(R_M - R_F)]$$

Assumptions of the CAPM:
- Investors only need to know expected returns, variances, and covariances in order to create optimal portfolios.
- All investors have the same forecasts of those measures.
- The market for assets is perfectly competitive.
- Investors are price takers whose individual buy and sell decisions have no effect on asset prices.
- Investors can borrow and lend at the risk-free rate, and unlimited short-selling is allowed.
- There are no frictions to trading, such as taxes or transaction costs.

Implications of the CAPM:
- Because all investors have the same expectations and use mean-variance analysis, they all identify the same risky tangency portfolio and combine that risky portfolio with the risk-free asset when creating their portfolios.
- Because all investors hold the same risky portfolio, the weight on each asset must be equal to the proportion of its market value to the market value of the entire portfolio.
- The security market line (SML), which is the graph of the CAPM, describes the relationship between the expected return and risk for all assets, both individual securities and portfolios.
- Systematic risk, measured by beta, is the only risk priced by the market.

LOS 57.f
The security market line (SML) is the graph of the CAPM, representing the cross-sectional relationship between the expected return for individual assets and portfolios and their systematic risk. The intercept equals the riskfree rate and the slope equals the market risk premium.

The market risk premium equals the expected difference in returns between the market portfolio and the risk-free asset. Using the CAPM, the market risk premium equals the additional return that investors require as compensation for additional units of systematic risk.

The formula for the beta (systematic risk) for a security i is:

$$\beta_i = \frac{Cov_{iM}}{\sigma_M^2}$$

The market portfolio Sharpe ratio is the slope of the CML:

$$\frac{E(R_M) - R_F}{\sigma_M}$$

LOS 57.g

The market model is a single-factor regression model that assumes there are just two sources of risk, unanticipated macroeconomic events (systematic risk), and firm-specific events (unsystematic risk). According to the market model, the return to Asset i is:

$$R_i = \alpha_i + \beta_i R_M + \varepsilon_i$$

The market model makes three assumptions: the expected value of the error term is zero, the errors are uncorrelated with the market return, and the firm-specific surprises are uncorrelated across assets. The market model greatly simplifies the forecast procedures needed for mean-variance analysis.

The market model makes the following predictions:

- The expected return on Asset i depends only on the expected return on the market portfolio, $E(R_M)$, the sensitivity of the returns on Asset i to movements in the market, β_i, and the average return to Asset i when the market return is zero, α_i.
- The variance of the returns on Asset i consists of two components: a systematic component related to the asset's beta, $\beta_i^2 \sigma_M^2$, and an unsystematic component related to firm-specific events, σ_ε^2.
- The covariance between any two stocks is calculated as the product of their betas and the variance of the market portfolio: $Cov_{ij} = \beta_i \beta_j \sigma_M^2$.

LOS 57.h

Historical betas may be very poor predictors of future betas. Therefore, we often employ the adjusted beta formula, which adjusts the future beta toward a value of 1 over time.

LOS 57.i

The instability in the minimum-variance frontier is a concern for a number of reasons:

- The statistical inputs (means, variances, covariances) are unknown, and must be forecast; greater uncertainty in the inputs leads to less reliability in the efficient frontier.
- Statistical input forecasts derived from historical sample estimates often change over time, causing the estimated efficient frontier to change over time (this is called time instability).
- Small changes in the statistical inputs can cause large changes in the efficient frontier (called the "overfitting" problem), resulting in unreasonably large short positions, and overly frequent rebalancing.

LOS 57.j

A multifactor model is an extension of a one-factor market model in which asset returns are a function of more than one factor. There are three types of multifactor models:

- Macroeconomic factor models assume that asset returns are explained by surprises (or "shocks") in macroeconomic risk factors (e.g., GDP, interest rates, inflation). Factor surprises are defined as the difference between the realized value of the factor and its consensus expected value.
- Fundamental factor models assume asset returns are explained by the returns from multiple firm-specific factors (e.g., P/E ratio, market cap, leverage ratio, earnings growth rate).

- Statistical factor models use multivariate statistics (factor analysis or principal components) to identify statistical factors that explain the covariation among asset returns. The major weakness is that the statistical factors do not lend themselves well to economic interpretation.

LOS 57.k

Using a multi-factor model, the portfolio expected return, factor sensitivities, and the error terms are calculated as the weighted average of the individual stock parameters.

LOS 57.l

The APT is an equilibrium asset-pricing k-factor model which assumes no arbitrage opportunities exist. According to the APT, the expected return on a diversified portfolio P is linearly related to its factor sensitivities:

$E(R_P) = R_F + \beta_{P1}(\lambda_1) + \beta_{P2}(\lambda_2) + \ldots + \beta_{Pk}(\lambda_k)$, where each λ stands for the expected risk premium associated with each risk factor

LOS 57.m

Active return is the difference between portfolio and benchmark returns ($R_P - R_B$), and active risk is the standard deviation of active return over time. Active risk is determined by the manager's active factor tilt and active asset selection decisions.

Active risk squared = active factor risk + active specific risk.

The information ratio is active return divided by active risk: $IR = \dfrac{\overline{R}_P - \overline{R}_B}{s_{(R_P - R_B)}}$

A factor portfolio is a portfolio with a factor sensitivity of 1 to a particular factor and zero to all other factors. It represents a pure bet on one factor, and can be used for speculation or hedging purposes.

A tracking portfolio is a portfolio with a specific set of factor sensitivities. Tracking portfolios are often designed to replicate the factor exposures of a benchmark index like the S&P 500.

LOS 57.n

The CAPM is a single-factor asset pricing model, in which only risk relative to the broad market is priced. The CAPM suggests that all investors should hold some combination of the market portfolio and the risk-free asset. In contrast, the APT captures multiple dimensions of risk besides the overall market risk, and suggests that investors make decisions relative to multiple sources of risk.

Investors who are independently wealthy and don't depend on their salary as a source of income can earn a substantial risk premium by increasing their portfolio allocation to cyclical stocks, even though they are exposed to less than average systematic recession risk.

CONCEPT CHECKERS

1. Assume the following information for stocks A and B.
    *   Expected return on Stock A = 18%.
    *   Expected return on Stock B = 23%.
    *   Correlation between returns of Stock A and Stock B = 0.10.
    *   Standard deviation of returns on Stock A = 40%.
    *   Standard deviation of returns on Stock B = 50%.

    The expected return and standard deviation of an equally weighted portfolio of stocks A and B are *closest* to:

	Expected return (%)	Standard deviation (%)
A.	20.5	33.54
B.	20.5	11.22
C.	33.5	11.22

Use the following data to answer Questions 2 through 4.

Assume the expected return on stocks is 18% (represented by Z in the figure), and the expected return on bonds is 8% (represented by point Y on the graph).

Minimum-Variance Frontier: Stocks and Bonds

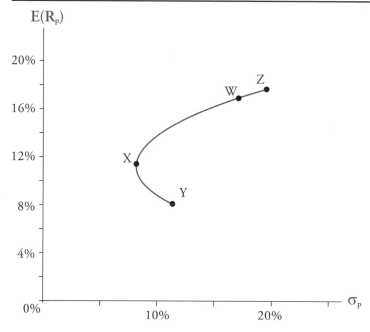

2. The graph shows the minimum-variance frontier for stocks and bonds. The point on the graph that *most likely* represents a 90% allocation in stocks and a 10% allocation in bonds is Portfolio:
    A. W.
    B. X.
    C. Z.

3. According to the graph, the point that *most likely* represents the global minimum-variance portfolio is Portfolio:
    A. X.
    B. W.
    C. Z.

4. The efficient frontier consists of the portfolios between and including:
    A. X and W.
    B. Y and Z.
    C. X and Z.

5. The benefits of diversifying from a 1-stock to a 2-stock portfolio will be greatest when the correlation between the two stocks is:
    A. −1.0.
    B. 0.0.
    C. +1.0.

Use the following figure to answer Questions 6 and 7.

Mean-Variance Analysis

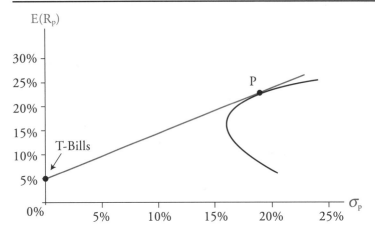

6. Portfolio P is the point where the straight line is tangent to the curve. It is also the market portfolio. The market price of risk is the:
    A. expected return on the minimum-variance portfolio.
    B. slope of the line connecting T-bills and Portfolio P.
    C. point at which the straight line intersects the expected return axis.

7. Portfolio P is the point where the straight line is tangent to the curve. It is also the market portfolio. The line that connects T-bills and Portfolio P is called the:
    A. capital market line.
    B. security market line.
    C. efficient market line.

Use the following data to answer Questions 8 through 12.

Samuel Perkins uses the capital market line (CML) to advise his clients. Current market expectations are as follows:

- Expected return on the market portfolio   12%
- Standard deviation on the market portfolio   20%
- Risk-free rate   4%

8. Perkins advises a client who would like to have a portfolio with a standard deviation equal to 10%. Using the CML, a portfolio meeting the client's risk tolerance will have an expected return *closest* to:
   A. 6%.
   B. 8%.
   C. 10%.

9. Perkins advises another client who currently owns a portfolio with an expected return of 8% and a standard deviation of 15%. The amount (percentage points) by which Perkins can improve his client's expected return by using the CML while maintaining the client's 15% standard deviation is *closest* to:
   A. 2%.
   B. 4%.
   C. 6%.

10. One of Perkins's clients has an expected return objective of 10%. Using the CML, Perkins can create a portfolio with a standard deviation as low as:
    A. 13%.
    B. 14%.
    C. 15%.

11. What is the appropriate allocation to the optimal risky portfolio for a Perkins's client who has a 10% standard deviation objective?
    A. 30%.
    B. 40%.
    C. 50%.

12. From the data provided, the intercept and slope of the CML are *closest* to:
    A. 4% intercept and a 8% slope.
    B. 4% intercept and a 40% slope.
    C. 8% intercept and a 40% slope.

13. At a recent analyst meeting at Invest Forum, analysts Michelle White and Ted Jones discussed the use of the capital asset pricing model (CAPM) and the arbitrage pricing theory (APT). White states that the CAPM implies that investors hold a risky portfolio of all assets weighted according to their relative market value capitalizations. Jones states that the APT implies that investors will make investment decisions by allocating their money between a risk-free asset and the market portfolio.

    Are the statements of White and Jones correct?
    A. Both statements are correct.
    B. Only one of the statements is correct.
    C. Neither statement is correct.

14. Analysts Linda Yarbrough and Pamela Burke recently discussed the application of the market model. Yarbrough comments that, assuming betas remain constant, the market model prediction of the covariance between any two assets rises during a period of rising market volatility. Burke states that the market model prediction of covariance will not be correct if the firm's unique components of asset returns are correlated.

    Are the statements of Yarbrough and Burke correct?
    A. Both statements are correct.
    B. Only one of the statements is correct.
    C. Neither statement is correct.

15. An equally-weighted portfolio is formed in which the average stock variance equals 9% and the average covariance equals 5%. As the number of assets included in this portfolio increases, portfolio risk will *most likely* fall at a(n):
    A. increasing rate and approach 9%.
    B. steady rate and approach 7%.
    C. decreasing rate and approach 5%.

16. Which of the following statements is *least likely* a prediction of the single-factor market model?
    A. The covariance between two assets is related to the betas of the two assets and the variance of the market portfolio.
    B. All investors hold the market portfolio, so the CML is defined as the capital allocation line with the market portfolio as the tangency portfolio.
    C. The expected return on Asset i depends on the market's expected return, the sensitivity of Asset i's returns to the market, and the average return to Asset i not related to the market return.

17. A multifactor model uses factors that are stock or company characteristics, such as price-to-book and price-to-earnings ratios, that have been shown to affect asset returns. This type of multifactor model would be called a:
    A. systematic factor model.
    B. fundamental factor model.
    C. macroeconomic factor model.

18. Jones Brothers uses a 2-factor macroeconomic factor model to evaluate stocks and has derived the following results for the stock of AmGrow (AG):
    - Expected return   10%
    - GDP factor sensitivity   2
    - Inflation factor sensitivity   −0.5

    Over the past year, GDP grew at a rate that was two percentage points lower than originally expected, and inflation rose two percentage points higher than originally expected. AG also experienced a large unexpected product recall causing a firm-unique surprise of −4% to its stock price. Based on the information provided, the rate of return for AG for the year was *closest* to:
    A. 1%.
    B. 2%.
    C. 3%.

19. Patricia Franklin makes buy and sell stock recommendations using the capital asset pricing model. Franklin has derived the following information for the broad market and for the stock of the CostSave Company (CS):
    - Expected market risk premium   8%
    - Risk free rate   5%
    - Historical beta for CostSave   1.50

    Franklin believes that historical betas do not provide good forecasts of future beta, and, therefore, uses the adjusted beta formula:

    forecast beta = 0.80 + 0.20 × historical beta

    After conducting a thorough examination of market trends and the CS financial statements, Franklin predicts that the CS return will equal 10%. Franklin should derive the following required return for CS along with the following valuation decision (undervalued or overvalued):

	Valuation	CAPM required return
A.	Overvalued	8.3%
B.	Overvalued	13.8%
C.	Undervalued	13.8%

20. A portfolio that has the same factor sensitivities as the S&P 500, but does not hold all 500 stocks in the index, is called a:
    A. factor portfolio.
    B. tracking portfolio.
    C. market portfolio.

21. A portfolio with a factor sensitivity of one to the yield spread factor and a sensitivity of zero to all other macroeconomic factors is *best* described as a:
    A. factor portfolio.
    B. tracking portfolio.
    C. market portfolio.

22. Factor Investments manages a tracking portfolio which claims to outperform the S&P 500. The active factor risk and active specific risk for the tracking portfolio are *most likely* to be:
    A. high active factor risk and high active specific risk.
    B. high active factor risk and low active specific risk.
    C. low active factor risk and high active specific risk.

23. Which of the following is the *most* important assumption underlying the market model?
    A. The expected value of the error term is not 1.
    B. The errors are uncorrelated to the probability distribution function.
    C. The firm-specific surprises are uncorrelated across assets.

24. The Sharpe Ratio is best formulated as:

    A. $\dfrac{\bar{R}_P - \bar{R}_B}{s_{(R_P - R_B)}}$.

    B. $\dfrac{E(R_T) - R_F}{\sigma_T}$.

    C. $R_F + \left[\dfrac{E(R_M) - R_F}{\sigma_M}\right]\sigma_C$.

ANSWERS – CONCEPT CHECKERS

1. **A** $E(R_P) = w_A E(R_A) + w_B E(R_B) = (0.50)(0.18) + (0.50)(0.23) = 0.205 = 20.5\%$

$$\sigma_p = \left[w_A^2 \sigma_A^2 + w_B^2 \sigma_B^2 + 2 w_A w_B \rho_{AB} \sigma_A \sigma_B \right]^{1/2}$$

$$\sigma_p = \left[\begin{array}{c} (0.5)^2 (0.4)^2 + (0.5)^2 (0.5)^2 \\ + 2(0.5)(0.5)(0.1)(0.4)(0.5) \end{array} \right]^{1/2} = 0.3354 = 33.54\%$$

2. **A**   Since the return to *W* is the nearest to *Z* (stocks), it is logical to assume that point *W* represents an allocation of 90% stocks/10% bonds. The return for *W* is lower than *Z*, but it also represents a reduction in risk.

3. **A**   The *global minimum-variance portfolio* is the portfolio on the minimum-variance frontier that has the smallest standard deviation (or variance). This portfolio appears as the farthest left point on the efficient frontier.

4. **C**   The *efficient frontier* consists of portfolios that have the maximum expected return for any given level of risk (standard deviation or variance). The efficient frontier starts at the global minimum-variance portfolio and continues above it. Any portfolio below the efficient frontier is dominated by a portfolio on the efficient frontier. This is because efficient portfolios have higher expected returns for the same level of risk.

5. **A**   As the correlation between two assets decreases, the benefits of diversification increase. That's because the separate movements of the stocks serve to reduce the volatility of the combination, leaving a portfolio that is less volatile than its individual components. As we combine the two stocks, the efficient frontier *bulges* up and to the left (i.e., northwesterly if you think of the plot as a map and north as up). This bulge is what creates the diversification benefits because we can develop portfolios above the global minimum-variance portfolio that dominate those below. The greater the bulge, the greater the benefits! The amount of bulge in the frontier is a function of the correlation between the two assets: the lower the correlation (closer to –1), the greater the bulge. The larger the correlation (closer to +1), the smaller the bulge.

6. **B**   The CML is the line connecting T-bills and Portfolio P. The market price of risk is the slope of the CML, which has the same interpretation as the slope coefficient of the CAL. Had risk been measured on the graph with beta, the graph would represent the SML. The market price of risk would still be the slope of the line.

7. **A**   Since risk in the graph is represented by standard deviation and P is the market portfolio, the line represents the CML. The CML is the CAL with the market portfolio as the tangency portfolio. Had risk been measured by beta, the line would be the SML.

8. **B**   The equation for the CML is:

$$E(R_C) = R_F + \left[\frac{E(R_M) - R_F}{\sigma_M}\right]\sigma_C \text{ , where } R_F = 0.04$$

$$\left[\frac{E(R_M) - R_F}{\sigma_M}\right] = \left[\frac{0.12 - 0.04}{0.20}\right] = 0.40$$

Therefore, the equation of the CML is:

$$E(R_C) = 0.04 + 0.40\sigma_C$$

Setting the standard deviation equal to 0.10:

$$E(R_C) = 0.04 + 0.40(0.10) = 0.08 = 8\%$$

9. **A**   The equation for the CML is: $E(R_C) = 0.04 + 0.40\sigma_C$. Setting the standard deviation equal to 0.15:

$$E(R_C) = 0.04 + 0.40(0.15) = 0.10 = 10\%$$

Therefore, Perkins can improve the client's expected return by two percentage points:

new expected return = 10%

old expected return = 8%

10. **C**   The equation for the CML is: $E(R_C) = 0.04 + 0.40\sigma_C$. Setting the expected return to 0.10:

$$E(R_C) = 0.10 = 0.04 + 0.40\sigma_C$$

Solving for σ_C:

$$0.40\sigma_C = 0.10 - 0.04 = 0.06$$

$$\sigma_C = 0.06 / 0.40 = 0.15 = 15\%$$

11. **C**   The standard deviation for the investment combination (of Treasury bills and the market portfolio) equals:

$$\sigma_C = w_M\sigma_M$$

The client wants $\sigma_C = 0.10$.

Therefore, $0.10 = w_M(0.20)$.

$$w_M = 0.10 / 0.20 = 0.50 = 50\%$$

Therefore, the portfolio should be allocated 50% to Treasury bills and 50% to the market portfolio.

12. **B**   The equation for the CML is:

$$E(R_C) = R_F + \left[\frac{E(R_M) - R_F}{\sigma_M} \right] \sigma_C$$

where the intercept is the risk-free rate, $R_F = 0.04$, or 4%, and the slope equals the market risk premium $[E(R_M) - R_F]$ per unit of market risk, σ_M.

$$\left[\frac{E(R_M) - R_F}{\sigma_M} \right] = \left[\frac{0.12 - 0.04}{0.20} \right] = 0.40, \text{ or } 40\%$$

13. **B**   The CAPM assumes all investors have identical expectations and all use mean-variance analysis, implying that they all identify the same risky tangency portfolio (the "market portfolio") and combine that risky portfolio with the risk-free asset when creating their portfolios. Because all investors hold the same risky portfolio, the weight on each asset must be equal to the proportion of its market value to the market value of the entire portfolio. Therefore, White is correct. In contrast, the APT places no special emphasis on the market portfolio. In fact, the APT does not even require that the "market portfolio" exist. Therefore, Jones is incorrect.

14. **A**   The market model makes a number of assumptions which lead to the prediction that the covariance between two assets equals the product of the asset betas multiplied by the market variance. Therefore, Yarbrough is correct. One of the assumptions of the market model is that firm-specific events are uncorrelated across firms. If this assumption is violated, then the market model predictions of the covariances will be wrong. Burke's statement is correct.

15. **C**   The formula for the variance of an equally-weighted portfolio is:

$$\sigma_P^2 = \frac{1}{n} \overline{\sigma_i^2} + \frac{n-1}{n} \overline{Cov}$$

where:

$\overline{\sigma_i^2}$ = the average variance of all assets in the portfolio

$\overline{Cov}$ = the average covariance of all pairings of assets in the portfolio

As *n* increases, the first term in the formula approaches zero, and the second term approaches the average covariance. That is:

- $(1/n) \times \overline{\sigma_i^2}$ gets closer to zero as *n* gets large.
- $[(n - 1)/n] \times \overline{Cov}$ gets closer to the average covariance as *n* gets large.

Therefore, as *n* increases, the variance of the equally-weighted portfolio approaches the average covariance (5%). There are limits to the benefits of diversification benefits. As more assets are added to the portfolio, the portfolio variance approaches that of the broad market variance. Therefore, as the portfolio size increases, the portfolio risk falls at a decreasing rate.

16. **B** The single-factor market model does not predict that all investors hold the market portfolio. The market model makes three predictions:
- The expected return on Asset i depends on the market's expected return, the sensitivity of Asset i's returns to the market, and the average return to Asset i not related to the market return.
- There are two components to the variance of the returns on Asset i: a systematic component related to the asset's beta and an unsystematic component related to firm-specific surprises.
- The covariance between two assets is related to the betas of the two assets and the variance of the market portfolio.

17. **B** *Fundamental factor models* focus on microeconomic factors. Each factor, whether a ratio or a *descriptor*, has unique factor values.

18. **A** The 2-factor model for AG is:

$$R_{AG} = 0.10 + 2(-0.02) - 0.50(0.02) - 0.04 = 0.01 = 1\%$$

The AG return was less than originally expected because AG was hurt by lower than expected economic growth (GDP), higher than expected inflation, and by negative company specific surprise events.

19. **B** The CAPM equation is:

$$E(R_i) = R_F + \beta_i[E(R_M - R_F)]$$

Franklin wants to use the adjusted beta formula which equals:

beta forecast = 0.80 + 0.20(historical beta)

beta forecast = 0.80 + 0.20(1.50) = 1.10

The CAPM required return for CostSave is: 0.05 + 1.1(0.08) = 13.8%. Note that the market premium, $E(R_M) - R_F$, is provided in the question (8%).

Franklin should decide that the stock is overvalued because she forecasts that the CostSave return will equal only 10%, whereas the required return (minimum acceptable return) is 13.8%.

20. **B** A *tracking portfolio* is a portfolio with a specific set of factor sensitivities. Tracking portfolios are often designed to replicate the factor exposures of a benchmark index like the S&P 500. In fact, a factor portfolio is just a special case of a tracking portfolio. One use of tracking portfolios is to attempt to outperform the S&P 500 by using the same factor exposures as the S&P 500, but with a different set of securities than the S&P 500.

21. **A** A *factor portfolio* is a portfolio with a factor sensitivity of 1 to a particular factor and zero to all other factors. It represents a *pure bet* on that factor. For example, a portfolio manager who believes GDP growth will be greater than expected, but has no view of future interest rates and wants to hedge away the interest rate risk in his portfolio, could create a *factor portfolio* that is only exposed to the GDP factor and not the interest rate factor.

22. **C** A tracking portfolio is deliberately constructed to have the same set of factor exposures to match ("track") a predetermined benchmark. The strategy involved in constructing a tracking portfolio is usually an active bet on asset selection (the manager claims to beat the S&P 500). The manager constructs the portfolio to have the same factor exposures as the benchmark, but then selects superior securities (subject to the factor sensitivities constraint), thus outperforming the benchmark without taking on more systematic risk than the benchmark. Therefore, a tracking portfolio, with active asset selection but with factor sensitivities that match those of the benchmark, will have little or no active factor risk, but will have high active specific risk.

23. **C** The market model makes three assumptions:
    - The expected value of the error term is zero. (Choice A is tempting, but not complete enough to be correct.)
    - The errors are uncorrelated with the market return.
    - The firm-specific surprises are uncorrelated across assets.

24. **B** The three formulas shown in the question are for (A) the information ratio, (B) the Sharpe ratio, and (C) the CML.

RESIDUAL RISK AND RETURN: THE INFORMATION RATIO

EXAM FOCUS

This reading introduces a framework for managing residual risk and return. Two key concepts are important: first, the information ratio is used to measure our investment opportunities, and second, residual risk aversion measures the degree to which we are willing to take advantage of those opportunities. These ideas help us to quantify our ability to add value. You should be able to compute an information ratio and recognize that the information ratio is independent of the level of aggressiveness of the manager. Be able to compute value added given residual risk and risk aversion of the investor.

Active management is justified only when the active manager can "beat" the appropriate passive benchmark, in other words, generate positive risk-adjusted returns in excess of the benchmark. In this topic review, we evaluate the concept of the information ratio and how it connotes opportunities available to an active manager.

LOS 58.a: Define the terms "alpha" and "information ratio" in both their ex post and ex ante senses.

LOS 58.b: Compare the information ratio and the alpha's T-statistic.

CFA® Program Curriculum, Volume 6, page 476

ACTIVE RETURN VS. RISK

Alpha or **residual return** is the return of a portfolio in excess of its benchmark (adjusted for risk difference between the portfolio and benchmark). The ex-post alpha (i.e., alpha measured after actual results become available) is the average realized residual return over a measurement interval. Ex-post alpha can be positive or negative. The ex-post alpha for a portfolio can be computed using a regression model:

$$R_{pt} = \alpha_p + \beta_p R_{Bt} + \varepsilon_t$$

where:
R_{pt} = excess return on portfolio p for time t (portfolio return minus the risk-free rate)
α_p = ex-post (actual or realized) alpha on portfolio p (regression intercept estimate)
β_p = portfolio beta (regression slope estimate)
R_{Bt} = excess return on benchmark portfolio (benchmark return minus the risk-free rate)
ε_t = random component of residual return

The alpha of a portfolio is simply the weighted average of the alphas of the individual securities in the portfolio. By definition, the alpha of the benchmark portfolio (and of the risk-free asset) is zero. *Ex-ante* alpha is a forward-looking *forecast* of residual return, while *ex-post* alpha is a backward-looking average of *realized* residual returns. The alpha referred to in the rest of the topic review is always ex-ante alpha.

INFORMATION RATIO

The information ratio of a portfolio is the annualized residual return of the portfolio divided by the annualized residual risk.

$$\text{information ratio} = \frac{\text{annualized residual return}}{\text{annualized residual risk}} = \frac{\alpha}{\omega}$$

$$\text{ex-post information ratio} = \frac{t_\alpha}{\sqrt{n}}$$

where:
t_α = t-statistic of α (i.e., the intercept term) in the regression model
n = number of years of data in the regression model

While the information ratio is computed using annual residual return and risk, we can also compute it over any horizon. However, the numerator (alpha) increases proportionately with time (annual alpha will be 12 times as high as monthly alpha), while the denominator increases by square root of the time horizon (annual residual risk will only be $\sqrt{12}$ = 3.46 times the monthly residual risk). Hence, the information ratio would increase with the time horizon. If we use quarterly data, the residual return would be one-fourth of the annual return and residual risk would be $1/\sqrt{4}$ or half of annual residual risk. Hence, the quarterly information ratio would be half of the annual information ratio.

A manager's personal information ratio is the highest information ratio that can be attained using all possible portfolios the manager can choose from.

Example: Residual return for a given level of residual risk

A manager can achieve an expected residual return of 2% with a residual risk of 5%. Compute the expected residual return given a risk tolerance of 8% for residual risk.

Answer:

manager's information ratio = 2% / 5% = 0.4

residual risk target = 8%

expected residual return = (0.4)8% = 3.2%

Example: Residual return of a portfolio

Consider five stocks that have non-zero alpha, and a benchmark portfolio that contains an equal weighting in each of these stocks:

Stock	Alpha	Benchmark Weight	Portfolio X Weight	Portfolio X Active Weight[1]	Portfolio Y Weight	Portfolio Y Active Weight
A	–1.0%	20%	15%	–5%	10%	–10%
B	–1.5%	20%	15%	–5%	10%	–10%
C	2.0%	20%	25%	5%	30%	10%
D	0.5%	20%	25%	5%	30%	10%
E	0.0%	20%	20%	0%	20%	0%

1. Active weight of a portfolio = portfolio weight – benchmark weight

Calculate the alpha of the Benchmark portfolio, and the alpha of portfolios X and Y.

Answer:

The portfolio alpha can be computed as the weighted average of individual security alphas:

$$\text{Benchmark } \alpha = (0.20)(-1.0\%) + (0.20)(-1.5\%) + (0.20)(2.0\%) + (0.20)(0.5\%) + (0.20)(0.0\%) = 0\%$$

$$\text{Portfolio X } \alpha = (0.15)(-1.0\%) + (0.15)(-1.5\%) + (0.25)(2.0\%) + (0.25)(0.5\%) + (0.20)(0.0\%) = 0.25\%$$

$$\text{Portfolio Y } \alpha = (0.10)(-1.0\%) + (0.10)(-1.5\%) + (0.30)(2.0\%) + (0.30)(0.5\%) + (0.20)(0.0\%) = 0.5\%$$

Portfolio alphas can also be computed using the active weights:

$$\text{For portfolio X } \alpha = (-0.05)(-1.0\%) + (-0.05)(-1.5\%) + (0.05)(2.0\%) + (0.05)(0.5\%) + (0.00)(0.0\%) = 0.25\%$$

Note that in the previous example, portfolio Y's active weights are twice as large as portfolio X's active weights; hence, portfolio Y is simply a more aggressive version of portfolio X. However, since both portfolios are relying on the same information set, the higher alpha for portfolio Y will come at a cost of higher residual risk leaving the information ratio unchanged. In other words, *a manager's level of aggressiveness does not affect her information ratio.*

A portfolio manager will choose, based on their aggressiveness, from all portfolios that are available to the manager. The plot of residual return versus risk for a given information ratio is called the **residual frontier**. Figure 1 shows an example of a residual frontier.

Figure 1: Residual Frontier for a Manager with IR = 0.5

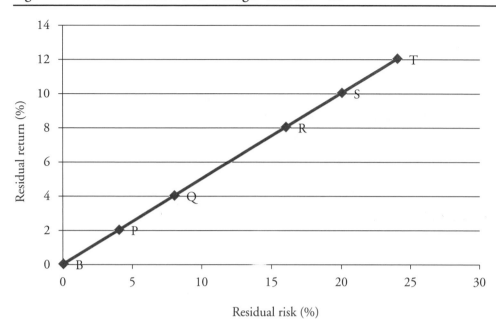

Portfolio B in Figure 1 is the benchmark portfolio (recall that the benchmark portfolio has zero alpha and zero residual risk). Portfolios P, Q, R, S, and T are other portfolios available to the manager; the manager's choice will depend on how much residual risk she is comfortable with. The slope of the residual frontier is the information ratio. A higher information ratio means a steeper residual frontier.

For an active manager, the information ratio can be viewed as a **budget constraint**: the manager can increase the active return only by increasing residual risk.

$$\alpha = IR \times \omega$$

LOS 58.c: Explain the objective of active management in terms of value added.

CFA® Program Curriculum, Volume 6, page 482

VALUE ADDED

The objective of active management is to maximize value added. **Value added** is a metric that attempts to capture the tradeoff between active return and active risk.

value added = $\alpha - (\lambda \times \omega^2)$

where:
λ = risk aversion parameter (a higher λ indicates higher risk aversion)

Professor's Note: While applying this formula, use the return and risk figures in percentage (not decimal) form.

Value added is higher for a manager with higher alpha, lower risk aversion, and lower residual risk. Value added can be thought of as risk adjusted excess return: alpha is discounted for higher residual risk or higher risk aversion.

Figure 2 shows three parabolas with different values of value added. All three curves are for moderate level of risk aversion ($\lambda = 0.10$). The top curve represents VA of 3%. Each point on this parabola differs in terms of alpha and residual risk but has the same VA. The middle and bottom parabolas represent VA of 2% and 1%, respectively. The three curves are parallel to each other. An investor would prefer the highest value for VA but is limited to the opportunities presented by their residual frontier.

Figure 2: Constant Value Added Parabolas

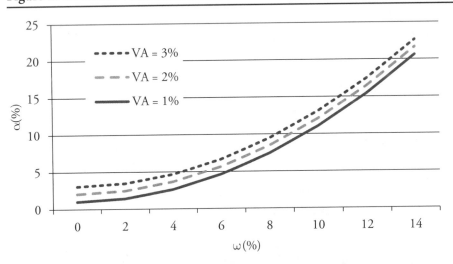

Example: Value added

Jackie Schroff is a value manager with First Partners, LLP. Schroff estimates that he can generate residual return of 3% annually. Schroff's residual risk is 6.5%.

Compute the value added for:

a. an aggressive investor ($\lambda = 0.05$).

b. a moderately risk-averse investor ($\lambda = 0.10$).

c. a conservative investor ($\lambda = 0.15$).

Answer:

$$VA = \alpha - (\lambda \times \omega^2)$$

a. Aggressive investor ($\lambda = 0.05$):

$$VA = 3\% - (0.05 \times 6.5^2) = 0.89\%$$

b. Moderately risk-averse investor ($\lambda = 0.10$)

$$VA = 3\% - (0.10 \times 6.5^2) = -1.23\%$$

b. Conservative investor ($\lambda = 0.15$)

$$VA = 3\% - (0.15 \times 6.5^2) = -3.34\%$$

Value added decreases as the investor's risk aversion (i.e., the price of risk) increases.

LOS 58.d: Calculate the optimal level of residual risk to assume for given levels of manager ability and investor risk aversion.

CFA® Program Curriculum, Volume 6, page 484

OPTIMIZATION

Figure 3 combines a residual frontier (IR = 0.9) with the three value added parabolas shown in Figure 2. Investors would prefer to be on the highest parabola (i.e., highest value added). Given the residual frontier, a VA of 3% is not achievable, while a VA of 1% is sub-optimal. The tangency point denoted by P ($\omega = 4\%$) is the optimal portfolio as it lies on the highest achievable VA curve (VA = 2%) and is achievable (i.e., lies on the residual frontier).

Figure 3: Combining the VA Parabolas with the Residual Frontier

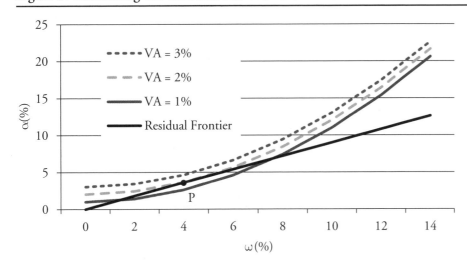

Earlier, we defined the budget constraint and value added to respectively be:

$$\alpha = IR \times \omega$$

$$VA = \alpha - (\lambda \times \omega^2)$$

Substituting the value of α from the first equation into the second equation, we obtain:

$$VA = IR \times \omega - (\lambda \times \omega^2)$$

From this expression we can see that value added initially increases with risk, but the penalty for risk eventually outweighs the gains from taking additional risk. Figure 4 shows value added (VA) for hypothetical values of $\lambda = 0.12$ and $IR = 0.5$.

Figure 4: Value Added vs. Residual Risk ($\lambda = 0.12$, $IR = 0.5$)

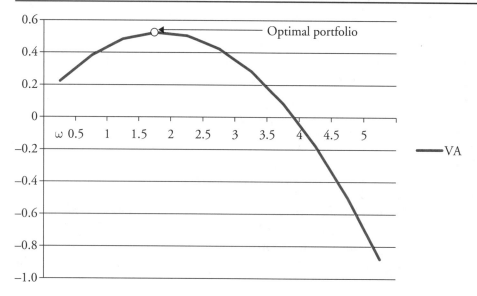

The optimal level of residual risk (ω^*) given IR and λ can be derived as:

$$\omega^* = \frac{IR}{2\lambda}$$

This equation tells us that the higher (lower) the information ratio and lower (higher) the risk aversion, the higher (lower) the optimal level of residual risk.

The optimal level of residual risk equation can also be used to derive the following expression for the implied level of risk aversion:

$$\lambda = \frac{IR}{2\omega^*}$$

LOS 58.e: Justify why the choice for a particular active strategy does not depend on investor risk aversion.

CFA® Program Curriculum, Volume 6, page 486

CHOICE OF ACTIVE STRATEGY

As illustrated in Figure 3, the optimal portfolio is the point where the residual frontier is tangent to the highest achievable value added parabola. As defined earlier,

$$VA = IR \times \omega - (\lambda \times \omega^2)$$

and

$$\omega^* = \frac{IR}{2\lambda}$$

Substituting the value of ω^* into the value added equation,

$$VA^* = \frac{IR^2}{4\lambda}$$

Which can be rewritten as:

$$VA^* = \frac{\omega^* \times IR}{2}$$

Note that risk aversion λ drops out of the last equation, which leads to an important conclusion: *Investors will choose the manager with the highest information ratio, independent of the investor's level of risk aversion. Risk aversion of the investor will only determine how aggressively (or conservatively) the investor will implement that manager's strategy.*

Figure 5 shows the amount of value added for different values of information ratio (IR) and risk aversion (λ) assuming that the manager takes the optimal level of risk (ω^*). We choose information ratios of 1.00 (extremely good), 0.70 (very good), and 0.45 (good). For risk aversion, we choose values of 0.15 (high risk aversion), 0.10 (moderate risk aversion), and 0.05 (low risk aversion).

Figure 5: Value Added

	Risk Aversion (λ)		
IR	0.05	0.10	0.15
1.00	5.00%	2.50%	1.67%
0.70	2.45%	1.23%	0.82%
0.45	1.01%	0.51%	0.34%

As can be seen in Figure 5, the value added increases with information ratio *regardless of the risk aversion.*

KEY CONCEPTS

LOS 58.a

Alpha is defined as the risk-adjusted, residual return over a pre-specified benchmark. Ex-ante alpha is a forward-looking forecast of residual return, while ex-post alpha is a backward-looking average of realized residual returns.

The information ratio of a portfolio is the annualized residual return of the portfolio divided by the annualized residual risk.

$$\text{information ratio} = \frac{\text{annualized residual return}}{\text{annualized residual risk}} = \frac{\alpha}{\omega}$$

LOS 58.b

The ex-post information ratio is related to the t-statistic one obtains for alpha in the regression of portfolio excess returns against benchmark excess returns:

$$\text{ex-post information ratio} = \frac{t_{\alpha}}{\sqrt{n}}$$

where:

t_{α} = t-statistic of α (i.e., the intercept term) in the regression model.

n = number of years of data in the regression model.

LOS 58.c

The objective of active management is to maximize value added (VA). Given the risk aversion parameter (λ):

$$VA = \alpha - (\lambda \times \omega^2)$$

Value added is higher for higher alpha, lower risk aversion, and lower residual risk.

LOS 58.d

$$\text{The optimal level of residual risk} = \omega^* = \frac{IR}{2\lambda}$$

LOS 58.e

The highest achievable level of value added is a function of the optimal level of residual risk and the portfolio manager's information ratio.

$$VA^* = \frac{\omega^* \times IR}{2}$$

Investors will simply choose the manager with the highest information ratio. Risk averseness of the investor will simply determine how aggressively (or conservatively) the investor implements that strategy.

CONCEPT CHECKERS

Use the following information to answer questions 1 through 6.

Yuri Abramovic is a high net worth individual with an extensive portfolio of investments in equities, fixed income, and alternative investments. Abramovic added the alternative investments allocation five years ago in order to increase his returns as his traditional investments were, in his opinion, underperforming.

However, after three quarters of poor performance from this new allocation, Abramovic is once again looking for new ways to increase returns, and is thinking about moving a substantial portion of his $7 million equity allocation. Currently, he is heavily invested in Blue Meadow Capital's Large Cap Tracker Fund. This fund is passively managed; its primary aim is to match the performance of a benchmark set of large cap U.S. equities. Despite a recent rally in the equity markets, Abramovic is concerned that the market is set for a period of uncertainty, and he is interested in switching to a more actively managed fund.

Abramovic has reviewed the prospectuses of several actively managed funds and extracted the data shown below in Exhibit 1.

Exhibit 1

Fund	Residual Risk	Total Return	Residual Return
XSEEK 100	5.2%	15.0%	4.0%
XSEEK 150	6.0%	16.0%	5.0%
XSEEK 180	5.5%	15.8%	4.8%

Each of these funds is managed by a different active manager. Abramovic is aware that the information ratio is often used to analyze the performance of active managers but is apprehensive because the information ratio is based on historical information. Abramovic expresses his main concern as follows:

"The information ratio is useful when assessing active managers, but if the manager increases the level of residual risk taken in a period, an information ratio that is greater than one will decrease while an information ratio of less than one will increase."

Abramovic knows that the information ratio can also be calculated using the t-statistic of the ex-post alpha from a regression of a fund's returns against its benchmark portfolio's returns. He intends to calculate the IR as the alpha's t-statistic divided by the number of years of data used in the regression analysis.

Abramovic is approached by an old college friend who has spent the past five years running an actively managed fund. The two discuss a potential investment. Abramovic asks for more detail about the asset allocations and is provided with the data shown in Exhibit 2.

Exhibit 2

Stocks	Alpha	Benchmark Fund Weighting	Clear Return Elevate Fund Weighting (CRE)
Technology	1.8%	25%	35%
Health care	−2.4%	25%	20%
Retail	2.1%	25%	30%
Mining	−1.5%	25%	15%

Abramovic decides to do some further analysis on the data provided and calculates the alpha of a theoretical fund that has active holdings twice the size of those of the CRE fund for each of the four sectors.

Abramovic is also interested in the concept of value added. He has taken the following notes after reading an investment journal article about the concept of value added but is unsure whether or not he has understood the details correctly.

Journal Extract:

"Value added is a function of residual return, residual risk, and the level of residual risk aversion. Value added is positively related to residual return and the investor's level of residual risk aversion but is negatively related to residual risk."

Abramovic also compiled the data shown in Exhibit 3 to calculate value added.

Exhibit 3: Selected Information on Active Managers A, B, and C

Manager	Residual Return	Residual Risk	Level of Risk Aversion
A	5.0%	5.5%	0.12
B	4.0%	5.0%	0.10
C	5.0%	7.5%	0.08

1. Which of the three funds in Exhibit 1 has the highest information ratio?
    A. XSEEK 100
    B. XSEEK 150
    C. XSEEK 180

2. Is the statement Abramovic makes regarding concerns about the information ratio accurate?
    A. Yes.
    B. No, the information ratio would remain constant.
    C. No, an information ratio of greater than one would increase with an increase in residual risk and an information ratio of less than one would decrease.

3. The calculation Abramovic intends to use to calculate the information ratio using the alpha's t-statistic is *most accurately* described as:
   A. correct.
   B. incorrect as the t-statistic should be divided by the square root of the number of years of data.
   C. incorrect as the t-statistic should be multiplied by the number of years of data.

4. Using the data given in Exhibit 2, the alpha of the theoretical fund described by Abramovic is *closest* to:
   A. 1.11%.
   B. 0.03%.
   C. 2.22%.

5. The notes taken from the journal by Abramovic regarding value added are best described as:
   A. correct.
   B. correct regarding residual return and the level of residual risk aversion but incorrect regarding residual risk.
   C. correct regarding residual return and residual risk but incorrect regarding the level of residual risk aversion.

6. Using the data from Exhibit 3, the manager who has the highest optimal level of residual risk is *most likely*:
   A. Manager A.
   B. Manager B.
   C. Manager C.

ANSWERS – CONCEPT CHECKERS

1. **C** Information ratio is calculated as residual return / residual risk.

   XSEEK 100 IR = 0.04 / 0.052 = 0.77

   XSEEK 150 IR = 0.05 / 0.06 = 0.83

   XSEEK 180 IR = 0.048 / 0.055 = 0.87

2. **B** Information ratio is independent of the manager's aggressiveness. If the residual risk is doubled so is the residual return. Information ratio, therefore, remains constant.

3. **B** The information ratio can be calculated as $IR = \dfrac{t_\alpha}{\sqrt{n}}$

   where:
   t_α = t-statistic of α (i.e., the intercept term) in the ex-post regression model.
   n = number of years of data in the regression model.

4. **A**

Stocks	CRE Active Weighting	Theoretical Fund (×2)	Alpha
Technology	35% − 25% = +10%	+20%	0.2 × 1.8% = 0.36%
Health care	20% − 25% = −5%	−10%	−0.1 × −2.4% = 0.24%
Retail	30% − 25% = +5%	+10%	0.1 × 2.1% = 0.21%
Mining	15% − 25% = −10%	−20%	−0.2 × −1.5% = 0.30%
			Total Alpha = 1.11%

5. **C** Value added is calculated as: $\alpha - (\lambda \times \omega^2)$

   where:
   α = residual (or active) return
   λ = risk aversion parameter
   ω = residual risk

   Value added is, therefore, positively related to residual return and negatively related to the level of residual risk aversion and residual risk.

6. **C** The optimal level of residual risk (ω^*) given the information ratio (IR) and level of residual risk aversion (λ) is:

   $$\omega^* = \dfrac{IR}{2\lambda}$$

Manager	Residual Return	Residual Risk	IR	Level of Risk Aversion	Optimal Level of Residual Risk
A	5.0%	5.5%	0.909	0.12	3.79
B	4.0%	5.0%	0.800	0.10	4.00
C	5.0%	7.5%	0.667	0.08	4.17

THE FUNDAMENTAL LAW OF ACTIVE MANAGEMENT

Study Session 18

EXAM FOCUS

The information ratio can be increased by increasing skill (accuracy of forecasts) or by increasing the breadth (without sacrificing accuracy). Be able to use the additivity principle, describe the relationship between the optimal level of residual risk and the components of the information ratio, and compute the information coefficient in a market timing scenario.

This topic review further explores the concept of the information ratio described in an earlier topic review where we defined the information ratio as the ratio of residual return (active return) to residual risk. We now explore a different way to compute the information ratio: as a product of the manager's skill (information coefficient) and the breadth of manager's information space (the number of independent investment decisions taken in a period).

LOS 59.a: Define the terms "information coefficient" and "breadth" and describe how they combine to determine the information ratio.

CFA® Program Curriculum, Volume 6, page 496

Information coefficient (IC) is a measure of a manager's forecasting accuracy (and, thus, skill). We can measure information coefficient as the correlation of a manager's forecasts with actual outcomes.

Breadth (BR) is the number of *independent* forecasts of exceptional return per year that the manager makes. Independent forecast in this context means that the forecasts should not be based on highly correlated (or identical) information sets. For example, suppose a manager has two pieces of information:

* value stocks are expected to outperform growth stocks.
* high dividend yield stocks are expected to outperform low dividend yield stocks.

Recognize that the two pieces of information are not independent as there is a significant overlap between value stocks and high-yield stocks. Similarly, if multiple analysts in a firm pick different stocks in the same industry, they may be relying on the same information and hence are not making *independent* bets.

Quantifying the breadth metric is fairly straightforward. If an analyst follows two stocks and makes monthly bets, the breadth of the analyst is:

BR = 2 forecasts/month × 12 months/year = 24 forecasts/year

INFORMATION RATIO

The **fundamental law of active management** relates breadth and skill to the information ratio with the following formula:

$$\text{information ratio (IR)} = IC \times \sqrt{BR}$$

Managers can increase their information ratios by improving their forecasting accuracy (IC) or by increasing the number of bets they make (BR) without shrinking their skills.

Example: Information Ratio

A manager has an information coefficient of 0.1 and makes quarterly bets on 100 stocks.

1. Compute the information ratio for the manager.

2. If the manager wants to achieve an information ratio of 0.4, how many stocks would the manager need to make quarterly bets on while keeping the information coefficient the same?

Answer:

1. IC = 0.1

   BR = 4 × 100 = 400

   $IR = 0.1\sqrt{400} = 2.0$

2. $IR = IC \times \sqrt{BR}$

   $0.4 = 0.1 \times \sqrt{BR}$

   $\sqrt{BR} = 4 \rightarrow BR = 16$

The manager would need to follow four stocks on a quarterly basis.

ADDITIVITY PRINCIPLE

Consider a hypothetical firm with two analysts: a fixed income analyst and an equity analyst. The firm's information ratio can be obtained using:

$$IR_F^2 = IR_{FI}^2 + IR_{EQ}^2 = IC_{FI}^2 \times BR_{FI} + IC_{EQ}^2 \times BR_{EQ}$$

where:
IR_F = information ratio for the firm
IC_{FI}, BR_{FI} = information coefficient and breadth of the fixed income analyst, respectively
IC_{EQ}, BR_{EQ} = information coefficient and breadth of the equity analyst, respectively

The additivity principle assumes that the firm follows an optimal implementation of alphas across both the asset classes.

 Professor's Note: Optimal implementation of alphas is one of the assumptions of the fundamental law of active management and is discussed later in this topic review.

Example: Combined information ratio

Dharmesh Thakur, equity analyst with Gupta Asset Management, currently follows 100 stocks and makes quarterly forecasts. Thakur's information coefficient is 0.05.

1. Compute Thakur's information ratio.

2. If Thakur chooses to follow an additional 100 stocks (with quarterly forecasts) but with an information coefficient of 0.04, what will be Thakur's new information ratio?

Answer:

1. Thakur's current breadth = 400. Current information ratio = $0.05 \times \sqrt{400} = 1.00$

2. New information ratio = $[1.00^2 + (0.04)^2(400)]^{1/2} = 1.28$

LOS 59.b: Describe how the optimal level of residual risk of an investment strategy changes with information coefficient and breadth, and how the value added of an investment strategy changes with information coefficient and breadth.

CFA® Program Curriculum, Volume 6, page 496

The previous topic review defined the optimal level of residual risk that a manager should take as ω^*.

$$\omega^* = \frac{IR}{2\lambda}$$

Substituting $IC \times \sqrt{BR}$ for IR, we get:

$$\omega^* = \frac{IC \times \sqrt{BR}}{2\lambda}$$

Hence, the optimal level of residual risk increases with information coefficient and breadth and decreases with risk aversion.

We can also incorporate the information ratio components into the value added (at optimal level of residual risk) equation discussed in the previous topic review:

$$VA^* = \frac{IR^2}{4\lambda} = \frac{IC^2 \times BR}{4\lambda}$$

LOS 59.c: Contrast market timing and security selection in terms of breadth and required investment skill.

CFA® Program Curriculum, Volume 6, page 500

Market timing is simply a bet on the direction of the market. If a manager makes N bets on the direction of the market and N_c of these bets are correct, the information coefficient of the manager is the covariance between the forecast and the actual direction of the market:

$$IC = 2\left(\frac{N_c}{N}\right) - 1$$

Note that if the manager is correct half the time (i.e., $N_c / N = 0.5$), the value of the IC (and the information ratio) will be zero.

Example: Market timer vs. security selector

Darsh Bhansali is a manager with Optimus Capital. Bhansali, a market timer, makes bets every quarter about the direction of the market. Bhansali's forecasts are right 55% of the time. Mike Neal is an equity analyst focusing on Asian stocks. Neal, a security selector, selects undervalued securities and typically makes 50 bets per year. Neal has an information coefficient of 0.04.

Compute the information ratios of Bhansali and Neal.

Answer:

Bhansali's IC = $2(0.55) - 1 = 0.10$

Bhansali's IR = $(0.10)\sqrt{4} = 0.20$

Neal's IR = $(0.04)(\sqrt{50}) = 0.28$

LOS 59.d: Describe how the information ratio changes when the original investment strategy is augmented with other strategies or information sources.

CFA® Program Curriculum, Volume 6, page 500

Imagine that a manager relies on one source of information with an information coefficient of IC. Further, suppose that the manager chooses to use an additional (second) source of information.

One of the assumptions used in measuring breadth is that the underlying information sources are uncorrelated. If the two information sources are correlated, the information coefficient (skill) of the manager does not increase proportionately with the amount of new information. Rather, the information from the second source is not entirely new and hence only enhances the manager's skill by an incremental amount. The combined information coefficient using the two sources of information (IC_{COM}) can be derived as:

$$IC_{COM} = IC\sqrt{\frac{2}{1+r}}$$

where:
IC = the original information coefficient
r = correlation between the two sources of information

Note that when the information is independent (i.e., r = 0), then $IC_{com}^2 = 2 \times IC^2$.

LOS 59.e: Describe the assumptions on which the fundamental law of active management is based.

CFA® Program Curriculum, Volume 6, page 502

ASSUMPTIONS OF THE FUNDAMENTAL LAW OF ACTIVE MANAGEMENT

The fundamental law of active management assumes that:

1. The manager has accurate knowledge of her skills and exploits this optimally. In other words, the manager recognizes what she knows and what she doesn't know and invests appropriately.

2. The sources of information used by the manager are independent so that each bet is based on new information.

3. The information coefficient is the same for each bet, meaning that the skill involved in making each forecast is the same. If not, we can categorize the bets into "skill buckets" and use the additivity principle.

KEY CONCEPTS

LOS 59.a

The information coefficient (IC) is a measure of the manager's forecasting accuracy or skill. Breadth (BR) is the number of independent forecasts of exceptional return that the manager makes per year.

The fundamental law of active management relates breadth and skill to the information ratio:

Information ratio (IR) $= IC \times \sqrt{BR}$

LOS 59.b

Given a level of investor risk aversion (λ), the optimal level of residual risk (ω^*) is given by:

$$\omega^* = \frac{IC \times \sqrt{BR}}{2\lambda}$$

And the value added for an optimal level of residual risk (VA^*) by the active manager can be quantified as:

$$VA^* = \frac{IR^2}{4\lambda} = \frac{IC^2 \times BR}{4\lambda}$$

LOS 59.c

Market timing is simply a bet on the direction of the market. The information coefficient for a market timer is given by:

$$IC = 2\left(\frac{N_c}{N}\right) - 1$$

where N is the total number of bets on market direction made by the analyst and N_C is the number of bets that were correct.

LOS 59.d

When a manager obtains an additional source of information that is correlated (correlation = r) with the manager's original information, the information coefficient IC_{COM} using the two sources combined is:

$$IC_{COM} = IC\sqrt{\frac{2}{1+r}}$$

LOS 59.e

Assumptions of the fundamental law of active management:
1. The manager has accurate knowledge of his skills and acts on information optimally.
2. Sources of information are independent.
3. Information coefficient (i.e., the skill involved in forecasting) is constant across bets.

CONCEPT CHECKERS

Answer questions 1 through 6 based on the following information.

Jon Deerson, CFA, currently works for Greenhill Capital, a small investment house in the United States. Deerson is currently assessing the performance of a portion of his firm's actively managed equity portfolio. Sumit Chowdhury, the chief investment officer at Greenhill, is a strong believer in active management. Chowdhury recommends that all clients be advised to keep at least 20% of their equity exposure in actively managed funds.

The results over the last decade have been largely positive with the actively managed portion of funds outperforming the passively managed portion eight years out of the last 10. Chowdhury believes this level of success is largely due to using active managers with a large breadth of investment forecasts. In an appendix to his monthly client update, Chowdhury states:

"Using active managers who have a wide breadth of investment forecasts is crucial to our aim of only using managers with an information ratio of at least 0.6. Doubling the number of forecasts made during a period will cause the information ratio to double."

Deerson has gathered information on two active managers in an attempt to assess their performance. Deerson is concerned that one of the managers, Williams, has taken on a level of residual risk that is too high. Deerson decides to compare the level of residual risk to which Williams is exposed to that of another manager, Basey. Deerson picked Basey for comparison for two reasons:

- Both managers have the same information coefficient and level of risk aversion.
- An analysis performed by Greenhill shows that Basey takes on the optimal level of residual risk.

The information that Deerson has gathered is shown in Exhibit 1.

Exhibit 1

Manager	Residual Risk	Number of Forecasts per Year
Williams	6.1%	250
Basey	6.0%	220

Deerson concludes that Williams has indeed taken on a more-than-optimal amount of residual risk. Deerson then calculates value added for both managers, and concludes that Williams's value added is greater than Basey's.

Deerson is also analyzing the performance of another active manager, Carlos Ruy. Ruy operates as a market timer, tracking stocks and classifying them as likely to increase or likely to decrease in value. Ruy undertakes a transaction on each of the stocks he follows every quarter. Ruy has historically been right 52% of the time.

Deerson intends to use this historical information to calculate Ruy's information ratio and compare this to the information ratio of another manager, Gupi, who last year had an information coefficient of 0.05. Gupi claims that this year his performance should be much better than prior periods as he intends to use a new second source of information. Deerson estimates that this new source of information has a correlation coefficient of 0.5 with Gupi's original source.

Deerson intends to present his findings regarding the active managers he has analyzed to Chowdhury. Regarding the fundamental law of active management, Deerson intends to state the following:

Assumptions Underpinning the Fundamental Law of Active Management
- Assumption 1: The manager has accurate knowledge of his skills and uses this information optimally.
- Assumption 2: The sources of information utilized by the manager are interdependent, and each bet is based on existing information.
- Assumption 3: The information coefficient is the same for each bet, meaning that the skill involved in making each forecast is the same.

1. Chowdhury's statement regarding breadth is *most likely* incorrect because doubling the number of forecasts made will:
    A. cause the information ratio to increase but not double.
    B. increase only the information coefficient and not the information ratio.
    C. not impact the information ratio as it is independent of the number of forecasts made.

2. Deerson's conclusion regarding Williams's level of residual risk is *most likely*:
    A. correct, as a manager with a greater breadth should have a lower optimal level of residual risk.
    B. incorrect, as a manager with a greater breadth should take on greater residual risk.
    C. incorrect, as the optimal level of residual risk depends on the information ratio and level of risk aversion and not on breadth.

3. Deerson's conclusion regarding Williams's value added is *most likely*:
    A. correct.
    B. incorrect because a higher level of residual risk reduces value added.
    C. incorrect because a larger breadth reduces value added.

4. Ruy's information ratio is *closest* to:
    A. 0.04.
    B. 0.08.
    C. 0.88.

5. Gupi's information coefficient after he combines two sources of information will be *closest* to:
    A. 0.050.
    B. 0.067.
    C. 0.058.

6. Which of Deerson's written statements regarding the assumptions of the fundamental law of active management is *least accurate*?
   A. Assumption 1.
   B. Assumption 2.
   C. Assumption 3.

ANSWERS – CONCEPT CHECKERS

1. **A** The fundamental law of active management tells us that:

   information ratio (IR) = $IC \times \sqrt{BR}$

   BR is the breadth so a doubling of the number of forecasts will increase the information ratio by a factor of about $\sqrt{2}$. IC is the information coefficient.

2. **B** The optimal level of residual risk increases with breadth, as given by:

   $$\omega^* = \frac{IC \times \sqrt{BR}}{2\lambda}$$

   Since Williams makes more forecasts than Basey, it cannot be concluded that Williams's level of risk is too high.

3. **A** Value added can be calculated as $VA = \dfrac{IR^2}{4\lambda} = \dfrac{IC^2 \times BR}{4\lambda}$

   We are told that both managers have the same information coefficient and risk aversion. We can see from this formula that the manager with the higher breadth should have a higher value added.

4. **B** $IC = 2\left(\dfrac{N_c}{N}\right) - 1$

   IC = 2(0.52) − 1 = 0.04

   information ratio (IR) = $IC \times \sqrt{BR}$

   IR = $(0.04)\sqrt{4} = 0.08$

5. **C** $IC_{COM} = IC\sqrt{\dfrac{2}{1+r}} = 0.05 \times \sqrt{(2/1.5)} = 0.058$

6. **B** Assumption 2 should state that the sources of information utilized by the manager are *independent* and each bet is based on *new* information, not *existing* information.

The following is a review of the Portfolio Management principles designed to address the learning outcome statements set forth by CFA Institute. This topic is also covered in:

THE PORTFOLIO MANAGEMENT PROCESS AND THE INVESTMENT POLICY STATEMENT

Study Session 18

EXAM FOCUS

This qualitative material on portfolio management revisits concepts first introduced at Level I and provides an introduction to the extensive treatment of the topic you'll see in Level III. Keep the following points in mind: (1) the investment environment is ever-changing, so investment decision making must recognize the potential for shifts in a variety of factors, and (2) every investment decision should be framed within a portfolio perspective—it is not enough to know the characteristics of a potential investment itself, you must be aware of how an investment affects the risk and return characteristics of your overall portfolio.

WARM-UP: ELEMENTS OF PORTFOLIO MANAGEMENT

Although specifying objectives and constraints and evaluating relevant economic and market conditions represent the beginning of the process, these decisions are also linked to the measurement, monitoring, and evaluation steps of the process. The integrative nature of portfolio management involves numerous feedback loops and allows managers to be as rigid or flexible (or as quantitative or qualitative) as they desire. There is no end point to the process, only evaluation of performance that may indicate a need for rebalancing. The following represents the elements of the portfolio management process.

Evaluating investor and market characteristics. The first step is to determine the objectives and constraints of the investor. Objectives are related to the risk and return expectations of the investor. Constraints are those factors that limit or restrict certain decisions or investment choices. The second step is to evaluate the economic environment. The factors relevant to an economic evaluation are mostly *macro* issues dealing with the overall state of the economy (growth prospects, inflation expectations, unemployment, and other considerations). An economic evaluation can also work down to *micro* issues, such as those related to sector-, industry-, and security-specific considerations.

Developing an investment policy statement. This next portion of the investment management process formalizes objectives and constraints into an investment policy statement (IPS), which will guide investment decisions and formalize the investment strategy (e.g., whether the portfolio will be actively managed or follow a more passive approach). Capital market expectations that take into account the economic evaluation conducted previously are also formalized in this step.

Determining an asset allocation strategy. After the formal documentation of the IPS is completed, decisions on how and where funds will be invested are completed, and a strategic asset allocation is created. Securities are evaluated as to how they might fit into a portfolio that meets the objectives and constraints of the investor. Portfolio decisions are implemented and then executed in a timely fashion so that the investor's funds can be put to use in attaining goals and objectives.

Measuring and evaluating performance. After a stated time period, which will be specified in the IPS, portfolio performance will be measured and an evaluation as to whether the portfolio attained investor objectives and followed the IPS will be prepared. Portfolio rebalancing may be indicated by the results of the evaluation. Connecting the evaluation step to the beginning of the process must occur to ensure portfolio decisions parallel investor needs and desires.

Monitoring dynamic investor objectives and capital market conditions. Continuous monitoring of both investor and marketplace characteristics takes place throughout the entire process. Multiple feedback mechanisms throughout the entire portfolio management process indicate where significant changes in either investor factors or marketplace prospects require adjustments to the portfolio. Remember, this is a dynamic, ongoing process. There are no end points, only continuous connections between objectives and constraints to portfolio monitoring and evaluation.

LOS 60.a: Explain the importance of the portfolio perspective.

CFA® Program Curriculum, Volume 6, page 510

The portfolio perspective is a key underlying principle of the entire CFA curriculum. The equity pricing models in the Level II curriculum are all based on the principle that only systematic risk is priced. Furthermore, one of the basic principles of the New Prudent Investor Rule is that diversification is expected of portfolio managers as a method of reducing risk.

Investors, analysts, and portfolio managers should analyze the **risk-return tradeoff** of the portfolio as a whole, not the risk-return tradeoff of the individual investments in the portfolio, because unsystematic risk can be diversified away by combining the investments into a portfolio. The systematic risk that remains in the portfolio is the result of the economic fundamentals that have a general influence on the security returns, such as GDP growth, unexpected inflation, consumer confidence, unanticipated changes in credit spreads, and business cycle.

LOS 60.b: Describe the steps of the portfolio management process and the components of those steps.

CFA® Program Curriculum, Volume 6, page 511

The ongoing portfolio management process can be detailed within the integrative steps described by **planning**, **execution**, and **feedback**. Each general step contains numerous components. The planning phase consists of analyzing objectives and constraints, developing an IPS, determining the appropriate investment strategy, and selecting an appropriate asset allocation. The focus of this topic review at Level II is the first step: planning.

LOS 60.c: Explain the role of the investment policy statement in the portfolio management process, and describe the elements of an investment policy statement.

CFA® Program Curriculum, Volume 6, page 511

The investment policy statement (IPS) is a formal document that governs investment decision making, taking into account objectives and constraints. The main role of the IPS is to:

- Be readily implemented by current or future investment advisers (i.e., it is easily transportable).
- Promote long-term discipline for portfolio decisions.
- Help protect against short-term shifts in strategy when either market environments or portfolio performance cause panic or overconfidence.

There are numerous elements to an IPS. Some elements that are typically included are:

- A client description that provides enough background so any competent investment adviser can gain a common understanding of the client's situation.
- The purpose of the IPS with respect to policies, objectives, goals, restrictions, and portfolio limitations.
- Identification of duties and responsibilities of parties involved.
- The formal statement of objectives and constraints.
- A calendar schedule for both portfolio performance and IPS review.
- Asset allocation ranges and statements regarding flexibility and rigidity when formulating or modifying the strategic asset allocation.
- Guidelines for portfolio adjustments and rebalancing.

LOS 60.d: Explain how capital market expectations and the investment policy statement help influence the strategic asset allocation decision and how an investor's investment time horizon may influence the investor's strategic asset allocation.

CFA® Program Curriculum, Volume 6, page 514

The final step in the planning stage is creation of a **strategic asset allocation**. This step combines the IPS and capital market expectations to formulate long-term target weightings for the asset classes to be included in the portfolio. The need for flexibility in the asset allocation to allow for temporary shifts (called tactical asset allocations) in response to alterations in short-term capital market expectations should also be considered.

Study Session 18

Cross-Reference to CFA Institute Assigned Reading #60 – The Portfolio Management Process and the Investment Policy Statement

There are three common approaches used to implement the strategic asset allocation:

- *Passive investment strategies* represent those strategies that are not responsive to changes in expectations. Indexing and buy-and-hold investment strategies are examples of passive investment strategies.
- *Active investment strategies* are much more responsive to changing expectations. These strategies attempt to capitalize on differences between a portfolio manager's beliefs concerning security valuations and those in the marketplace. Generating *alpha* and investing according to a particular investment style fall into the active investment strategy category.
- *Semi-active, risk-controlled active,* or *enhanced index strategies* are hybrids of passive and active strategies. Index tilting, where portfolio managers attempt to match the risk characteristics of a benchmark portfolio, but also deviate from the exact benchmark portfolio weights in order to earn higher returns, is one example of this approach to strategic asset allocation.

Forecasts of risk-return characteristics are required for asset classes that are included in the investor's portfolio so that the portfolio's expected risk-return profile is well understood. The role played by this step is to connect realistic market expectations to the objectives and constraints of the investor. Should the portfolio's risk-return profile diverge significantly from the investor's objectives, the strategic asset allocation may need to be reviewed.

The length of the time horizon may also influence the investor's asset allocation. An investor with a shorter investment time horizon will often choose a strategic asset allocation that is relatively less risky, with a smaller allocation to equities, for example.

LOS 60.e: Define investment objectives and constraints, and explain and distinguish among the types of investment objectives and constraints.

CFA® Program Curriculum, Volume 6, page 517

Investment objectives relate to what the investor wants to accomplish with the portfolio. Objectives are mainly concerned with risk and return considerations.

Risk objectives are those factors associated with an investor's willingness and ability to take risk. Combining willingness and ability to accept risk is termed *risk tolerance. Risk aversion* indicates an investor's inability and unwillingness to take risk.

For an individual, willingness and ability to take risk may be determined by behavioral or psychological factors, whereas for an institution, these factors are determined primarily by portfolio constraints. Some specific factors that affect ability to accept risk are as follows:

- *Required spending needs:* How much variation in portfolio value can the investor tolerate before being inconvenienced in the short term?
- *Long-term wealth target:* How much variation in portfolio value can the investor tolerate before it jeopardizes meeting long-term wealth goals?

- *Financial strength:* Can the investor increase savings (or decrease expenditures) if the portfolio is insufficient to meet spending needs?
- *Liabilities:* Is the investor legally obligated to make future payments to beneficiaries, or does the investor have certain set spending requirements in retirement (i.e., pseudo liabilities)?

If the investor's portfolio is large relative to spending and obligations, a greater ability to take risk is apparent. Appropriately connecting willingness to ability may require educating the client in risk-return principles, as shown in Figure 1.

Figure 1: Willingness vs. Ability to Take Risk

Willingness to Take Risk	Ability to Take Risk	
	Below Average	*Above Average*
Below average	Lower risk tolerance	Education/resolution required
Above average	Education/resolution required	Higher risk tolerance

Professor's Note: When the investor's ability and willingness to assume risk are in conflict, resolution is required. If ability exceeds willingness, the investor should be counseled that the assumption of more risk may be appropriate, with the ultimate decision up to the investor. If willingness exceeds ability, ability should define the maximum risk tolerance.

There are two risk objective measurements: absolute and relative risk objectives. Standard deviation of total return represents an example of an absolute risk objective, whereas deviations from an underlying index, or *tracking risk*, represent an example of a relative risk objective. Relative risk measures are often easier to quantify from an individual investor's perspective, but absolute risk objectives are also referred to, even if only stated in qualitative forms.

Individuals often state their willingness to assume risk in broad terms; for example, "I have a moderate level of risk tolerance." Although institutions may state specific quantitative risk measures, such as "The level of portfolio volatility should not exceed 25% in any given year," their risk objectives can also be ranked along a qualitative risk objective spectrum. It is important to incorporate whatever level of specificity is mentioned when analyzing the risk objective.

Return objectives can be classified as either a *desired* or a *required return*. A desired return is that level of return stated by the client, indicating how much the investor wishes to receive from the portfolio. A required return represents some level of return that must be achieved by the portfolio, at least on an average basis to meet the target financial obligations. As such, required returns serve as a much stricter benchmark than desired returns.

In either case, the level of return needs to be consistent with the risk objective. Desired or required returns might be unrealistic, given available market conditions or risk objectives. Educating the investor as to disconnections between return and risk may be required. Some additional considerations in calculating return levels are differentiating between *real* and *nominal* returns, and distinguishing *pretax* and *after-tax* returns.

Whatever the return level generated, one factor to remember is that the return objective should be considered from a *total return* perspective. Even if a substantial income (or spending) component is required from the portfolio, the return objective should be evaluated by the total return, the return from both income and capital gains, and the characteristics of the portfolio. The assumption is that spending needs can be met through both investment income and capital appreciation.

INVESTMENT CONSTRAINTS

Investment constraints are those factors restricting or limiting the universe of available investment choices. Constraints can be generated either internally (those determined by the investor) or externally (those determined by some outside entity, such as a governmental agency). The five main classes of constraints relate to liquidity, time horizon, legal and regulatory concerns, tax considerations, and unique circumstances.

Liquidity constraints relate to expected cash outflows that will be needed at some specified time and are in excess of available income. In addition, it is ordinarily prudent to set aside some amount (e.g., three months living expenses) to meet unexpected cash needs. Often, liquidity is required over multiple time periods. A down payment for a home, funding for children's education, and providing for special needs during retirement are all liquidity concerns. The reason liquidity constraints are important to consider is that, depending on marketability, certain assets may generate only a portion of their fair value if they must be sold quickly. Attention must be paid to an asset's ability to be turned into cash without significant impact on portfolio value or asset allocation.

Linkages between liquidity and risk objectives are also apparent. Higher liquidity requirements usually indicate a lower tolerance for risk taking. Sensitivity to liquidity is a factor potentially affecting the willingness to take risk.

Time horizon constraints are associated with the time period(s) over which a portfolio is expected to generate returns to meet specific future needs (e.g., paying for retirement or childrens' college education).

Tax constraints depend on how, when, and if portfolio returns of various types are taxed. Some institutional investors (e.g., pension funds and endowments) have tax-exempt status. However, income and realized gains generated by personal portfolios are taxable and attention must be paid to the taxing environment when formulating the IPS. Often, differential tax treatments are applied to investment income and capital gains, which may be taxed at a lower rate. On the other hand, returns on certain types of retirement accounts are tax deferred until withdrawals are made.

Depending on which investment vehicle is chosen for the portfolio, tax consequences may adversely impact the after-tax returns. Estate taxes can also affect portfolio decisions. As a result, investment choices must be made with careful consideration of how a portfolio's returns will be taxed.

Legal and regulatory factors are externally generated constraints that mainly affect institutional investors. These constraints are usually associated with specifying which investment classes are not allowed or dictating any limitations placed on allocations to particular investment classes. Trust portfolios for individual investors may also be subject to substantial legal and regulatory oversight, which must be considered when establishing the IPS. Otherwise, this constraint does not usually affect individual investors. An example of a legal constraint that affects the management of trust assets for an individual is the New Prudent Investor Rule.

Unique circumstances are internally generated and represent special concerns of the investor. University endowments and philanthropic organizations, for example, might not allow investments in companies selling tobacco, alcohol, or defense products. Individuals might wish to have their portfolios fund specific activities (e.g., grandchildren's education, cancer research, or support for the arts), or they might be unfamiliar or inexperienced with certain investments. These, as well as any special investor circumstance restricting investment activities, must be considered in the formulation of the IPS.

A brief summary of return objectives and risk tolerance for individual and various institutional investors is shown in Figure 2.

Figure 2: Investment Objectives of Individual and Institutional Investors

Investor	Return Requirement	Risk Tolerance
Individual investor	Depends on life-cycle stage and financial position	Depends on life-cycle stage and financial position
Defined benefit pension plan	Sufficient to fund pension liability while accounting for inflation	Depends on plan features, age of workforce, and funding status of plan
Defined contribution pension plan	Depends on life-cycle stage of beneficiaries	Depends on risk tolerance of beneficiaries
Endowments and foundations	Sufficient to cover spending needs, expenses, and inflation	Generally average or above average
Life insurance companies	Function of policyholder reserve rates	Below average because of significant regulatory constraints
Non-life insurance companies	Function of policy pricing and financial strength	Below average because of significant regulatory constraints
Banks	Function of cost of funds	Depends on business model and financial strength

©2013 Kaplan, Inc.

LOS 60.f: Contrast the types of investment time horizons, determine the time horizon for a particular investor, and evaluate the effects of this time horizon on portfolio choice.

CFA® Program Curriculum, Volume 6, page 522

The time horizon for an investment portfolio may be short, as with a couple saving to purchase a home in two years, or long, as in the case of a couple in their 30s saving for retirement. Investors may also have a combination of short and long investment time horizons, as in the case of a couple who are saving both to fund their children's educations in five years and for retirement in 30 years.

The importance of the time horizon as an investment constraint is based on the idea that the longer the investment time horizon, the more risk an investor can take on. For time horizons of ten years or more, the fact that returns will average over economic and market cycles is generally believed to justify a greater allocation to equities and perhaps to riskier equities. The uncertainty about returns and the inability to make up for poor results over a short investment horizon leads many short-term investors to select relatively low-risk (predictable) securities. For a specific investor, however, a low *willingness* to take risk may constrain portfolio risk because of sensitivity to interim results, even when the investment horizon is relatively long and the *ability* to take on risk is greater.

LOS 60.g: Justify ethical conduct as a requirement for managing investment portfolios.

CFA® Program Curriculum, Volume 6, page 525

The investment professional who manages client portfolios well meets standards of competence and standards of conduct. It is important to recognize that the portfolio manager, who is an expert in the field with presumably more knowledge of investment principles than the client, is in a position of trust and so must meet the highest standards of ethical conduct in order to truly serve clients. The appropriate standard of conduct is embodied by the CFA Institute Code and Standards of Practice.

KEY CONCEPTS

LOS 60.a

Because different economic factors influence the returns of various assets differently, the risk of one asset is only somewhat correlated with the risk of other assets. If we evaluate the risk of each asset in isolation and ignore these interrelationships, we will misunderstand the risk and return potential of the investor's total investment position. The portfolio perspective tells us that our fundamental concern is to understand the risk and return in a portfolio context.

LOS 60.b

The three phases of the portfolio management process are planning, execution, and feedback; the Level II curriculum focuses on the planning phase.

- The planning phase consists of analyzing objectives and constraints, developing an IPS, determining the appropriate investment strategy, and selecting an appropriate asset allocation.
- The execution process relates to portfolio construction and revision.
- The feedback process consists of monitoring, rebalancing, and performance evaluation.

LOS 60.c

The IPS is a written document providing guidelines for portfolio investment decision making. The IPS does the following:

- Provides guidance for current and subsequent investment adviser decisions.
- Promotes long-term discipline in investment decision making.
- Protects against short-term shifts in strategy when either market conditions or portfolio performance cause panic or overconfidence.

There are several elements to a suitable IPS: a description of the client's situation; the purpose, as well as identification, of responsibilities; formal statements of objectives and constraints; schedule for portfolio performance and IPS review; asset allocation ranges; and guidance for rebalancing and adjustment activities.

LOS 60.d

While the investment policy statement will outline the appropriate risk-return characteristics for an investment portfolio, the strategic asset allocation to provide these characteristics will depend on capital markets expectations (risk, returns, and correlations) for the various asset classes. Typically, a longer investment time horizon will lead investors to tolerate more portfolio risk and employ strategic asset allocations more heavily weighted toward asset classes with greater risk and greater expected returns, such as equities.

LOS 60.e

The two investment objectives to consider are:

- Return objectives.
- Risk objectives.

The five common constraints are:

- Liquidity.
- Time horizon.
- Legal and regulatory concerns.
- Tax considerations.
- Unique circumstances.

Differences between an investor's willingness and ability to take risk create additional education/resolution responsibilities for the portfolio manager with regard to formulating the risk objectives.

LOS 60.f

Investors may have short or long investment horizons, or some combination of the two when multiple investment goals are identified. Investors with longer horizons (>10 years) have the ability, but not necessarily the willingness, to employ strategic asset allocations with more risk since returns will be averaged over economic and market cycles and investors have more time to recover from periods of relatively poor returns.

LOS 60.g

The investment professional who manages client portfolios well meets standards of competence and standards of conduct. It is important to recognize that the portfolio manager, who is an expert in the field with presumably more knowledge of investment principles than the client, is in a position of trust and so must meet the highest standards of ethical conduct in order to truly serve his clients. The appropriate standard of conduct is embodied by the CFA Institute Code and Standards.

CONCEPT CHECKERS

Use the following information to answer Questions 1 through 3.

Jane Smith has an investment portfolio of $5 million. She is 68 years old, retired, and has no children. After her death, she wishes to leave her portfolio to a local art museum that has given her relatively free access to art exhibits over the past decade. Her health is better than average, and she maintains an active lifestyle consisting of frequent swimming, biking, and playing tennis with friends at her country club. Smith estimates that to maintain her standard of living, she needs approximately $250,000 per year. Expenses are expected to grow at an expected inflation rate of 2%. She states that as a retiree, her tolerance for risk is "below average." Smith has come to you for assistance in investing her assets.

1. Smith's return objective is *closest* to:
    A. 3%.
    B. 5%.
    C. 7%.

2. Smith's ability to take risk is *most appropriately* characterized as:
    A. below average.
    B. average.
    C. significantly above average.

3. In terms of Smith's time horizon and liquidity constraints, Smith *most likely* has:
    A. a short-term time horizon and no significant liquidity constraints.
    B. a short-term time horizon and significant liquidity constraints.
    C. a long-term time horizon and no significant liquidity constraints.

Use the following information to answer Questions 4 and 5.

Joe Farmingham is 38 years old, married, and has two children, ages 12 and 7. He recently received an inheritance of $300,000 and is considering investing "real money" for the first time. Farmingham likes to read the financial press and indicates that if he had money to invest in the past, he could have taken advantage of some undervalued security opportunities. Farmingham believes he has an average tolerance for risk-taking in investment activities, but he also enjoys skydiving every other weekend.

4. Farmingham's ability to take risk is *most appropriately* characterized as:
    A. below average.
    B. average.
    C. above average.

5. The *most appropriate* investment strategy for Farmingham to take advantage of his stated propensity for finding undervalued investments is a(n):
    A. active investment strategy.
    B. risk-controlled active investment strategy.
    C. enhanced index strategy.

CHALLENGE PROBLEMS

6. Lanaster University's endowment fund was recently estimated to be around $200 million. The university's endowment investment committee oversees numerous asset managers and is responsible for creating the investment policy statement (IPS). Ellen Hardinger and Will Smithson have been discussing the many factors that go into an IPS and are somewhat perplexed as to how to state the fund's risk objective. Hardinger and Smithson make three statements regarding the risk objectives of the endowment fund:

   Statement 1: The fund is relatively conservative in its investment approach.
   Statement 2: The fund performance should not exhibit more than a 20% standard deviation in any given year.
   Statement 3: The fund should not exhibit performance differences of more than 5% from the Wilshire 5000 over any 3-year period.

   They need assistance in understanding how to combine those risk statements into a risk objective. How many of the statements represent absolute risk?
   A. One.
   B. Two.
   C. Three.

Use the following information for Questions 7 through 9.

William and Elizabeth Elam recently inherited $500,000 from Elizabeth's father, Abraham, and have come to Alan Schneider, CFA, for assistance. Both William and Elizabeth are 30 years old. William is employed as a factory worker with a salary of $40,000. Elizabeth is a teacher's aide and has a salary of $18,000. Their four children are ages 6, 5, 4, and 3. They have no other investments and have a current credit card debt of $60,000. When interviewed by Schneider, William made the following statements:

- I love being on top of the latest trends in investing.
- My friend Keith told me that the really smart investor holds stocks for no more than a month. After that, if you haven't made a profit, you probably won't.
- Technology stocks are hot! Everyone has been buying them.
- Can you believe that my mother still has the same portfolio she had a year ago? How boring!

7. The Elams' ability and willingness to take on risk are *most appropriately* characterized as:
   A. above average willingness and ability.
   B. below average ability and average willingness.
   C. average ability and above average willingness.

8. The Elams' time horizon constraint can be *best* characterized as:
   A. long-term and single stage.
   B. long-term and multistage.
   C. variable term and single stage.

9. The Elams' liquidity and legal/regulatory constraints are *best* characterized as:
   A. significant.
   B. insignificant.
   C. liquidity significant and legal/regulatory insignificant.

ANSWERS – CONCEPT CHECKERS

1. **C** Smith states that she needs $250,000 annually to maintain her standard of living. This amount of annual expenditures represents 5% ($250,000 / $5,000,000) of the current portfolio. Accounting for an expected increase in expenses at the anticipated level of inflation indicates a return objective around 7%.

2. **B** Although her stated willingness to take risk is below average, the size of her portfolio, her good health, and relative long time horizon indicate an ability to take average risk. As a retiree, sensitivity to substantial declines in portfolio value is probably a concern.

3. **C** Barring any unexpected health-related costs, the inflation-adjusted income needed will probably not change dramatically. Smith's concern for liquidity primarily relates to unusual cash outflows (e.g., health care costs, emergency spending) that might take place during her retirement years and hence, she has no significant liquidity constraints. Smith has essentially a long-term time horizon for her portfolio: until the end of her life, which could be another 20 years.

4. **C** Farmingham appears to have the ability and willingness to take risk. He frequently enjoys risk-seeking activities, such as skydiving. His relatively young age indicates a somewhat long time horizon for his investment portfolio. These facts couple ability and willingness to take an above-average level of risk.

5. **A** Farmingham indicates that he follows the financial press and has spotted what he considered to be undervalued securities. This activity indicates that Farmingham pays attention to security valuation issues and that he probably will do so in the future. His portfolio, therefore, should follow an active investment strategy.

ANSWERS – CHALLENGE PROBLEMS

6. **A** The statement of "20% standard deviation in any given year" is an absolute risk measure because it quantitatively states a specified level of total risk not to be exceeded. Conversely, the statement "performance differences from the Wilshire 5000 of more than 5% over any 3-year period" is a relative risk measure. Comparing measures of portfolio risk to another investment vehicle is an indication of relative risk.

    Institutional investors tend to be more quantitative in their assessments of risk, but the statement that the fund "is relatively conservative in its investment approach" also specifies a qualitative component to the risk objective.

7. **A** Because of their long time horizon and their situational profile, the Elams have the ability to tolerate an above-average level of risk. Based on the interview with William, the Elams have stated a willingness to tolerate an above-average level of risk. Therefore, the portfolio can be constructed based on an above-average level of risk.

    Based upon their lack of investing experience and rather aggressive attitude toward portfolio risk management, however, the financial services professional should be certain that the Elam's have a clear understanding of the concepts of risk and return.

8. **B** The Elams' time horizon is long term and at least two-fold: the time until retirement and their retirement years. It is possible that a third time horizon could develop should the Elams decide to support their children through post-secondary education. Should they decide to retire at age 60, their pre-retirement time horizon would be 30 years.

9. **C** The main liquidity constraint presented in the case is immediate and significant (the $60,000 in credit card debt). Schneider should recommend that the Elams eliminate this liability with the inheritance funds immediately. No special legal or regulatory problems are apparent. Prudent investor rules apply if William is interested in creating a trust fund.

18 minutes

Use the following information to answer Questions 1 through 6.

Figure 1 represents capital market opportunities as estimated by two analysts at Ruger Bank, Jim Henshaw, CFA, and Jill Ponder, CFA Level III Candidate. They assume that all assets are priced at their equilibrium levels consistent with the CAPM.

Figure 1: Mean Variance Analysis

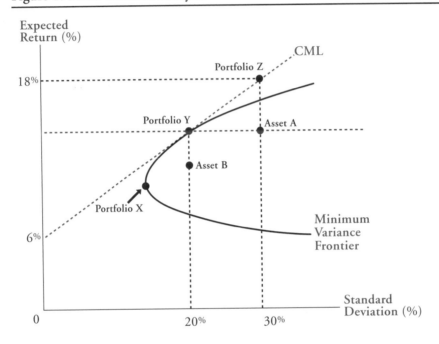

Ralph Cimins, a client of Henshaw and Ponder, is fairly risk averse and insists on keeping 40% of his portfolio in U.S. Treasury bills, which are yielding 6%. Henshaw believes Cimins's ability to tolerate risk is greater than that and would like to see Cimins invest 80% of his portfolio in risky assets. Ponder suggests that Portfolio X would be suitable for Cimins as this is the portfolio of risky assets with the least standard deviation and the least systematic risk.

Ponder is concerned about instability of the minimum variance frontier for the risky assets. Henshaw suggests that improving their historical market-model estimates of next period's risky-asset betas could reduce problems of instability, but Ponder believes the instability is just a result of changing capital markets conditions and that using only the most recent data can improve the stability of the efficient frontier.

They also consider a multi-factor model of securities returns and the use of factor portfolios. Henshaw states that they might be able to improve the Sharpe ratio of the portfolio they are constructing for Cimins by using a tracking portfolio to match a benchmark portfolio's risk along several dimensions. Ponder suggests that they use their firm's research to construct a tracking portfolio that has a Sharpe ratio greater than that of Portfolio Y in Figure 1.

1. Assuming the CAPM holds and that Portfolio Y in Figure 1 is a proxy for the market portfolio, its Sharpe ratio is *closest* to:
    A. 0.30.
    B. 0.40.
    C. 0.50.

2. Ponder claims that Asset A is too risky with a standard deviation of 30%, and none of Asset A should be included in Cimins's portfolio. Henshaw claims that Asset A will plot on the Security Market Line and that including some of Asset A in Portfolio Y will not increase its risk. With respect to these claims:
    A. Ponder is correct and Henshaw is not.
    B. Ponder is incorrect and Henshaw is correct about Asset A plotting on the SML but not about the effect of adding it to Portfolio Y.
    C. Ponder is incorrect and Henshaw is correct in both his claims.

3. If Ponder and Henshaw construct Cimins's portfolio with his desired allocation of 40% to T-bills and the remainder invested in Portfolio Y, the beta and expected return on Cimins's portfolio will be *closest* to:

	Beta	Expected return
A.	0.40	9.6%
B.	0.60	9.6%
C.	0.60	10.8%

4. With respect to their claims about the instability of the efficient frontier:
    A. both Henshaw and Ponder are incorrect since the instability of the efficient frontier cannot be improved by either method.
    B. Henshaw is correct but Ponder is not.
    C. Ponder is correct but Henshaw is not.

5. Assume that Portfolio Y is the market portfolio, that the research department at Ruger Bank can identify a number of stocks that are priced either above or below their equilibrium levels, and that a multi-factor model rather than the CAPM describes returns on risky assets. Ponder and Henshaw could increase the expected return of Crimins's portfolio without altering its risk by:
    A. using a factor portfolio that is overweight the underpriced stocks combined with an allocation to T-bills.
    B. constructing a tracking portfolio for Portfolio Y that has none of the stocks identified as overpriced.
    C. constructing a portfolio that is long the overpriced stocks and short the underpriced stocks and hedging its additional risk with a factor portfolio.

6. Ponder and Henshaw are estimating the beta of Asset B in Figure 1 and feel that adjusting their estimate of historical market-model beta is appropriate. This adjustment to their calculated beta, assuming that Asset B is priced at its equilibrium value according to the CAPM, would *most likely* be to:
    A. increase the historical market-model beta.
    B. decrease the historical market-model beta.
    C. not change the historical market-model beta for this asset.

SELF-TEST ANSWERS: PORTFOLIO MANAGEMENT

1. **B** The Sharpe ratio is the slope of a line (the CML) from the risk-free rate to Portfolio Y, which can be calculated from the values for Portfolio Z. (18 − 6) / 30 = 0.40.

2. **C** According to the CAPM, at least some of all tradable risky assets are in the tangency (market) Portfolio Y. Since all assets are assumed to be priced at their equilibrium values, they will all plot on the SML. Since Asset A has the same expected return as Portfolio Y, it must have the same beta as the market portfolio, which is one.

3. **C** The portfolio beta will be a weighted average of the beta of T-bills (= 0) and the beta of Portfolio Y (= 1), (0.4)(0) + (0.60)(1) = 0.60. Given that the slope of the CML in Figure 1 is 0.40, the market risk premium is 0.40 × 20% = 8% and the expected return according to the CAPM is 6% + (0.60)(8%) = 10.8%.

4. **B** The instability of the efficient frontier is due to estimation (sampling) error in historical betas (or asset returns parameters) as well as the fact that historical estimates are not forecasts; that is, they are not forward looking. Better historical estimates will reduce sampling error, while use of a forecasting model can yield forward looking estimates. Either of these can reduce instability of the estimated efficient frontier. Using less data, as Ponder suggests, will aggravate the instability problem as it will lead to greater estimation error and not address the problem of changing betas over time.

5. **B** A tracking portfolio is constructed to match the factor risks of a benchmark portfolio such as the market portfolio, Portfolio Y. By going either overweight the underpriced stocks or underweight the overpriced stocks within a tracking portfolio (relative to their benchmark weights), the portfolio manager can increase the expected returns of the portfolio of risky assets, while still matching the risk characteristics of the benchmark portfolio. Since Portfolio Y is the market portfolio and contains all stocks in some positive amounts, omitting the overpriced stocks will increase the expected portfolio return. The long-short portfolio may have quite different risk characteristics from those of Portfolio Y and unsystematic risk as well. A single factor portfolio cannot be expected to hedge away these risk differences.

6. **A** Assuming assets are priced according to the CAPM, Asset B must have a beta less than one since it has a lower expected return than Portfolio Y, the market portfolio. Because betas are mean reverting toward one, the adjustment to the historical market-model beta for Asset B is to increase it toward one.

FORMULAS

definition of the futures price:

$$\text{futures price} = \text{spot price} \times (1 + r)^{(T-t)}$$

forward contract price: $FP = S_0 \times (1 + R_f)^T$

forward contract value of long position:

at initiation: zero, because priced to prevent arbitrage

during life of contract: $S_t - \left[\dfrac{FP}{(1 + R_f)^{T-t}} \right]$

at expiration: $S_T - FP$

equity forward contract price:

$$FP(\text{on an equity security}) = (S_0 - PVD) \times (1 + R_f)^T$$

$$FP(\text{on an equity security}) = \left[S_0 \times (1 + R_f)^T \right] - FVD$$

equity forward contract value: $V_t(\text{long position}) = [S_t - PVD_t] - \left[\dfrac{FP}{(1 + R_f)^{(T-t)}} \right]$

equity index forward contract price:

$$FP(\text{on an equity index}) = S_0 \times e^{\left(R_f^c - \delta^c\right) \times T} = \left(S_0 \times e^{-\delta^c \times T} \right) \times e^{R_f^c \times T}$$

equity index forward contract value:

$$V_t(\text{of the long position}) = \left(\dfrac{S_t}{e^{\delta^c \times (T-t)}} \right) - \left(\dfrac{FP}{e^{R_f^c \times (T-t)}} \right)$$

fixed income forward contract price:

$$FP\left(\text{on a fixed income security}\right) = \left(S_0 - PVC\right) \times \left(1 + R_f\right)^T$$
$$= \left[S_0 \times \left(1 + R_f\right)^T\right] - FVC$$

fixed income forward contract value: $V_t\left(\text{long position}\right) = \left[S_t - PVC_t\right] - \left[\dfrac{FP}{\left(1 + R_f\right)^{(T-t)}}\right]$

currency forward contract price: $F_T\left(\text{currency forward contract}\right) = S_0 \times \dfrac{\left(1 + R_{DC}\right)^T}{\left(1 + R_{FC}\right)^T}$

currency forward contract value:

$$V_t\left(\text{currency forward contract}\right) = \left[\dfrac{S_t}{\left(1 + R_{FC}\right)^{(T-t)}}\right] - \left[\dfrac{F_T}{\left(1 + R_{DC}\right)^{(T-t)}}\right]$$

continuous time price and value formulas for currency forward contracts:

$$F_T\left(\text{currency forward contract}\right) = S_0 \times e^{\left(R_{DC}^c - R_{FC}^c\right) \times T}$$

$$V_t\left(\text{currency forward contract}\right) = \left[\dfrac{S_t}{e^{R_{FC}^c \times (T-t)}}\right] - \left[\dfrac{F_T}{e^{R_{DC}^c \times (T-t)}}\right]$$

generalized no-arbitrage futures price:

$$FP = S_0 \times \left(1 + R_f\right)^T + FV\left(NC\right)$$

$$FP = S_0 \times \left(1 + R_f\right)^T - FV\left(NB\right)$$

Treasury bond futures contract price: $FP = \left[\text{bond price} \times \left(1 + R_f\right)^T - FVC\right] \times \dfrac{1}{CF}$

put-call parity for European options: $C_0 + \left[\dfrac{X}{\left(1 + R_f\right)^T}\right] = P_0 + S_0$

put-call parity for European options with cash flows:

$$C_0 + \frac{X}{\left(1 + R_F\right)^T} = P_0 + \left(S_0 - PVCF\right)$$

binomial model:

$$D = \frac{1}{U}$$

$$\pi_U = \frac{1 + R_f - D}{U - D}$$

$$\pi_D = 1 - \pi_U$$

expiration value of caplet $= \dfrac{\max\ \{0,\ [(\text{one-year rate} - \text{cap rate}) \times \text{notional principal}]\}}{1 + \text{one-year rate}}$

expiration value of floorlet $= \dfrac{\max\ \{0,\ [(\text{floor rate} - \text{one-year rate}) \times \text{notional principal}]\}}{1 + \text{one-year rate}}$

delta and dynamic hedging:

$$\text{delta}_{call} = \frac{C_1 - C_0}{S_1 - S_0} = \frac{\Delta C}{\Delta S}$$

$$\Delta C \approx N(d_1) \times \Delta S$$
$$\Delta P \approx \left[N(d_1) - 1\right] \times \Delta S$$

forward put-call parity: $C_0 + \dfrac{X - F_T}{\left(1 + R_f\right)^T} - P_0 = 0$

fixed swap rate (with four payments): $C = \dfrac{1 - Z_4}{Z_1 + Z_2 + Z_3 + Z_4}$

payoff to cap buyer:

$$\text{periodic payment} = \max\left[0,\ (\text{notional principal}) \times (\text{index rate} - \text{cap strike}) \times \left(\frac{\text{actual days}}{360}\right)\right]$$

payoff to floor buyer:

$$\text{periodic payment} = \max\left[0,\ (\text{notional principal})\times(\text{floor strike}-\text{index rate})\times\left(\frac{\text{actual days}}{360}\right)\right]$$

upfront premium % (paid by protection buyer) $\approx$ (CDS spread – CDS coupon) × duration

price of CDS (per \$100 notional) $\approx$ \$100 – upfront premium (%)

profit for protection buyer $\approx$ change in spread × duration × notional principal

STUDY SESSION 18: PORTFOLIO MANAGEMENT

expected portfolio return (two assets): $E(R_p) = w_1 E(R_1) + w_2 E(R_2)$

portfolio variance (two assets): $\sigma_P^2 = w_1^2 \sigma_1^2 + w_2^2 \sigma_2^2 + 2w_1 w_2 \text{Cov}_{1,2}$

correlation: $\rho_{1,2} = \dfrac{\text{Cov}_{1,2}}{\sigma_1 \sigma_2}$

variance of equally-weighted portfolio: $\sigma_P^2 = \dfrac{1}{n}\overline{\sigma_i^2} + \dfrac{n-1}{n}\overline{\text{Cov}} = \overline{\sigma_i^2}\left(\dfrac{1-\rho}{n}+\rho\right)$

reward-to-risk ratio $= \dfrac{E(R_T)-R_F}{\sigma_T}$

CAL: $E(R_C) = R_F + \left(\dfrac{E(R_T)-R_F}{\sigma_T}\right)\sigma_C$

CML: $E(R_C) = R_F + \left[\dfrac{E(R_M)-R_F}{\sigma_M}\right]\sigma_C$

SML: $E(R_i) = R_F + \beta_i\left[E(R_m)-R_F\right]$

Beta: $\beta_i = \dfrac{\text{Cov}_{i,M}}{\sigma_M^2} = \dfrac{\rho_{i,M}\sigma_i\sigma_M}{\sigma_M^2} = \rho_{i,M}\left(\dfrac{\sigma_i}{\sigma_M}\right)$

market model: $R_i = \alpha_i + \beta_i R_M + \varepsilon_i$

$$\sigma_i^2 = \beta_i^2 \sigma_M^2 + \sigma_\varepsilon^2$$

$$Cov_{ij} = \beta_i \beta_j \sigma_M^2$$

adjusted beta: $\beta_t = \alpha_0 + (1 - \alpha_0)\beta_{t-1}$

Arbitrage Pricing Theory (APT): $E(R_P) = R_F + \beta_{P,1}(\lambda_1) + \beta_{P,2}(\lambda_2) + \dots + \beta_{P,k}(\lambda_k)$

$$\text{information ratio} = \frac{\text{annualized residual return}}{\text{annualized residual risk}} = \frac{\alpha}{\omega}$$

$$\text{ex-post information ratio} = \frac{t_\alpha}{\sqrt{n}}$$

value added $= \alpha - (\lambda \times \omega^2)$

$$\omega^* = \frac{IR}{2\lambda}$$

$$VA^* = \frac{IR^2}{4\lambda}$$

$$VA^* = \frac{\omega^* \times IR}{2}$$

information ratio (IR) $= IC \times \sqrt{BR}$

$$IR_F^2 = IR_{FI}^2 + IR_{EQ}^2 = IC_{FI}^2 \times BR_{FI} + IC_{EQ}^2 \times BR_{EQ}$$

$$\omega^* = \frac{IC \times \sqrt{BR}}{2\lambda}$$

$$VA^* = \frac{IR^2}{4\lambda} = \frac{IC^2 \times BR}{4\lambda}$$

$$IC = 2\left(\frac{N_c}{N}\right) - 1$$

$$IC_{COM} = IC\sqrt{\frac{2}{1+r}}$$

INDEX

©2013 Kaplan, Inc.

Notes

Notes

Notes

Notes

Notes

Notes

Notes

Notes